THIS IS
YOUR OWN
TIME YOU'RE
WASTING

THIS IS
YOUR OWN
TIME YOU'RE
WASTING

Classroom confessions, calamities
and clangers

**LEE PARKINSON
AND ADAM PARKINSON**

Illustrated by Tim Sadler

HarperCollins*Publishers*

HarperCollins*Publishers*
1 London Bridge Street
London SE1 9GF

www.harpercollins.co.uk

HarperCollins*Publishers*
Macken House, 39/40 Mayor Street Upper
Dublin 1, D01 C9W8, Ireland

First published by HarperCollins*Publishers* 2022
This edition published 2023

10 9 8 7 6 5 4 3 2 1

A catalogue record of this book is available from the British Library

ISBN 978-0-00-850841-8

Printed and bound in the UK using 100% renewable electricity at CPI
Group (UK) Ltd

MIX
Paper | Supporting
responsible forestry
FSC
www.fsc.org   FSC™ C007454

This book is produced from independently certified FSC™ paper to
ensure responsible forest management.

For more information visit: www.harpercollins.co.uk/green

To each and every person who works within education, thank you for the incredible job you do, day in day out, to help and support the next generation.

To everyone who has listened to and supported the podcast and to those of you who have contributed stories that have featured on previous episodes or in this book, thank you.

Contents

Good morning, Class!

GOOOOOOOOOD MOOOORRRRNIING, Mr P!

Sorry, force of habit. Welcome everyone.

Yes, indeed. Welcome.

Can you believe that we have been asked to write another book?

Actually, I can't, but we were so chuffed with the response from everyone, and our amazing publishers also agreed to let us have a second bite of the cherry.

Honestly, we received a HUGE amount of positive feedback and so much love for our tales from the classroom. Try to think of this book as a second helping of your favourite school dinner.

Mmm, spag Bol ...

Fish fingers ...

Wednesday roast ...

School pizza (not the corner piece) ...

Turkey Twizzzlerrrrrrssssss ...

Adam! You're drooling over your keyboard.

Oops, sorry. I just love me a bit of school dinners. Basically, any school dinner served with beans and smiley faces.

Not quiche, though.

HELL NO! I'm pretty sure you can be sentenced to eating quiche as punishment for tax fraud in some countries.

They say the second project can always be a tricky one; the dreaded second album. Very rarely do movie sequels live up to the first one. You can count them on one hand usually; *Toy Story 2* is arguably decent, *The Godfather: Part II* and probably *Terminator 2: Judgment Day*. We want this book to be held in the same esteem. To be fair, this book isn't a direct sequel. Instead, this is more of an emulation of book one, which drew back the curtain on the modern-day classroom. The bits you don't see. It was more of a 'deep dive' (ticking that Ofsted box early doors) into our experience and our careers.

One thing we didn't really delve into was the way our profession dealt with the Covid-19 pandemic. The reason for this was that we wrote it before and during the first lockdown. At the time of writing this introduction, we have just come out of lockdown 3.0. I sincerely hope that the world will be a much more normal place by the time this book hits the shops (providing shops are open). I equally hope that schools will be open (even though they never bl**dy closed) and looking like they are going back to some sort of normalcy. Therefore, it feels like now is the right time to speak about our experience of teaching during the pandemic and give you a real, insiders' experience of what it was like working in a primary school (in and out of lockdowns) but also how teaching may be changed forever, as a result.

Our first book laid the foundations of life inside modern-day teaching, just like the brilliant EYFS (Reception class/ pre-school) staff do day in day out. Anyone using the lazy stereotype that these Early Years teachers simply babysit or get their kids to sit and do colouring-in should be ashamed of themselves. These superheroes do an incredible job in transitioning near-toddlers into young learners and should be highly admired and respected. I have spent time teaching down in EYFS, but I've never done it full-time. While I enjoy my occasional trip into Reception class, I'm totally out of my depth; give me Year 6 any day! Nothing angers me more than seeing EYFS (and teachers in general) being undermined, either within a school or outside of it.

The ignorance shown by many outside of education can leave you seething, needing to stay calm and biting your tongue (yours, not theirs, obviously ...). It's crazy the attitude towards teachers that would never be held towards people in any other profession. You would never say to a zookeeper, for example:

'So, I take it you just babysit the penguins all day?'

Or respond to a doctor:

Doctor: 'I am afraid after the colonoscopy there seems to be an issue with your colon.'

Patient: 'Well, my colon doesn't behave like that at home, could it be that you don't like my colon?'

Right, rant over ... for now, but you'll be hearing a lot more on this theme later on!

Just as we did in our *Sunday Times* bestselling (I can't believe I'm typing that either) first book *Put a Wet Paper Towel On It*, we promise to deliver plenty more of the school-based laughs that kept people giggling last time.

Since launching the podcast in 2018, we have been inundated with thousands – and I mean thousands – of stories from teachers and school staff all over the UK and beyond. All these hilarious tales (mostly primary based but plenty from secondary teachers, too) have then been re-told by us with permission from both the school staff and parents all over the UK and beyond. We love sharing these stories on the podcast, on our live episodes and even on our nationwide tour. Some of our favourites will be retold here alongside other anecdotes we've handpicked for your enjoyment. Everything we receive and share with you is kept completely anonymous, of course – to protect the identities of everyone involved, and to ensure the teachers and school staff keep their jobs!

I am sure there will be some who read the shocking stories in this book and claim they can't possibly be true. But let me reassure you that teachers are some of the most trustworthy professionals out there; they are not the type of people to say one thing and actually mean something different. This obviously doesn't apply, of course, if they are writing end of year reports, in which case, it has been known for teachers to embellish the truth (if your teacher said you were a 'lively character', that means you were an annoying and gobby little turd). What we have done with some of the stories, though, is rewritten them a little – for artistic effect, to potentially earn ourselves a sticker and so that maybe, just maybe, we can finally get our pen licences too! We also have a whole lot more to share with you as we delve into the treasure trove of podcast features, including plenty of **confessions**, **catastrophes** and ...

POO STORIES!

... Adam, I was trying to be alliterative!

Ok then. CRAP STORIES!

Let's go for **clangers**.

Clangers it is! But don't worry, readers, there'll be plenty of tales about poop. After all, there's not a classroom in the UK where some child doesn't leave an unpleasant present in the bog that could sink a battleship!

I can't believe you've gone straight for the toilet humour.

Gotta play to my strengths!

And for any weirdos who are reading this book without having enjoyed our first one, what are you doing? Who would jump straight into a sequel? No one watches *Die Hard 2* without watching the original *Die Hard* film – which, I want to make clear in written text, **IS** a Christmas film. But if you did read and enjoy *Put a Wet Paper Towel On It*, there'll be plenty in this book for you, including a few appearances by folks like Big Mike (our dad), the Geordie PE teacher and Adam's mate, former work colleague and epitome of teaching professionalism (yeah right) a certain ... Mr Cockney John. Big Mike, Geordie and old CJ aren't the only interesting characters in this book, though, as we've plenty more brilliant staff and children who, just like Adam, 'don't always make the right choices'.

Anyway, if this *is* your first rodeo with the Two Mr Ps, for reference throughout this book, if you are seeing this font, it is Mr P (Lee) speaking – or should I say writing ...

And if you see this font, it is the Other Mr P (Adam).

Life is pretty sweet when you're a kid. Even if all your childhood memories aren't perfect, it was hopefully a simpler, less stressful time for you than adulthood.

When you consider how much the world has changed from when Adam and I were children, you sometimes need to take a step back and appreciate how far things have come, especially since the dawn of the internet. I mean, can you imagine trying to survive the pandemic with the technology we had when we were at school? Stuck in your house with nothing but your Nokia 3210? No World Wide Web and therefore no social media – no Instagram, Facebook, Twitter, YouTube or TikTok? It would have just been non-stop Snake! Imagine the high score you could SMS your friend — if you had credit — followed by an image made purely from letters and symbols available on your number keypad. I would spend hours desperately trying to compose the latest Dr. Dre tune on the phone keypad. Only true millennials would be able to work out which tone this one is:

```
5 5 5 2 8
6 6 # 9 9 6
2 # 8 2 # 2 #
2 # 2 2
2 2 5
6 # 2 5 0
6 0 6 # 5
6 # 2 5 0
6 0 6 # 5
6 # 2 5 0
6 0 6 # 5 9
0 8 2 8 8 6 6 # 9 9
6 8 6 # 8 6
```

You mean that anyone reading this book needs to not only break out their old Nokia phone to try this, but they'll have to hunt down their old charger as well?!?

Potentially.

Can't wait to see how this pans out when we record the audiobook!

Indeed! You'd best find your charger, mate! Anyway, after this most random start to a chapter, it must be time for us to explore the utterly random things that are, or were, quintessentially part of a primary school classroom yet can seldom be found outside of it! Overhead projectors, anyone? You get where I'm going with this one ...

Many years ago, before we even had phones, TV was king. With only four channels until 1997 for most (unless you had cable), many kids would have to plan their social lives around the TV schedules. If you wanted to watch *Gladiators* on ITV, you couldn't watch whatever was on BBC unless you were videoing it in a different room. There was no pausing the TV, either. My kids will never understand the challenge of the mad dash during the ad break to get to the toilet, stick the kettle on and sort myself out with a Club biscuit.

Technology moves on – and thank goodness it does – can you even imagine having remote teaching when we were kids? It would have been impossible in 1995, as barely anyone was online. You would think that all the advancements in technology would have vastly impacted the classroom. Come on, after all that was promised in *Back to the Future Part II* (ahem ... hoverboards, anyone? No, I mean real ones, not the electric skateboards that are awesome but don't actually, you know, hover), you would think that the kids would all be learning while wearing virtual-reality helmets, with personal robot teachers. The 80s lied to us!

The old adage is true, though; the more things change, the more they stay the same. If you haven't already guessed, this chapter will hopefully take you on a little journey into the random things we take for granted and explore how some have stood the test of time, whereas others are definitely best forgotten.

Let's kick off with another thing my kids' generation will never understand, which is the majesty of the Classroom TV Stand.

There was no better feeling if you were a child of the 80s and 90s than hearing the ear-offending screech of wheels as the TV stand rolled into the classroom and you got to tune in to the classic BBC *Look and Read* series, *Through the Dragon's Eye* (on VIDEO/VHS, no less). Just hearing Derek Griffiths (the voice of many people's childhood, and the unmistakable voice of SuperTed, amongst others) and his dulcet tones as he began: 'North or South, East or West, the quest ...'. It was absolute dream stuff because you got to sit there and do bugger all work for the duration of the 20-or-so-minute episode. It was meant to be a writing stimulus, whereby children would engage with the video and then use the themes to help them create their own epic literary masterpieces. It all depends on your vintage as to whether you remember *Through the Dragon's Eye*, *Badger Girl* or even the much-loved *Geordie Racer*, of course.

The masterful TV stand would transport the class on a journey to a magical place where regional stereotypes, mulleted child actors (spouting *Star Wars'*-quality dialogue) and frankly terrifying wardrobe choices. Seriously, google an episode of *Through the Dragon's Eye* and you'll see the stuff of nightmares: bright orange and green humans, a cardboard dragon that sounds a bit like Gandalf and a villain that looks like a love child of Skeletor and Charles Dickens on steroids, wearing a bubonic plague mask.

Now, with interactive whiteboards, it is a case of sticking a DVD into the teacher's computer. Although I have to admit, with streaming services, I don't even own DVDs any more. I've lived through two revolutions – man, I am getting old.

Other than that, pretty much everything we did at primary school still happens now. Granted, we don't tend to back our books. Remember that? That was a huge primary school trend whereby you would cover your exercise books in wrapping paper or, for full protection, wallpaper. It was a real skill to master and yet it made no difference to your books because, ultimately, if your drink bottle leaked, no wallpaper was going to save it. You might have tried to add another layer of security with sticky-backed plastic (eat your heart out, *Blue Peter*), but even that wouldn't survive the dreaded leak from the crappy water bottle you had.

Although most children are allowed to bring in their own bag, in a lot of schools they have their own merch range, like they are famous YouTubers or influencers, so as you remortgage your house to pay for school uniform you can accessorise with a school bag with the school emblem embroidered on it. On a side note, as a teacher, I think the prices of some school uniforms are absolutely ridiculous. That's not something that we as staff all decided together, but while the month of August is great for me as a teacher, it is terrible as a parent because I have to fork out hundreds to kit out my kids (I forgot to mention, I have triplets) with uniform that when washed shrinks to a size that wouldn't fit a two-year-old.

Back in our day, school bags were a real statement, whether you went for the leather Head bag that had a detachable book bag, straps, handles and enough room to fit your homework and PE kit, or one of the shopping bags that became very popular – from the Jane Norman pink bag to the JD Sports drawstring plastic bag. There were also some bags that came with matching lunch boxes and pencil cases, but come secondary school it would spell social disaster if you rocked up with one of those.

Stationery has become more restricted in a lot of schools, too. Either the basics are provided or a list will be sent home to parents of what to buy if the school budget cannot stretch to it. As a child, the back-to-school anxiety never existed, as the excitement of the trip to WHSmith, Woolworths (RIP) or Stationery Box (RIP) was just around the corner. Do you go for the Gul pencil case or mix it up with a Pepsi Max can-shaped pencil case? Or do you upgrade and get a pencil case with the full mathematical set, which included protractors you only used in two lessons, a couple of weird triangle rulers that to this day I have never used and a set of compasses that in primary school would be confiscated as a weapon? Do you go for a bendy ruler or a ruler that folds and can easily be used as a nunchuck, knowing that if you do need a long straight line you will always get a little kink where the ruler folds? Or do you go down the rene-gade route and get gel pens or felt tips when the teacher made it clear that only colouring pencils are allowed? Should I get a double-edged rubber where one side rubs out pencil and the other states it erases ink but instead just rips the paper? What about pencils; do you go for the standard HB or one of the clickable propelling ones that allow you to press the top to push out more lead? The clicky pencil had an extra bonus, because it provided a very quick magic trick where you could make it look like the lead could disappear by pressing and holding the rubber end and pretending to stab your finger. One drawback of these, though, was that you couldn't sharpen them and therefore missed out on gathering around the bin having what your teacher calls 'a mother's meeting' where you chat sh*t instead of getting on with your activities.

If you were older you could finally invest in a fountain pen, which was when the biggest decision of your young life had to be made: do you go for Parker or LAMY? Whatever you went for, one thing was for sure, you couldn't be without the famous double-ended eraser pen – you know, those brilliant creations where one end erases the ink, while on the other there's a pen that allows you to correct the mistake. Those were the days!

It's amazing how so much of the stuff you did when you were at school still happens now.

Papier-mâché, junk-modelling, tea-bagging ...

... TEA-BAGGING!? WTF? This is a family-friendly book ...

No, you pilchard, I mean the art of ageing a piece of paper by smearing a used tea bag all over the surface and when it's dry, writing Egyptian hieroglyphics on it or making a treasure map. Putting crisp packets into the oven so they shrink into badges isn't as popular as it once was; it died out when conkers were no longer safe to play with. God, I miss conkers. What a game! I know we mentioned conkers in the last book, but there is a conker tree near our house and I regularly see kids walk past it, ignoring some grade-A, guaranteed destroyers just lying there. I went and got some with my kids recently and was picking them up saying, 'This is definitely a six-er', then had to explain what this meant. I still remember all the nights I would spend soaking them in vinegar and leaving them in the freezer (wrapped in a tea towel) in the hope I could take down the three-er that dominated in the playground that day.

Speaking of tea towels, those humble drying rags are still used in every nativity as headwear for Joseph and the shepherds. Of course, some enthusiastic parents prefer to grab a fairly decent nativity costume from B&M that gets worn for about three performances in December of their child's Reception year before being bundled into the back of their wardrobe, never to be seen again (unless the sibling is cast as the same part, but even then you can't bloody find the headpiece so it's back to using a tea towel). If you're going for the tea towel option, any one will suffice; even those that have a drawing of every child in the school on them make an occasional appearance. That's because this is still the go-to PTA fundraising idea; we are talking about tea towels that feature a hand-drawn portrait of every child in the class or school. If you ever wanted the inside scoop of how these masterpieces work, it involves every child being given a small piece of white paper and asked to draw a self-portrait. That's it.

If the children involved in creating a school tea towel are from lower down the school, you can bet your bottom dollar that one of them will have chicken pox just before the deadline so the grown-ups on hand will either select another child to draw their friend or do it themselves. The child will have no recollection either way and their grandparents will fork out for the finished tea towel regardless. What always makes me laugh with any class or school-portrait tea towel is that 99 out of the 100 are – how can I put this kindly? – a bit crap. Let's be fair, none of these kids would get a job as a police sketch artist. Yes, there's always that one child who is decent at drawing and will create something impressive that stands out like a sore thumb, which is interesting because at least two children's portraits will look more like an actual thumb. It is the only drawing that looks like a human face and not a collection of extras from the *Lord of the Rings'* final battle.

Once the tea towel has been purchased, it will probably be used once, then washed and, to avoid it becoming permanently stained, popped away into a cupboard or drawer for all eternity as just another example of the amount of stuff that comes home from school to fill up parents' storage spaces. Now, this might sound harsh, but I guarantee any parents reading this know exactly what I am talking about here. On behalf of the whole teaching profession, I can only apologise for the amount of crap we have cluttered your house with. Unless the particular artwork is going to go on display in the school corridor, the paintings, charcoal, water-colours, papier-mâché, clay and, worst of all, pasta-shell art has one destination and that is your home. It is like a never-ending conveyor belt of, well … sh*te!

We all go through the same process as parents. In the beginning, we cherish everything, including the finger paint-ings that are so abstract they would probably sell for millions that clog up our fridge door to the point where you are considering investing in another fridge just to put up more pictures. But once you've had your fourth pasta-shell picture of a dinosaur in one week, you have to call it a day. Would you believe that pasta can be actually cooked and eaten rather than wasted on woeful pictures or, even worse, jewellery?

One saving grace for parents is that the volume of artwork that comes home decreases the older your children get, apart from in the week before Christmas. All the way through primary school, you can bet you'll be receiving a decoration that will ruin the aesthetic and colour scheme of your tree but your child will want it on there no matter what. You'll get a Christmas card, too, which goes from the basic collage of a cotton-wool snowman, including twigs for arms, all the way to the elaborate 3D pop-up cards (depending on whether the teacher can be arsed or not). And, of course, there is the calendar – a Christmas image with the cheap matchbox-size calendar that gets stuck on or stapled at the bottom. It is the most impractical calendar you will ever have, there is no space to note down reminders, and the likelihood is by the time it makes it home the actual calendar bit will have become disconnected from the picture. Lower down the school, there's every possibility you may end up with another child's artwork, because the little ones seldom put their names on things. A rushed job of a TA quickly scrawling names on the back may mean that little Alice will go home with Sam's handprint snowflake. Fortunately, neither Sam nor Alice will remember which one is theirs anyway!

The amount of unwanted artwork heading home might increase at Christmas, but you can also guarantee that a week when there's been a few wet-break times will result in a high volume of questionable masterpieces in the school bags. After children have raided the scrap-paper drawer and spent their break or lunchtime using the plethora of lidless felt-tip pens creating their own artwork (with no input from teachers), a parent's fridge may be adorned with a few new pictures that have yellow, brown and grey as their main colours, mostly due to those being the only pens that still work. From noughts and crosses to paper aeroplanes and even those fortune-telling devices where you have to select numbers and colours in order to learn that 'U R a poo head', kids will always manage to entertain themselves as best they can when they can't get outside. In my day, my go-to activity involved mastering the ability to draw that graffiti-style letter S. I still do it in staff meetings when I'm bored.

There's a huge sense of relief that a teacher feels when a child asks at the end of a wet break time, 'Can I take these home?' while pointing to a pile of pictures they have just created. Who in their right mind would refuse that request? They don't realise that their artworks will be going home whether they like it or not. A little tip for parents: use the old 'green filing cabinet'. In every classroom there is usually a paper recycling bin, which more often than not is coloured green to symbolise the recycled element and which is what teachers refer to as the green filing cabinet (I'm making a winking face as I type this). Come to think of it, this relates to pretty much any sort of paper in the class; if there is work produced that isn't going to be assessed, go on display or be referenced again, you can bet your bottom dollar it will be stored in the green filing cabinet. It is also where most handouts from staff meetings go.

I say all this, but you may be the parent of *that* child – the child who is so gifted at art that as a teacher you feel embarrassed creating anything in front of them. For me, I feel embarrassed modelling anything when it comes to drawing and art – I am dreadful at it. While most teachers have go-to lines such as, 'This is your own time you're wasting' and 'Put a wet paper towel on it' (see what I did there), my most common go-to line during sketching lessons is: 'Remember, children, I am not an artist,' as I draw yet another awful stick man monstrosity. But there is nothing more impressive than having a pupil who can create a piece of artwork that is truly breathtaking. If I was that parent, every piece of artwork would be framed, or, in fact, auctioned to the highest bidder. If you ever wonder which child I am talking about here, it's the aforementioned tea-towel artist. Perhaps I should pay them in house points or dojos to teach my art lesson for me.

One thing that's for sure when it comes to doing any art in class is that you will need to get the paint shirts – a tub full of old school shirts with a few random T-shirts that have been donated to school. One golden rule of wearing the paint shirt is that you *have* to wear them back to front. Within the tub of shirts will also be some old newspapers to cover the desks before you get the paint out. An important tip now from an 'experienced' teacher here, do steer clear of using certain newspapers! Definitely don't use right-wing periodicals when covering your tables for art; the last thing you need following a citizenship lesson on **tolerance** is for little Susie to start reading about which celebrities are being body-shamed this week and for little Nikal to be reading how immigrants are stealing British jobs. Even worse if there's an old tabloid from years gone by when page 3 still featured topless ladies.

Thanks for the mammaries!

Question. Did you even go to school in the UK if you didn't spend at least a year of your education in a 'temporary' portacabin? I put the word temporary in inverted commas as they are most often anything but temporary; the fact that they have been there longer than most staff have been alive will tell you how temporary they are. If you are a millennial, like myself, and did indeed learn in one of these shacks, I guarantee they will still be there. I remember doing a placement 18 years ago in a portacabin – the same one that since last year my own children have called their classroom – and putting up a display, only for my whole hand to break through the structure as I stapled the wall. The worst is when the weather takes a downward turn; I have taught in these portacabins when there has been a storm and you and your class are fearing for your collective lives, expecting the building to be swept away like the farmhouse in the *Wizard of Oz*. I used to keep the huge PE parachute in there just in case we needed a safe landing after being swept away. And by parachute I mean the massive multicoloured one that put Joseph and his Technicolour Dreamcoat to shame – the one that for children of the 90s onwards, when they became commonplace, it was the most fun you could have at primary school. In fact, it is the most fun you've probably ever had in your whole life. For most of us, it would go something like this:

3) Getting married.
2) Seeing the birth of your children.
1) The PE lesson with the parachute.

According to legend, the parachute is not something that can be purchased, they just magically started appearing in schools post World War II. They are pretty much inde-structible – apart from the black handles, which didn't last the first term. To locate the parachute, just step into the PE stock cupboard and there, underneath the box of coits (those flipping solid rubber rings) and bean bags, it will be. Due to the sheer size of the parachute it has never once been cleaned so there's probably the germs of at least three generations of one family on there.

There's only one other place that has more germs than the parachute and that is the lost property box. It's the most random collection of uniform items that have a wealth of bacteria festering amongst them. I always wonder why there is often just one shoe, too. There's never a pair, just one random shoe, meaning that at some point a child has waltzed out of school with just one shoe on but even the parent didn't realise as there is no mention of it.

The lost property accumulates during the school year until it becomes a small mountain. I make no bones about who is to blame for the Mount Everest of lost uniform … that's right, the bloody parents who fail to label their child's clothes.

How hard is it to do, really? Yet these parents are the first to moan and complain when an item goes missing. The amount of conversations I have had that go along the lines of:

'Mr P, Callum has lost his jumper.'

'Did he have his name in it?'

'Yes.'

'With what?'

'Machine-washable pen!'

'Brilliant! Ok, Callum, do you want to go and check in the class for it, otherwise, check the lost property box.'

'Found it!'

'Where was it?'

'In my bag!'

Another tactic to use when a jumper is missing an owner and it has no name on is to get the sniffer on the case. Every class will have a child who has a superpower, which, let's be fair, wouldn't defeat Thanos but does mean they can smell a jumper and instinctively know which child it belongs to.

A truly desperate moment for any primary school child is the day you forget your PE kit and have to somehow create one from the lost property box. This results in you wearing a pair of shorts made for a toddler with a vest or shirt that would be too big on The Mountain from *Game of Thrones*. Seriously, there is always uniform in that lost property box that is so big it could double up as a parachute.

But there was no way you were going to miss your PE lesson, especially if it involved the blue climbing frame – you know, the one that was folded up against one of the walls but would be brought out then pinned into the holes on the wooden floor and the teacher would allow you to simply climb it. Some schools were lucky enough to have ropes as well. Alongside the wooden benches, the padded coloured trestle tables and, of course, the blue PE mats, it made for one hell of a lesson. Those blue mats ... you got more cushion and protection from concrete; I swear the knee problems I've had as an adult all stem from landing on those. Although, having the task of putting them away at the end of the lesson was a good flex as everyone knew only the strongest children could do that job. Nowadays the climbing frame does little but gather dust. Is this down to schools developing a much better PE curriculum with more focus on skills, technique and tactical play? No, it's more the health-and-safety-obsessed risk-assessment world we live in. You don't dare let children climb and fall, as explaining that alongside the plethora of wet paper towels you would need just isn't worth it. Shame really, I love that climbing frame.

Saying that, I remember in my first year of teaching having a very enthusiastic PE teacher who came into school to try to spruce up our PE lessons, not that I felt we needed it, and as a new teacher we had to observe them (who took themselves very seriously) teach a lesson. They wanted to ensure I made the most of the equipment, so they got out the blue climbing frame and set it up and they were demonstrating how to manoeuvre through the circles of the contraption when all of a sudden they got stuck. I thought they were joking to begin with, as I didn't think it was possible that as a fully grown adult you could somehow get stuck in an apparatus built for children, but here we were. It was when the teacher was going more and more red in the face that I decided I ought to intervene, but they had already established repeatedly that I was the student, I shouldn't interrupt when they were in full flow and I was there to simply watch and learn. Eventually I realised they clearly needed some help, so while trying not to laugh at the sight of a fully grown adult trapped in a school climbing frame, biting my tongue as I threw daggers at my class, who were also sniggering, I managed to untangle the teacher, who quickly thanked me before moving on to show us how to balance by turning the wooden benches upside down.

Talking of accidents, another random thing is the school accident book. Now, accident books themselves are not random, as you find these in most workplace environments, but what is random and unique to primary schools is bump notes. These are little slips of paper that explain to parents that their child has had a head injury, no matter how severe — or not. Children love getting a bump note as they can sometimes mistake these for other more positive acknowledgements, such as star of the week certificates. Children also know that with a bump note comes the wet paper towel that they will make last the rest of the afternoon.

The other thing that separates primary school accident books from other official books are the more peculiar entries you find. Don't just believe us, here's a sample of some:

Testicles stuck in the shaft of a tennis racket.

Poked himself in the eye with a banana!

A child was hit round the face with a panini and his tooth fell out.

Pulled a muscle in his leg trying to sniff his toes.

Finger stuck in sink trap. Had to remove the trap and send her to A&E with it still attached.

Tried to sharpen their own finger with a pencil sharpener.

A child hit their head on the sink after slipping on a turd in the middle of the bathroom floor left by another child.

A child swallowed a ruler.

Cut tongue licking shoe sole, which had a drawing pin attached.

Ice pack applied after a child was kicked in the head by the class teacher, who tripped on the carpet and landed on top of them.

Child had skidded on the bark play area, bark went straight up his shorts and boxers and into his rectum.

A child was bitten by his friend as his friend thought he was a banana.

Nothing wrong with him, but the child had a cold compress as he felt he was missing out.

A child swallowed a 10p coin because he was pretending to be a vending machine.

A pheasant flew through the window of the corridor and she got glass in her eye.

A child put his tie in chilli powder and later rubbed it in his eyes to see if it would hurt. He can conclude that it does indeed hurt.

Put sweetcorn and peas in their ears and nose. Taken to the hospital to be removed.

I had to put myself in the accident book for sticking a cherry stone up my nose at lunchtime. I don't know what I was playing at. My mum had to come and take me to the hospital. I was 39 at the time.

And my personal favourite:

Poked in the eye with the accident book ... A child came into the first aid room with a tiny, minor (nonsense) scrape and went out with a genuine injury. The accident record folder was slightly hanging off the side of the shelf and the child walked right into it.

If you enjoyed these little accident book entries, then you'll be delighted to learn that we've got an entire chapter dedicated to school-related injuries later in the book!

Somewhere else in the school hall will be the most pathetic sight in most primary schools – the music trolley. Yes, I'm about to pick a fight with the school music co-ordinators, but it's got to be said: what is the point of it? A trolley made up of broken instruments with bits missing; a glockenspiel with no wooden sticks or half the keys missing, a triangle with no string to hold it, a tambourine with ripped skin, wood blocks to scrape and maracas, to name but a few. What in the world can you possibly do with it? There are never enough instruments on it for every child in your class anyway, so it simply occupies a corner of the hall, and the instruments on it never really get used, either. Don't get me started on the random wooden frog instrument that somebody picked up on their holiday to the Caribbean!

If you think the music trolley is random, remember trundle wheels? A walking stick with a circle on the end that clicked every time you rolled a metre. You may not remember these brilliant measuring tools as you only used them once in your whole primary school career, usually during the maths topic of area and perimeter. I vaguely remember using it in science, but since being a teacher, this has never been the case. I must be getting it confused with the science investigation of drawing silhouettes around our shadows throughout the day to show how the Earth moves. This is a stalwart of a science investigation that every child did and continues to do during primary school, alongside growing a flower and making an electrical circuit (providing you miraculously have enough batteries). But I want to let you into a little secret, a confession that could lead to an onslaught from fellow educators ... we rig most science investigations. We have to! You would not believe the amount of science lessons where I look at the planning and think, this should be straightforward, then I have a practice run of the investigation – as failing to prepare is preparing to fail – only for the investigation to be a load of codswallop. Don't get me wrong, the logic is correct and the desired outcome should work, however, for some strange reason it rarely does.

I will give you an example of how my quick wit managed to salvage the lesson. We were learning about how air is a material. The investigation was simple: to prove air exists. In order to prove this theory, we would attach two balloons to a hanger, one of which would be inflated, the other deflated. With the air compressed the inflated balloon should weigh more than the deflated one. Simple, right? Well, no. No matter how many times I tried, I could not make the inflated balloon appear to weigh more. My lesson was going to be a disaster! Thinking quickly on my feet, I decided to put a blob of Blu Tack in the neck of the inflated balloon, which seemed to do the trick. The inflated balloon could clearly be seen to be heavier, demonstrating to my class that air was in fact a material, because when compressed it weighed more.

I guarantee, if you ask any teacher they will all admit to rigging a science investigation. In other words, at primary school there is no such thing as a fair test. If you are growing flowers in your classroom under different conditions – one in the dark, one with no water, one with no soil, etc. – and the flower under the 'perfect' conditions doesn't grow the way the teacher expected, you can bet your bottom dollar the teacher nips to the local florist to ensure they have the perfect bloom to prove the correct conditions plants need to grow.

So there you have it, once you've finished rigging science experiments, you can grab your trundle wheel, put it together with a parachute, a TV trolley and an unclaimed school jumper and realise that there are few places more random than a primary school. Good luck finding a charger for a Nokia 3210, though!

During initial teacher training and throughout their careers, many teachers (depending on where their careers take them) will get the opportunity to spend time in a number of different schools. The more schools you visit, the more you realise there's always a range of different characters that are so similar. There's always a child that never learns their spellings, there's always a child that never has their PE kit, and there's always a child that brings in boring crap for show and tell. As you read these words, it's easy to think of someone you went to school with who was THAT kid. If you can't, it might be you!

With this chapter, we are taking you on a little trip through the rogues' gallery of children you may know or have known during your time at school. These are obviously generalisations and not based on any specific children. No children are being mocked based upon their ability, gender, ailments, insecurities, etc. The children we've identified are hopefully almost archetypes of the crazy gang we've been lucky enough to be involved with.

If you're a fan of the podcast, you'll have come across David with his Donkey, Bobby with his Helix ruler and, of course, Adji with his Rick Astley news report. If you're not already a listener of the podcast, we've just recorded our 200th episode (at time of writing) so there's a wealth of funny stories about even funnier children and their shenanigans for you to enjoy. Right then, let's kick off with the keenest human you may come across in a primary classroom.

Sports-Mad

At the end of every lunchtime, without fail, he asks 'Are we doing PE?'

Uber-competitive. Rushes his maths work and never shows his workings.

Represents the school at football, tag-rugby, cricket, netball, rounders and athletics.

Doesn't need a captain's armband on the pitch, he leads by example.

Brilliant stagehand during school performances. Can remove a bench in 20 seconds.

Includes multiple semi-colons in his writing with no idea what they are for.

NEVER underlines the date and title with a ruler... NEVER!

Guaranteed to come back and volunteer at the school to complete his sports-leader qualification.

Every school has a boy or girl that can just try their hand at anything, and as long as there's a ball, field, bat or racquet involved, they are up for a game. Some schools have a wealth of sporting superstars, and some have just a few that stand out. I suppose it might boil down to the schools' priorities and dedication to sports, but also the size of their talent pool.

It's not always the tallest child or the one with particularly active parents. Those factors might help, but some children might just have a particular aptitude for sport and the school is always glad to have them. These kids have the potential to become elite sportspeople and they will, more often than not, regularly attend clubs and competitions outside of school that help them to hone their skills.

From a teaching perspective, these kids are great to have around because they usually have a real drive to succeed but also the leadership qualities to bring others with them. In a game of cricket or rounders you can spot them giving a little bit of coaching to their teammates. Whether advising on fielding positions or ways to retrieve the ball, they don't boss anyone around, they just give them a few pointers to help their game. You can see the look on their face when their mates manage to catch someone out because they were in the right place at the right time. Smart teachers will exploit their level of skills and experience and get the particularly capable sporting children to model good examples. Teachers in their fifties who don't fancy breaking out their own version of a forward roll will be glad they have a county-level gymnast to give some great examples, and why on earth not? It avoids rupturing a dodgy hamstring and empowers the children to be sports leaders.

Plenty of the super-sporty kids do have a competitive streak. It's what puts them on another level. This competitive streak needs to be channelled, especially as it often means that they finish their work in record time. Sadly, it may be barely legible, full of mistakes and containing none of the required punctuation or structure.

Slowing them down is tricky, but if it can be turned into some sort of sporting metaphor involving goals or targets with a reward at the end of it, their enthusiasm can be concentrated in the correct way.

Another key attribute of a sports-mad child is that they are very quick learners and will join in with anything. They may not be as keen to have a speaking or singing role in a school performance, but they'll be the best backstage crew ever. They won't miss a single stage direction, can prompt a forgotten line and should probably be trusted with the music cues more often than the staff. They keep the production moving brilliantly and shift sets with great ease, yet carefully enough that they don't injure anyone in the process.

Sports-mad kids are always great to have in the class. They may wind up teachers by constantly asking if they have spontaneous bench ball sessions on the timetable or trying to bargain in the summer months that if they finally bother to show their working out in maths, can they get out the rounders equipment? Little do they know that the teachers would prefer to be doing those activities anyway. As soon as some children leave primary school, you know they'll be back, a few weeks into starting Year 7. Some returning visitors will be more welcome than others, but teachers will always be happy to see kids like these popping in to say hi and will be even happier if they go on to great success.

From one school stalwart to another dependable member of the class. Now, most teachers at some point have thought or even said the following statement at parents' evening about this type of child: 'If I could have 30 of [insert name of particularly sensible child] in my class it would be an absolute dream.' In truth, 30 of the same child would be weird, but if it was 30 kind and reliable ones, it would definitely make life less stressful. There's no way you'd want 30 non-compliant ruffians, but by goodness me, a class of

Sensible Sally

No child is perfect... But this kid makes life so much easier.

She's not a toady, she genuinely likes to help.

30 of her in a class could be boring, but at least the date and title would be underlined.

Always selected to sell red noses, poppies and Pudsey bears during charity appeals.

It's hard not to treat her as a personal assistant.

She'd probably be more use in a staff meeting than half of the teachers!

How does she always know where everything is? Including the elusive metre stick!

These kids make parents' evenings worth doing.

Sensible Sallies would be so much easier to plan for, teach and mark their work.

No child is perfect, and any that you think are will have plenty of flaws that they either don't want to expose or try hard to cover up. Many teachers will want children to make mistakes, because mistakes are great for children's development of thinking skills and resilience. A sensible Sally is not perfect, but she is perfect to have around and always makes a day in the classroom worthwhile. You know that a sensible Sally will go on to do great things and make a positive contribution in the world.

Let's be quite honest, a sensible Sally has many roles to play in the class and teachers will happily exploit her willingness to fulfil them all. For example, if there is a new child joining a class (sometimes with little notice) you can bet that they will be paired with a sensible Sally for their first week. She will absolutely thrive in the role and consider it her mission to make the newcomer feel as welcome as humanly possible. Another important role she absolutely excels at is that of the class Mary Poppins. Always on the lookout in the playground for a younger child in need that could do with her help, if a little one looks lonely, has fallen over or has got their skipping rope all tied up, her radar for younger schoolmates starts beeping and within seconds she's spotted said child in need. Almost like the scene in *Mrs Doubtfire* where she rushes to perform the Heimlich manoeuvre on Pierce Brosnan's character when he starts choking – 'HELP IS ON THE WAY, DEAR!', a sensible Sally is there as quick as a flash and seeking out the nearest lunchtime supervisor to help the Year 2 that fell arse-first in the muddy puddle and was starting to cry. She'll happily reassure the child and distract them with a funny joke to help the little one feel OK.

This also applies to helping a teacher when they are clearly under immense pressure and about to lose their sh*t because guided reading overran again, their PPA (Planning, Preparation and Assessment) time has been cancelled and someone had just used a Sharpie on the class whiteboard. Sally will take time to calm the teacher down and, amazingly, her suggestion of using hand sanitiser on the permanent-pen daubings has actually worked. Everyone needs a sensible Sally; teachers will be very sad when she goes up a year in the summer. I genuinely know of teachers that have actively campaigned to stay with the same class for the following year because they enjoyed teaching one particular cohort of children so much. I also know teachers that have flat-out refused to have the same class twice, but that's a different story altogether.

Billy Big Boll**ks

Definitely 'doesn't always make the right choices'.

Anytime there's a visitor in assembly, they always pick him to help them.

He's not all bad... his armpit farts are quite impressive.

Mocks everyone's insecurities but he's a Year 6 and still has Velcro shoes.

Insists on being first in the line and will kick off if he isn't.

Must always have the last clap in assembly.

Growth spurt in Year 4 means he's taller than 50% of school staff – including his teacher.

Purveyor of the finest...
◄

Basically, Adam.

Oi!

Let's be honest, you were a typical Billy Big-Boll**ks during your time at school. We've documented it in the last book and had it confirmed by none other than the legendary Mr Tyrell (our former headteacher, who amazingly turned up to our book launch party in a Manchester night club).

All right, fair enough, I guess I'm the person best placed to write about this character, then. I mean, every school has got one. Some schools have plenty and even multiple versions in each year group – usually boys, but I've definitely met some female versions that could give any teacher headaches at the mention of their names.

A Billy Big-Boll**ks is your standard class nightmare. If there's a wrong choice to be made, he'll be the first in line. The kids' toilets with the wet green tissue that has been ripped into pieces, scrunched into a ball and thrown on the ceiling? That was him. Those things are hard to get down and may even turn into crusty green stalactites. Is it stalactites or stalagmites, Lee?

It's stalactites. As in 'tites (tights) go down.

Oooh er! I bet old Billy would appreciate that joke. Actually, he might not understand it. Billy Big-Boll**ks can be a good laugh, but it is dangerous to encourage him, so don't do it.

The disclaimer at the start of a WWE wrestling show where they make it very clear that the viewers should 'not try this at home' will completely fly over his head and he's quite often missing his lunch-time to perform a dangerous move on his mates. If he's asked to write a letter of apology to his poor victim, at least he'll make sure he tries to spell 'sunset-flip powerbomb' correctly.

If there's a visitor in school and they are delivering an assembly, you can bet your bottom dollar that they'll ask for a volunteer or two. Why oh why on earth do they always pick him? As he gets to his feet and struts to the front of the hall with a huge smile, all the staff in the hall are crapping themselves as to what carnage awaits the visitor. If the school sings 'Oil in My Lamp/Sing Hosanna' during their assembly, you can bet he'll be the annoying turd that has to randomly sing 'of kings' at the end. You know, despite the 100 times the entire school has been instructed not to. Or during a celebration assembly where he'll be competing with the alpha male from the other class to be the last person clapping before the headteacher goes nuts. If he hears someone coughing, he'll join in, and so will his mates. Basically, he's a pain in the ASS-embly.

One huge saving grace for our Billy is that he can often surprise people, so don't write him off. One teacher told us about the time when an Ofsted inspector came into the school and decided they would very randomly select children. Of course, they picked his school's version of Billy for a pupil interview. Mr Big-Boll**ks emerged from the chat with a big smile on his face. Dreading his response, the teacher thought he would be given a verbal bashing by his arch nemesis, but it turned out that Billy had really gone to bat for him, the school and the teaching staff. Billy was even quoted in the feedback as saying, 'Even when I'm naughty, my teacher never gives up on me. He always believes I can make good choices.'

Fair play to Billy Big-Boll**ks, he really can show the best of himself sometimes.

Sadly, the next day he drew a moustache on one of the Year 2s in permanent pen and we're back to bloody square one!

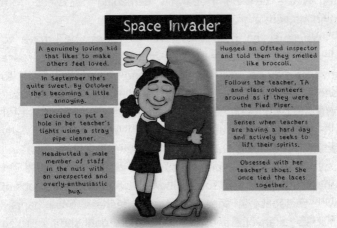

Space Invader

A genuinely loving kid that likes to make others feel loved.

In September she's quite sweet. By October, she's becoming a little annoying.

Decided to put a hole in her teacher's tights using a stray pipe cleaner.

Headbutted a male member of staff in the nuts with an unexpected and overly-enthusiastic hug.

Hugged an Ofsted inspector and told them they smelled like broccoli.

Follows the teacher, TA and class volunteers around as if they were the Pied Piper.

Senses when teachers are having a hard day and actively seeks to lift their spirits.

Obsessed with her teacher's shoes. She once tied the laces together.

One thing children learn as part of their development, and anyone that works in Early Years will explain it far better than either of us can, is boundaries – an understanding of their own personal space and appreciating and respecting that of others. Plenty of children learn about this early on, some take a while to grasp it, but the space invader knows what is appropriate in a polite school setting ... she just doesn't care. IT'S CUDDLE TIME!

Whether it's her parents, classmates, teacher, TA or just a random classroom visitor, our little space invader will zone in on someone (anyone) and become their new best friend (even if they see her every day). She's a hand holder, too. If the human she is near is at least above 4ft 9, then they are fair game for a bit of hand holding. Imagine the poor male student teacher, all 6-foot-3 of him, being brought into his placement class of 29 Year 1 children. Even worse, the story for the term is *Jack and the Beanstalk*! The little ones think they are being taught by a genuine, bonafide GIANT. Our space invader will sense his fear, knowing that for the next ten weeks he'll be irreparably damaging his knees from working with a group on the carpet daily.

Wherever he goes, whatever he does, he'll have to develop a sixth sense to keep check on where the space invader may be. Will she be standing behind him, ready to show affection? Sitting on a chair that he's about to use? Will she be untying his shoelaces while he is mixing paint for an art lesson he's about to teach? Wherever she is, any adult in the vicinity needs to make sure they aren't carrying anything that may spill, because the chances are she'll get under their feet and something will go flying. The problem with the space invader is that she's fearless! She'll happily trot up to anyone and just stand there until she's knocked over. You almost need to attach a bell to her so you have some idea where the hell she is!

The affection shown by the space invader is genuine. She has a great affinity for being around people and could almost be recognised as a class pet, purring away and hoping to get an adult's attention. She just likes people, which can be slightly annoying when another three or four children join in the game, and a teacher finds themselves startled by a collection of children standing next to them, staring with a rather menacing look as if they were part of Stephen King's *Children of the Corn*. The teacher or TA may do a double-take as they line up, smiling, waiting to pounce for a completely unnecessary mass cuddle.

As the children grow older, their need to show affection to the adults in their class diminishes, almost to the point where they fear being picked on for being a toady. The space invader will struggle to shake the habit and will still follow their teacher around like Little Bo Peep, except this sheep is never lost.

During a class game of tag-rugby, she'll still be shadowing the teacher attempting to referee the match. One teacher of our acquaintance was in full flow officiating, and when attempting to award a try he lifted his hand quickly and caught a particularly enthusiastic space invader in the mouth, giving the little girl a fat lip and the teacher teeth marks in his hand. There was blood a-plenty, and the trained first-aider had the unenviable task of working out which blood was coming from which person. Fortunately, the parents of the child were quite sympathetic to the situation when the teacher informed them that their child was a vampire. They even gave the teacher a pair of plastic Dracula fangs as part of his Christmas present.

Even in her later primary years, the space invader will represent the last bastion of kids that have no regard for personal space and will still love to hug the adults in her class until the final day of Year 6. Not sure the secondary science teacher will appreciate her proximity as he's demonstrating a Bunsen burner, though!

Comedian

Studies crap joke books to ensure he has one for every occasion.

Unlike Billy Big Boll**ks, this kid is actually funny.

His teacher is also partial to a pun. Sometimes it gets rather competitive!

Always cast as the 'comic relief' in school productions.

Once he's learnt a new joke, it'll be repeated plenty of times.

Every Christmas, he receives a brand-new whoopee-cushion in his stocking.

Manages to sneak a slightly rude joke into his talent show performance.

Always stays the right side of the line between cheeky and rude.

Most kids are at least a bit funny. All human offspring have the ability to make others laugh, sometimes on purpose and quite often by accident, but the giggles and laughter during a school day will definitely be a reflection of what the kids get up to or what comes out of their mouths.

This kid, the comedian, is very much a deliberate humorist. A student of comedy, he knows the difference between Russell Brand

and Russ Abbot (I'll let you decide if that's a good thing or not). Yes, he's still a primary-aged child, but there is no doubt that he has the potential to be a successful comedy writer in the future. Unlike Billy Big-Boll**ks (who just blurts out random things to make a scene and laughs at them) he strikes a decent balance between getting on with his work and trying to make others laugh. If he was cranking out jokes all the time, he wouldn't be half as funny and would be potentially twice as annoying.

His greatest gifts are having a wide-ranging vocabulary (for the purpose of delivering top-quality puns) and timing – which is widely appreciated to be the secret of great comedy. The comedian knows when to bust out a rib-tickler and when it may be worth staying quiet. There's no point trying to make the teacher laugh when there's a whole class boll**king in full swing for missing glue-lids. Don't get me wrong, he's desperate to comment that it's a rather 'sticky situation' but the beetroot-red teacher probably would appreciate the interjection. He needs to keep the teacher onside.

He'll have a few jokes ready for certain situations, but rather than deliver them out of context he'll wait as long as he needs to in order to deliver his zinger. If he's got a decent Halloween joke, he recognises it'll be wasted if he blurts it out halfway into Christmas activities. Yes, it means he'll have to wait nearly 11 months, but if the joke is good enough, he'll happily wait for the optimal moment. Proof of this occurs after a cookery lesson with the TA that loves watching *The Great British Bake Off*. They've just made cakes, covered them with tin foil and arrived back in the class. His teacher will make eye contact as he returns and wait for the comedian to start. He talks about how they were going to make cakes, but their plan was 'FOILED again'. The class will groan and laugh in equal measure, but the teacher starts playing along, enquiring what was under the foil, the comedian will reply 'It's got MUFFIN to do with you!' If the joke fails to land, at least he can finish it off with 'oh CRUMBS!'

Around 90 per cent of the staff find him hilarious, although that one time in Miss Nettleton's Year 3 class was a bit of a comedy damp squib. The jokes weren't quite as appreciated ... neither were the impersonations of Miss Nettleton when she accidentally ripped her skirt during geography. Tough crowd! This child is an absolute hoot during school trips. So much so that the driver let him tell jokes for 15 minutes over the bus microphone when they were stuck in traffic coming back from the Roman villa.

As long as he remembers to get all his work done, most teachers will let him keep busting out the funny stuff. Many teachers rely on children like the comedian to keep them ticking along during the day, and the classroom is always a better place for it.

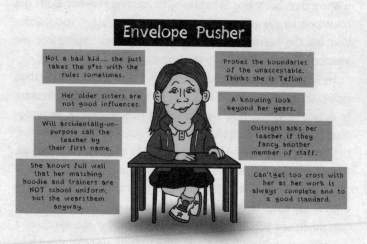

Envelope Pusher

Not a bad kid ... she just takes the p*ss with the rules sometimes.

Her older sisters are not good influences.

Will accidentally-on-purpose call the teacher by their first name.

She knows full well that her matching hoodie and trainers are NOT school uniform, but she wears them anyway.

Probes the boundaries of the unacceptable. Thinks she is Teflon.

A knowing look beyond her years.

Outright asks her teacher if they fancy another member of staff.

Can't get too cross with her as her work is always complete and to a good standard.

Some kids just don't know where the line is. This child, however, knows exactly where the line is ... she just doesn't care!

Let's state from the off that this child is not particularly badly behaved. She works hard, gets her activities done and produces a decent standard of work. If a teacher was tracking her school data, progress or test scores, she'll always be able to reach her expected level and more. Annoyingly, schools rely on children like this to keep Ofsted from paying them a visit. She knows her times tables, remembers to learn her spellings and reads every night. The real issue at the end of the day is she just doesn't think the rules apply to her.

Like a politician caught fiddling their expenses, they totally know what they are doing is wrong, they just didn't expect someone would find out and tell them to stop. If the teacher asks the class to stop talking so they can explain the instructions for the next task, she'll still be chatting away to her neighbour nonchalantly. If she is asked to end her conversation and pay attention just like everyone else, she'll give that look of, 'Oh, you mean me as well?' Even worse, she'll almost roll her eyes as if it's a giant inconvenience for her to delay her chat until break time, but she will do it in a way that irks the teacher rather than completely disrespects them.

One trick that teachers use to check whether children are listening is to ask them to repeat the instructions they have just been given for a task. Usually, a child will apologise for not listening or will respond with completely incorrect information. That's the teacher's way of making sure they listen next time. Unfortunately, you can't pull that trick with this child; if she is asked to repeat the input for the benefit of the rest of the class, she'll reproduce the teacher's instructions ... verbatim!

Verb-what?

Verbatim, it means 'word-for-word'. She'll arrogantly be able to tell the teacher exactly what they were expecting her to have missed while she was chatting away to her pal.

That's frustrating as hell.

Absolutely. Can't catch this kid out with tactics used on mere mortals. If a teacher stands any chance of winning against her, they'd best bring their A-game.

Another issue with the envelope pusher is that she doesn't adhere to school uniform requirements. School staff will politely remind her that certain attire is not appropriate, but I suppose it depends on how strict the school is with wardrobe violations. At the end of the day, she'll take the p*ss so often that many teachers will just give up and not question it any more. Her persistence will be rewarded, sadly, as she is continuously backed up by her parents.

Think of the poor office staff ringing home to say that young Jenny is wearing a bright-pink designer hoodie rather than her school-branded jumper or cardigan. Mum will automatically reply that her previous school tops were lost, ruined in the wash or that Jenny had had a growth spurt and they no longer fit her. Pretty sure her mum would've played the same games when she was at school herself and was equally backed up by her parents if the school took issue with her fashion statements.

The envelope pusher will also sport funky but pristine trainers that need to be worn because her school shoes broke earlier in the term when the class were made to run their 'daily mile' and didn't have time to change their footwear. Putting the blame on the school for ruining her shoes will present another argument to be had with her parents that will no doubt cause more grief, so the trainers reluctantly stay. If they were simple black pumps as replacements they wouldn't stand out so much, but the monstrosities that the envelope pusher insists on wearing wouldn't be out of place being worn by the Spice Girls in the mid-90s. Once again, her fashion choices aren't harming her learning, but it's another thing she seems to be getting away with.

This kid knows how to push buttons, but she's methodical and carries out her dirty deeds diligently. Actively listening in on adults' conversations and regurgitating information that she thinks will make sure her teacher stays on HER good side. When a teacher and TA might be having what they think is a private conversation, our envelope pusher may interject with: 'I didn't think Miss Kay and Mr Davey were still dating!?' In normal circumstances, a child would be admonished for being so impolite and intrusive, but the teacher and TA were quite clearly the source of the gossip so they can hardly ask where the rumour came from. Make no mistake, the envelope pusher has the goods on everyone. She knows which parents have fallen out, when Miss Griffiths' next lesson observation will be and why Sam's mum resigned as chair of the PTA in a huff. Pretty sure she has the investigative skills to work for the British Intelligence Services as a career, although I'm not sure the Official Secrets Act would keep what she uncovers even slightly secret.

One to watch out for, the envelope pusher is not necessarily malicious, but she is highly skilled and potentially dangerous for a teacher's career. You definitely have to get up early in the morning to catch her out. Many teachers will be determined to show her who's boss, but the smart ones often avoid that battle as it's one they may rarely win. Call a truce, early doors, and she may just prove to be an asset.

Muck Magnet

Undiscovered bird poo in his hair.

Slipped in a huge puddle on the way to school. Had to change uniform.

Sunjit chucked a blackberry yoghurt over him after a football argument.

Blue lip from chewing on a handwriting pen.

Mystery brown stain from dinnertime (hopefully gravy).

Leaned in paint and accidentally put a handprint on his top.

Bloody knee and grass stains from lunchtime ruckus. White pumps a write-off!

Tiny Year 1 replacement shorts, odd socks from lost property (including 1996 Aston Villa one).

If you are a parent and you are reading this AND you are the poor soul that does the washing in your household, then you'll appreciate that the muck magnet is the bane of your existence. All primary-age children will have the potential to get a little messy, sure – some rogue glue, a bit of glitter on the jumper or some spag Bol on a white collar. It's a perfectly acceptable fact that mess happens in primary schools; even the most sensible children will sometimes come a cropper in a muddy puddle. This child, however, seems to have the ability to be inexplicably drawn to anything that may render his uniform impossible to clean. At the start of the year, when the new uniform has just been purchased, when families are taking their first-day-back-after-summer photos (with school badge deliberately blurred out for safeguarding) the muck magnet's uniform and hair is pretty much pristine. Creases in trousers and skirts, shiny shoes, neat collars and jumpers almost fresh out of the cellophane. Posted to all and sundry on social media with random friends of friends feeling obliged to give the photo that all-important thumbs up with a comment about 'I can't believe it's been a year since they were in ... (insert year group)'. Within minutes of the photo being snapped, however, the muck magnet will have toothpaste, milk and, inexplicably, a bleach stain on his top.

He seems to almost be in a cartoon or slapstick Chuckle Brothers sketch. If there's something messy nearby, you can guarantee it'll be the muck magnet that will somehow end up covered in it. In the autumn term, this kid will have ruined four pairs of trousers by October – all ripped at the knees and covered in grass stains. As a result, he'll be wearing the shorts that were purchased for the summer term during wintertime. You would think that would put off the young scallywag from destroying his trousers through football-related shenanigans in the first few weeks ... it doesn't!

The muck magnet does Forest School on a Wednesday, and despite being bought some heavy-duty waterproofs and weapons-grade wellies (do they even exist?) to keep his under-clothes usable, he always manages to tread in fox poo, cut his finger on a thorn bush and drown his underpants on the mudslide. It wouldn't be too much of an issue if he had his Forest School activities at the end of the day, but considering his Wednesday session starts at 9:15am, there's a significant chance that he'll be squelching around for the rest of the day in damp socks and crusty underpants.

In the winter months he will come home with muddy shoes EVERY SINGLE DAY! With snow days being such a novelty in the UK, if the school stays open, you can bet he'll be on the field launching snow-balls at anyone and everyone, to the point where there is no longer any snow on the ground. There's the mixture of slush, mud and muddy slush, which will no doubt still be turned into what he thinks constitutes a snowball and launched at his fellow snowball fighters. Definitely not a good day for anyone to wear a cream or white jacket!

The final weeks building up to Christmas will be mostly joyful for the children in his class, but the calendars, cards and crêpe-paper monstrosities will mean that there is every chance his jumper will look like something so covered in paint, glue, tinsel, sequins and glitter that it wouldn't look out of place in Elton John's wardrobe or on display in the Tate Modern. I hope Santa brings him a change of outfit for Christmas!

Spring term and the freshly cut grass will somehow find its way onto this lad's uniform. Despite being warned not to go onto the school field until after the Easter holidays, the grass stains this term are significantly harder to get out of his uniform. The person in charge of uniform in his household is at the point of wondering if it will cost more to buy hardcore stain remover or to just buy new clothes. Either way, it's going to cost a packet.

During the summer, the weather should be drier and therefore the possibility of mud should be minimal. Don't worry, the muck magnet will find a way to get messy – especially as there will be athletics, rounders and cricket on the field, he's bound to discover something. Whether that's chewing on fountain-pen cartridges, rubbing out his class whiteboard on his shirt, ready-mix paint explosions or just pasta sauce from his rushed school dinner, the jumper is off, so the school polo shirt is fair game.

These kids are usually rather likeable and energetic folks, but they seem to just have an affinity for getting covered in filth, grime, grot and mess without a care in the world!

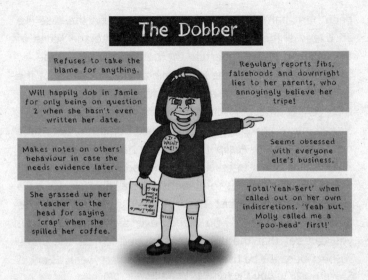

There's always one child that just can't help themselves; they are completely preoccupied with everyone else's activities and affairs.

Someone else's business is apparently HER business, and by golly gosh, goodness me, she is going to stick her nose in. If her own behaviour was perfect she'd at least have the moral high ground, but the fact that she tells on other children over tiny things while causing a world of problems at her end should tell you everything you need to know.

If Peter doesn't push his chair under the table before lunchtime, the dobber will let you know. If Tilly forgets to put her book away, the dobber will report it. If Isaac drops pencil sharpenings on the floor, funnily enough you'll be hearing about it straight away. Whether it's a minor error or a massive misdemeanour, rather than checking who has been hurt, harmed or upset, the dobber is on the case like an overly enthusiastic news reporter. First to the scene of the incident, she is reporting the details of what happened to all and sundry. As she keeps explaining the nature of the issue, she will add more and more details to the point where the event is unrecognisable. Rumours of a grazed knee have turned into a broken leg. A small head bump has become a near decapitation. A slip into a puddle has now required the RNLI to be called to rescue the poor soul lost at sea. With every tale she decides to embellish there must always be a culprit and blame must be attributed. Poor Richard was nowhere near Rosina who tripped over a skipping rope, but you can bet that the dobber has framed him as the prime suspect because he used a skipping rope, last week ... once! She'd make a great tabloid journalist!

She once ran up to a teacher because somebody had stolen Abigail's shoes and she started describing how cruel and unkind the person who did it must be. Abigail's parents were obviously concerned that their child came home wearing her PE trainers. Pretty understandable to expect your children to go to school wearing shoes and to return home at the end of the day wearing the same shoes. The problem is, the dobber was protesting a little too much, and with the help of the school site manager, a quick review of CCTV made it very apparent that the shoes were hidden behind the PE equipment shed. Closer inspection showed that there was a child in particular that was responsible for the gross act of footwear thievery and hiding the evidence. Funnily enough, the culprit looked incredibly similar to the dobber ... BUSTED!

Of course, the dobber's response was predictable as hell when confronted with the proof of her actions:

'Yeah, but Sienna told me to do it!'

Dinner Monster

Always hungry. If he doesn't tell you, his stomach definitely will!

Will pretty much eat anything. If it's edible, he'll have it.

Offers to return mugs to the staffroom purely to see if there are any biscuits worth nicking.

Perfect child to take on a school trip. Will hoover up remaining packed lunches to avoid waste.

Has cravings for the most random culinary combinations.

His rather active digestive system does require plenty of trips to the lavatory.

Always asks for seconds ... if possible, thirds as well.

Packs extra breaktime snacks just in case. Why wouldn't he?

There are some children that cannot wait for dinner times.

Is this another pop at me?

No, but you were probably one of them. You used to love dinner times, though. I could hear your stomach rumbling from our Year 6 classroom when you were in third year infants ... it was that loud! I mean, you probably weren't that enthusiastic after Dad decided to switch from school dinners to packed lunches.

I was bloody fuming! Especially towards the end of the week when I was clearly getting the last scrapings of the fish paste jar in my

sandwiches and crap-flavoured Nik Naks! The Nice 'N' Spicy and Rib 'N' Saucy flavours had already gone to you and Ryan on Monday and Tuesday. You know you're the least-favourite child when you are on the scampi and lemon ones.

Aside from Adam's bitterness towards 'the lunchbox years', it's pretty obvious that he could be considered a dinner monster.

The most annoying thing about the dinner monster is their amazing metabolism. Some teachers avoid the staffroom in case they accidentally smell some chocolate cake and put on half a pound. Seriously, this kid can process carbs like a Premier League footballer or elite-level athlete. They could turn up to the buffet at Pizza Hut, eat twice their body weight (including garlic bread and salad) and manage to store it all in their *hollow legs. (*Science geeks, we know this is impossible.) Potentially there's a career in competitive eating for this child, although he'd be that annoying person that stands out a mile because of his svelte physique, not looking anything like the rest of the competition. His metabolism may slow down as he gets older, but for now he's an eating machine.

Primary-aged children can be the fussiest eaters in the world. Parents are often concerned about their child's dietary habits and whether they'll be OK popping to a friend's house for tea. Some children will only be comfortable eating a certain type of pizza, shape of chips and brand of baked beans. You'll never have this issue with a dinner monster. If it's on a plate and edible, it's down the hatch and he's ready to get back to playing Lego, football or on his Nintendo. He'll probably have indigestion and impressive farts afterwards, but at least his plate is clean.

If the school's Modern Foreign Languages (MFL) co-ordinator decides that there should be a food-tasting experience related to the language the children have been learning about, then you can bet that the dinner monster is game. Picture the scene: there's a French banquet sprawled across a few school tables featuring a range of meats and cheeses for the children to try. Most kids will give it a go, but after one sniff of Gruyère they are sticking to the pieces of baguette for the rest of the session. As you'll be able to guess by now, the dinner monster has no qualms about trying the lot! Ten minutes later and he's already sampled half a pig plus enough Brie, Roquefort, Boursin and Emmental to clog his bowels for a week.

To honour our friend the dinner monster, we need a quick look at our Top Ten primary school dinners:

10 - Purely for balance and making healthy choices, I am going for the mixed veg side of peas, sweetcorn and diced carrot. It is number 10 for a reason: we needed one of our five-a-day on the plate and technically this was three with the combo, so it is there. I am not happy it is in the list, but we shall move on.

9 - Jacket potato – Always an option but never anyone's first choice, and it's all about the filling for me. Beans and cheese are always top of the pile, tuna mayo is bottom. My favourite part was the hard bottom of the potato skin.

8 - Fish fingers – another standard lunch option, usually on a Friday. Alongside chips and beans, it was a standard hearty meal.

7 - Unidentified meat pie – one for us Northerners. No one ever knew what the meat was from as it was always served as meat pie. Now, 14 years into teaching and I am still no

wiser, but when it's drowned in gravy I'm happy as Larry (unless Larry is the name of the mystery creature the meat came from – he'll be less keen).

6 - The veggie option – the cheese whirl. Decent substitute for anyone who didn't like the meat option, could also be served as a cheese flan.

5 - Bangers and mash – Still a staple meal for me as an adult. Were the sausages as overcooked and wrinkly as my nan's fingers? Yes. Was the mash so suspiciously smooth you questioned how much potato was actually in it? Sure. Was the mash perfectly scooped onto your plate like ice cream? Absolutely. But am I complaining? No!

4 - The turkey dinosaurs – Was Steven Spielberg inspired to create one of the biggest-grossing films of all time – *Jurassic Park* – after tucking into a plate of these delicious turkey dinosaurs? Well, no, but you can't tell me he'd turn these down.

3 - Potato smileys – Nothing turned your frown upside down like these bad boys. Curly fries were close, but these just trump it for me. Picture the scene: you've just entered the dining room after spending some time on the playground, you're fuming as if you were out first during 'bulldog'. You spot in the corner of your eye a tray of these smiling faces and suddenly life makes sense once again.

2 - Turkey Twizzlers – You can never keep a good Twizzler down – back from the brink and making a huge comeback in 2020. This was a different level back in the day, until Jamie Oliver ruined all our childhoods, but now they are back, and we can all get that hit of nostalgia as nothing tastes more like the 90s than some undercooked Twizzlers.

1 - My ultimate school dinner must be school pizza. A masterpiece I have tried all my adult life to recreate but to no avail.

Where some teachers get into this career to make a difference, others do it for the holidays, for me it was to rekindle my love with the delicious school pizza. Square pizza on the tray, especially the middle pieces oozing with so much cheese you had nightmares for days.

Well, from what goes in, to what comes out ...

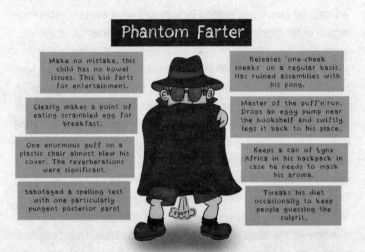

Phantom Farter

Make no mistake, this child has no bowel issues. This kid farts for entertainment.

Clearly makes a point of eating scrambled egg for breakfast.

One enormous guff on a plastic chair almost blew his cover. The reverberations were significant.

Sabotaged a spelling test with one particularly pungent posterior parp!

Releases 'one-cheek sneaks' on a regular basis. Has ruined assemblies with his pong.

Master of the puff'n'run. Drops an eggy pump near the bookshelf and swiftly legs it back to his place.

Keeps a can of Lynx Africa in his backpack in case he needs to mask his aroma.

Tweaks his diet occasionally to keep people guessing the culprit.

Toot!

Children have many talents. Plenty that should be put to good use and celebrated, and some hidden ones that can be encouraged to help them to reach their full potential. This child's talent should never be encouraged and certainly not celebrated. This is the class phantom farter! We are in no way mocking a child with constant tummy issues, because the phantom farter is perfectly able to control himself in the bottom burp department; he just chooses to use his malodorous flatulence for comedy purposes. If Billy

Big-Boll**ks lets out a mighty guffaw, he's doing it for maximum effect and hopefully (in his mind) a round of applause. The phantom farter is more interested in watching the response to his work. Almost like Heath Ledger's The Joker in the Batman film *The Dark Knight*, the phantom farter will cause chaos purely for his own enter-tainment and enjoy the reaction of everyone else. Michael Caine's Alfred comments: 'Some men just want to watch the world burn ...', and while a burning world is not his intention, the phantom farter will usually drop a particularly vicious air biscuit then wait in antici-pation as his classmates react one by one to a face full of unpleas-antness!

We've used 'he' and 'his' so far purely because many of the school farts we've been hit with have come from boys, but make no mistake, girls toot just as much; they just seem to be less proud of them! The moral of the story is, don't just assume that the child guffing and legging it is a lad, there will be plenty of wind-ninjas that are female. In fact, teachers, ask yourself if the pong-meister in your class is actually a child, or could it be sweet little old Mrs Jeffries the TA? It's probably best not to walk around smelling elderly members of staff, but don't rule her out of the list of possible suspects.

Whoever the class phantom farter is, you know that they take great pride in causing a room to smell like the undercovers of the bed that the grandparents from *Charlie and the Chocolate Factory* shared. And those old codgers mostly lived on cabbage soup, so you can imagine the pong! However bad the smell is, though, the phantom farter needs to ensure that he (or she) knows their limits. Regularly letting off toot parps after a decent portion of fruit salad at lunchtime may result in the very-much-dreaded 'shart' (for the uninitiated, it's a mixture of a fart with a bit of sh*t in it) and after years of successful undercover cheese-cutting, it would be disas-trous to reveal their true identity by waddling to the toilet like John Wayne because they were touching cloth!

I swear I've written about this character to see how many euphemisms for breaking wind I could sneak into this chapter. Anyway, kudos to the phantom farter, your epic skills are clearly well practised, just please don't do it when I've got my headteacher observing me. I'm not sure my lesson on coordinates would survive if you chose to stink out the joint with a gas deposit of epic proportions.

And, dear readers, if you think this part is a little childish, don't worry, we've got an entire chapter dedicated to toilet humour later in the book!

So that's our rogues' gallery; just a little whistlestop tour of some of the characters you may have met at primary school. However you behaved at school, and whether you made a positive contribution or were a bloomin' nightmare, there are plenty of people that never grow out of the traits they had as a child. Some will use them to their advantage, and some will end up on the wrong side of the law.

Ask yourself these questions: What were you like at school? Were you a sensible Sally? A dobber? I doubt you'll admit to being the phantom farter, but I suppose that's all part of the mystique. Well, that and the smell!

Ask any teacher or school staff member for their funniest story from the classroom and you can guarantee that many will tell a tale of something inappropriate that a child has brought into school to share during show and tell, or (even better) something that has had to be confiscated. So many readers told us that one of their favourite parts of *Put a Wet Paper Towel On It* involved the strange things children have proudly showcased during show and tell sessions. The reality is, we barely scratched the surface, there are literally thousands of stories that school staff have shared with us containing everything you can possibly imagine, so we thought we needed to dedicate a whole chapter to the weird, worrying and disgusting objects that children have brought onto the school premises. Not only will this chapter scare many parents when they realise that the secret drawer with Mum's special toys isn't actually that secret, we will also be sharing some very surprising verbal contributions from their little darlings.

So, if you haven't read our first book (again, really?), during a show and tell session students are encouraged to either 'show' something they have made, been rewarded or discovered, but also share some good, important news – which constitutes the 'tell'. And you would not believe how willing primary school children are to reveal the most embarrassing and disturbing things about what Mum and Dad get up to. It makes for an interesting parents' evening when you can put a face to the stories the children have revealed. This chapter is definitely a little bit of a cheeky one, so perhaps don't listen to this section on the audiobook during a family road trip to Devon, as there's potential sauciness afoot. You have been warned!

First of all, we will get the most obvious one out of the way. Of all the stories we have received, one of the most embarrassing (yet strangely common) objects that has been brought into school is a vibrator. If I had a penny for every story we've had that featured a child bringing in Mummy's special toy to show, I would have enough money to buy a really big ... sandwich. We have yet to have a show and tell where children know what the object actually is – they always think it is something else, like a fidget toy, laser pen, a lipstick, wobbly pen or a device that is really good for headaches (which, you know, isn't far off), and even a weapon – given that one child brought in a double-edged dildo with the sole intention of hitting his brother in the head with it. My favourite description was a child who brought his mum's 'lightsaber'. He was only five and had found it under her bed! 'It lights up and spins round and everything,' were the child's words, I understand.

Now, I believe I was very naive to the clearly booming sex-toy industry after seeing how many incidents there have been where children have brought these in, but nothing compares to this story a teacher shared:

As a student teacher many moons ago, I was on placement in a lovely little village Catholic school with a real old-school-type teacher. If you imagine Mrs May, the teacher from the Biff, Chip and Kipper books, she was like her in human form. The short white perm, pearl necklace, jumper and skirt – you can just picture her, very religious. She was lovely but was also very stern. The children knew that she was never to be crossed, but she created such a loving and caring atmosphere in her class and I learned so much from her.

But I will never forget this fateful day during show and tell. I was busy at the back of the class marking books from the lesson I had taught that day, while the teacher started show and tell after promising the class all week. A boy had brought in his mother's vibrator and was sharing it with the rest of the class. I was expecting the teacher to immediately stop the child in their tracks; however, to my shock, the teacher indulged the child and started asking questions. The child had explained that the massive, silver, shining affair was in fact a massager. The old-school class teacher then proceeded to test the so-called 'massager' on her own neck while commenting on how relaxing and soothing it was. I felt so bad I didn't intervene, but it was one of those moments where I couldn't actually believe she was being serious, plus as a student teacher I didn't want to come across as undermining the teacher. It was only after we had dismissed the class that I had explained to the teacher what the item actually was. The colour drained from her face, and she was apologising profusely while panicking about how to go about reporting it to the headteacher. I would have been more worried about whether the 'massager' the teacher had been rubbing all over her neck was in fact disinfected and clean after the last use.

I think this is my favourite story involving a vibrator.

You have a favourite?

Erm, well, my favourite show and tell story involving a vibrator, purely for the fact that it shows that as teachers we are always learning. When children have brought sex toys in for show and tell, there is the initial shock followed by an awkward explanation and excuse as to why we need to put it away and move swiftly on. Then comes the uncomfortable phone call home and even this can lead to more embarrassment. This sort of occurrence isn't exclusively for naive primary-aged children, however ...

I used to be a Head of Year and one of my lads in Year 8 brought in a vibrator that he kept showing to all of his mates, and which upset the sensibilities of a number of the other staff. I rang his mother to let her know what had been going on. She was all 'Oh, that's terrible, I'll come into school for a meeting to discuss his behaviour, etc.' then suddenly stopped and exclaimed, 'Oh, by the way, it's not mine, mind!!' Turned out that it belonged to his older sister who had just left our Sixth Form the year before. Can't imagine how mortified she must have been to have both her parents know she had a vibrator (Dad came with Mum to the meeting to collect it) as well as most of her ex-teachers.

What a whirlwind. And if you thought that was bad, this one is another cracker:

A child once brought in a vibrator. They had taken it out of their bag and decided to chase other children around the playground screaming, 'Expelliarmus!' The child in question was going through a Harry Potter-obsessed phase at the time. I had to confiscate the purple wand and report it to my headteacher. My headteacher at the time told me to ring his mum about it. It was the most embarrassing phone call I've ever made. She denied it was hers. I was trying to be understanding but continued to explain that the contraband in question was obviously inappropriate and this can't happen again. The parent continued to protest their innocence to the point where they became rather agitated and ended the phone call. I put it down to the situation being rather embarrassing until the child then told me his friend had given it to him, so I rang his mum too, assuming it was now hers, but there was no answer. So I handed her the vibrator at the end of the day. She was mortified and told me it wasn't hers! So, I was back to square one. I gave it back to the original child and later found out it belonged to his grandma!

That's not the only story where grandparents have turned out to have a lot more going on than you'd have thought:

I found an Ann Summers catalogue in a Reception child's book bag. A week later I found a pair of pink fluffy hand-cuffs. I had to speak to Mum privately at the end of the day, she was mortified but explained that the handcuffs weren't hers, they were her own mother's. She exclaimed,

'She had a sleepover at granny's house!' I thought, cool granny!

Cool indeed, but I don't think I know whether my parents have pink fluffy handcuffs? I certainly wouldn't want to know either. Pink fluffy handcuffs seem to be another popular feature in many households and are clearly not hidden well enough. They often find their way into school, where children will use them to chain their peers to the radiator in the corridor. To be fair, if you're not going to walk sensibly down the corridor, justice will be served.

If, as a parent, you ever wonder why your underwear seems to magically disappear from the washing pile, chances are your darling little cherub has decided to bring it along to school.

I had to confiscate a pair of silky knickers that turned out to be the child's mother's. He loved the texture against his face and I caught him snuggled up in the book corner with a lovely pair of bloomers!! The conversation at the end of the day with the parents was priceless!

I suspect the conversation went something like, 'Where did you get them from? I really need something a lot softer on my skin as these cotton ones are chafing my legs rotten!'

Other similar interesting items that teachers have had to quickly confiscate include: cock rings, a bell that said 'ring for sex', a wind-up willy that the Reception child thought was a pink aeroplane, a stress reliever in the shape of a boob, a g-string found because a child was limping when it was lodged in their wellies, a tube of KY Jelly that the Year 6 pupil was using like lip balm, condoms that were being blown up like balloons in the toilets and a gimp mask.

A GIMP MASK? What was their safe word?

Now a staple of most show and tell sessions will be children sharing medals or trophies that they might have won in their extra-curricular clubs, such as football, dancing, swimming, etc. But you can imagine the shock when a child brought in some plastic trophies for show and tell. Turns out they were his mother's 'Ann Summers' party rewards, with a few obscene phrases on. I can't imagine teachers and fellow students asking the usual questions when it comes to medals, 'How long have you been doing it?' 'Do you practise a lot?' 'How often do you do it?'

One benefit of advances in technology is that everything is now becoming cloud-based. Only a few years ago, everything from lesson plans to end of year reports would be stored on a USB stick. Alongside the ID badge, the USB stick was a staple of most teachers' lanyards, in fact, I reckon it still is. They were a technician's nightmare as they were a cesspool for viruses to make their way onto the school server and cause mayhem. Teachers who were still downloading 50 Cent's *Get Rich or Die Tryin'* album on Limewire were prime suspects for who infected the school laptops with another Trojan horse virus. But it wasn't just viruses that USB sticks caused pandemonium with.

A colleague of mine had a child bring in a USB stick of photos of his daddy, who was away in the army. She assured him she'd let him show some photos at the end of the day. As promised, at the end of the day my colleague inserted the USB into her laptop to show photos of 'Daddy being a soldier', but in reality were photos of Daddy standing to attention in a very different way. Needless to say, my colleague was so relieved she hadn't put the interactive whiteboard on yet ...

If you're wondering if the child's father was in fact a soldier or this was a bit of role play, it was a cheap dressing-up outfit from Smiffy's.

If you thought that was bad, there was a teacher who had been applying for a number of different jobs when they finally landed an interview at a dream school. They had impressed in the interview and had to then be observed teaching a class for 30 minutes. Upon receiving the instructions, they had prepared a lesson, and on entering the classroom put their USB stick into the teacher's laptop. When the USB drive loaded up, it was pretty clear that the image thumbnails in the folder were rather graphic photos of the teacher and their partner being intimate. The candidate was clueless to it but alongside their English lesson PowerPoint were images of his partner's parts and his bits. Needless to say, when the headteacher spotted those thumbnails in the observation, the candidate didn't end up getting the job.

When it comes to residentials, children will need to bring a suitcase or holdall for their clothes and belongings for the couple of days away. While away on a residential, one teacher was being contacted by the school office to say that a worried parent had been calling the school non-stop to say that something very important had been placed in the holdall that their child had taken to the trip and was insisting on driving to come and pick it up. The teacher investigated only to discover that in the bag were several rolled-up bank notes which at a glance looked like around £10,000. It was like a scene out of *Breaking Bad*. That was all that was shared, so I don't know what happened after that, whether the school allowed the dad to come and pick it up or they reported it and allowed the police to sort it out. But that child could have had a field day at the gift shop with that amount of cash. That's a hell of a lot of bouncy balls and pencil sharpeners!

And that's not the only criminal-related story: a kilo bag of weed was found in a Reception child's backpack. On another occasion, when cannabis was confiscated from another child, the parent, when informed, was more upset that he wasn't getting the drugs back than his son being permanently excluded. So here's another story that shows how little teachers know about the world of drugs:

Many moons ago, a head (now retired) accepted a gift of a plant from a child. This plant was proudly displayed in the head's office, just on the window overlooking the playground. It remained there until a member of staff pointed out that it was probably best to keep that 'type' of plant out of school and confiscated it from the head's office!

Class A drugs were innocently brought in by a child in a makeup bag that she'd been using as a pencil case. She was using her pencils to shade in a diagram when she shouted, 'Miss, I've found my mum's headache powder. She hides it from my dad sometimes so he doesn't use it up on her.' Pencil case with a bag of white powder and pencils were confiscated. That was a fun day. Safeguarding referral, police, forensics and an arrest. So sad, but up there with the most memorable items I've confiscated.

I had to confiscate a ring from a five-year-old. Turns out he'd taken all his mother's rings to give to his friends as 'ThunderCats rings of power!' It took a few days to retrieve them all.

I can just imagine the teacher trying to collect the rings like Thanos in *The Avengers*. In Year 2, one child brought their mum's diamond engagement ring in to give to his girlfriend. The mum was very relieved to get it back.

Now for the more random and questionable objects that have featured in a show and tell session.

A child opened her pencil case and pulled out a positive pregnancy test. She had no idea what it was. When I passed it on to Mum that afternoon, she was baffled at first then swore loudly and gave the name of her eldest daughter!

Two Tampons that were worn by a six-year-old as a pair of earrings.

A bag of hair that had been shaved from the child's dead cat.

A universal projector remote – genius kids kept switching everyone's whiteboards off.

A student was eating raw OXO cubes in my lesson, and even though I asked him to put them away he carried on, so I had to confiscate them.

A snowball. It had been hidden in the child's drawer for show and tell at the end of the week. The child was devastated when they opened the drawer to see a puddle of water.

I suppose it created a perfect learning opportunity for changing states of matter, though.

A child came in with their dad's teeth for show and tell.

I wonder if the child was chattering away about them, and thoughts for poor Dad who had to go the whole day toothless.

A child brought in an unspent World War I hand grenade to show and tell. The bomb squad had to do a controlled explosion over on the field.

Other weapons include:

A ball-bearing gun that had to be locked away until the police came for it.

A bear trap, which I hope wasn't brought in because the class were reading Michael Rosen's classic We're Going on a Bear Hunt.

An unexploded World War II mortar, which again resulted in a visit from the bomb squad.

A live bullet a Year 5 had found while making a den in the woods the evening before. A quick call and 15 minutes later two very large armed police confirmed the bullet I'd been throwing around was indeed a live NATO-issue bullet. Needless to say, we didn't get to keep it.

Nunchucks. Darling pupil was about to go on a D of E trip. Had to explain that the 'pen knife' suggestion in the kit list didn't mean 'weapon of choice'.

But I think some of my favourites involve a range of different animals, both dead and alive. I have to admit that I am not great with animals myself and I am lucky to say these have never happened to me, as I would not have handled these situations with as much grace as the teachers involved did.

My colleague once confiscated a dead squirrel that a boy was pushing around in a role-play pram.

A stick insect that a Year 5 pupil had transported to school in his glasses case.

A backpack full of five-week-old Persian kittens! A Reception child's family cat had kittens and I'd said how much I like kittens. She brought them in so I could pick one.

The weirdest thing a child brought into my classroom was when a five-year-old snuck a pet ferret in with her. I noticed it 30 minutes into the school day when we were gathered on the carpet. She was a bit fidgety and I noticed her school jumper moving about. She denied there was anything there at first and said it was her tummy rumbling! She later admitted she'd brought her pet to school so it wasn't lonely. Speedy phone call to parent who unfortunately informed us they were over an hour away in a business meeting! I had to improvise so we had a lesson about what makes a good school pet. Needless to say, I made sure ferrets weren't on the list!

A child once brought in a snake in their PE bag.

Another hid a snail in their swimming costume to take to the pool.

A hedgehog. She'd found it on the school field at lunchtime and smuggled it into my class wrapped in her scarf so she could take it home and keep it as a pet. I teach secondary. She was 14.

One of my friends who is a secondary school teacher had a student beckon her over and show her a baby marmoset monkey she'd got stashed down her top that she was hand-rearing.

A dead shark they caught while fishing with Dad. I've also had to confiscate a dead bat.

Live worms! It was carpet time in Reception. One of our boys was sitting quietly, paying attention, while a couple of worms wriggled out of his trouser pocket. He claimed he didn't know how they got there.

An imaginary bird in a cage. He went and hung it on his peg to wait for him until playtime.

My son's headteacher rescued the family hamster from my son as he had taken it to school in his pocket. That was a pretty interesting conversation I had in the headteacher's office as he struggled to keep a straight face.

Now the next story I have to say you need to take with a pinch of salt, as it is one that has been submitted numerous times and feels almost urban legend. I even remember this story floating around when I was at school, but I will share it nonetheless:

In the 1970s, Paignton Zoo only had a low wall around the penguin enclosure. When they got back from the trip, an irate parent phoned the school to say she had a penguin in her bath! Child's excuse was, it was sitting on its own and was lonely. He popped it into his rucksack and it was quiet in the dark. School got banned from the zoo.

So that is the show part of the chapter done, and if you haven't already been sick or taken a break to compose yourself we will now move on to the tells. Let's just say after reading this you will never trust a child with any sort of secret; they are the biggest gossips and the most unreliable sources of information. That is why the thought of Ofsted inspectors basing so much of their inspections on speaking to children about what they learned a year ago sends nothing but shivers down the spine of any adult that works in a school.

Here are things children have said — or should I say over-shared — that have revealed a little too much about what happens behind closed doors.

Way back in the 80s, a nursery child was going to have a medically needed circumcision. The next day he was a bit worried about going into hospital. We'd been all bright and positive about it and said he could open the door to the parents at the end of the morning (very coveted job!). He flung open the door, saw his dad amongst all the other parents and yelled, 'I'm not worried about my willy now, Dad, and Mum said you had the same operation!'

A Reception child brought in a lovely colourful picture for me. As I held it up for the other children to admire, I realised it was drawn on the back of her grandad's bail conditions.

A Year 1 child came to school in floods of tears. 'My daddy's gone to prison.' It turned out he was the prison chaplain!

'My mum won a beauty contest at the weekend,' said one of my pupils. His mum wasn't known for her looks so I asked which one. 'The owner looks like their dog competition.'

'Aww, what dog have you got?'

'A bulldog.'

'Daddy, a doctor, was fixing Mummy's sore tummy on the kitchen table and she was making a lot of noise.'

'You know my dad ... he's ever so funny. When he's on nights, he leaves a cucumber in Mum's bed.'

My child proudly announced to his classmates one day that 'Mummy did a trump in the bath that was so loud it made all the lights downstairs shake!' The worst part was that I was the TA in his class at the time, standing in the back corner of the classroom, washing the paint trays ... waiting for the ground to swallow me up.

About ten years ago, a Reception child said: 'My daddy is having his tubes tied today because Mummy is sick of him making babies fall out of her.' I will never forget that one.

During circle time: 'Me and Mam came back from the caravan early because she walked into the bedroom and Dad had her clothes on.'

A Year 1 child: 'My daddy has broken his leg. He jumped out a window.'

'Oh, dear, was there a fire?' I enquired.

'No, his girlfriend's husband came home.'

In my very first job talking about the 'people you live with' one Year 5 boy tells the class he's got a new dad. Goes on to say he's great, he has tickets for the football, a SEGA

Mega Drive (it was more than 20 years ago!) and he's called Steve. Another boy in the class piped up, 'He's good. We've had him.'

I thought the child in question had been off for the previous two weeks with badly infected chicken pox. I asked if they felt better when I took the register. 'What's chinkinpops? I've been Butlin's with me nan, Miss.' They then looked horrified and loudly exclaimed, 'Shit, that was supposed to be a secret.'

'My daddy has gone to hospital today ... he's got these things hanging out his bottom.'

"My daddy has a shed in the garden. It's always really warm in there. Lots of his friends come round to buy his special plants.'

Year 2 child: 'We went to a wedding on Saturday and we were late home because my dad got his thing stuck in his zip and had to go to hospital!'

'The man who brought me to school today was Nick. That's one of Mummy's boyfriends. There's another man called Jack. He's Mummy's other boyfriend.'

'My mummy is not Daddy's friend any more because Daddy had a sleepover at Bob's mummy's house.' (Both children were in the same class.)

A little boy today (Year 1) walked in during the register (so all is quiet and focused) and I said, 'Oh hello, are you feeling better?' His response was, 'I wasn't ill, I just pooed when I farted!' And continued to put his coat on his peg.

'My daddy dries his bum with a hairdryer!'

It certainly seems like the dads are the ones who get the brunt of the oversharing. It truly is never a dull moment when you are teaching and this chapter has certainly proved that point.

As we know, teaching is hard but incredibly rewarding, and when we take away all the crappy paperwork, the time spent with children can be a real gift. However, at the end of the academic year or before Christmas teachers may well be given a present or gift as a token of appreciation. I want to make it clear that teachers will always appreciate gifts but they will never expect them. Although, one thing I would say from experience is to maybe just drop subtle hints. In my NQT year, I ended up with 20-plus bottles of wine. I don't drink wine – in fact, I hate it. I think I still have some of those bottles in my cupboard somewhere. The next year, I just dropped a couple of subtle hints that my tipple of choice is beer. You know the odd maths question might be along the lines of, 'If Mr P had 12 beers, which he really likes, and drinks 11 beers after the Ofsted visit, how many beers will he have left?' It worked a treat; my Christmas break was fully stocked. If any parents are ever wondering what present teachers tend to like, my answer would always be … alcohol. While 'world's greatest teacher' mugs are great and when you get your first one it feels like a rite of passage in your teaching career, that novelty soon wears off. I've been spoiled with gifts in the past. One of my favourites was the summer when I was getting married, all the parents in the class got together and gave me a load of dollars for spending money for my honeymoon. It was class.

We have also received numerous examples of more unusual and unique gifts, so here are some of our favourites:

When my colleague was going on maternity leave, she was given the gift of a DVD of the birth of a little girl in her class.

That is a no-win situation for the teacher; surely you couldn't bring yourself to watch that, but then at the next parents' evening things could get quite awkward. 'So did you manage to watch the DVD we gave you?' 'Erm, not yet, I've been quite busy.' Or 'Yeah, a riveting watch and can I check is everything OK down there? Have the stitches sorted themselves out? Are we all healed and fixed up?'

A child took a spoonful of ice cream from their freezer and carried it all the way to school for my Christmas present.

One can only hope it wasn't chocolate-flavoured ice cream, otherwise that would be panic stations as the melted brown liquid was presented to the teacher: 'Here's your Christmas present!'

A plastic analogue clock with the student's face as the clock face!

I don't know how many TIMES I have to say it, time after time – that wouldn't be the best gift. One thing is for sure, the teacher wouldn't be clock-watching. They say time is precious but I am not sure it would be.

A gold model of a rocking horse with a bear riding it covered in gold glitter. I 'think' it was designed to go on a child's grave. When I thanked the mum for my lovely gift, she had no idea what I was talking about.

You know it is bad when the staff can compare random presents they've received: breast-firming cream, a six-pack of Müller Corners, a dress that was three sizes too big and a mother's actual, real jewellery. That list can only be topped if it was followed with 'and that was only for the male members of staff'.

A half-used Mum's Rollette deodorant stick!

A box of Roses. But when I opened it, the child had eaten them all except the coffee ones (which is bang out of order, I mean, what sort of mug eats the coffee ones?). *To add insult to injury, they left the empty wrappers. Also in the box was a note from the young man saying the temptation was too great and, seeing as it was Christmas, could I use a bit of Christmas spirit and not tell his mum?*

With my teacher hat on I can only be proud of the fact that the child in question threw in the word temptation. That would be slap bang in the middle of my vocabulary display on my working wall.

Teeth. Yes, real teeth. The little girl in Year 3 said, 'Did you find the special gift I've hidden in your handbag?'

Thank you! What am I supposed to do with actual human bones? It's not like you can put that on your teacher desk and look like you're a serial killer from *The Silence of the Lambs* and you just keep trophies of your victims. Although, for behaviour management it could be a winner.

'Mr P, what are those things on your desk?'

'These are the teeth of some of my last class who didn't bother to underline their title!'

Two rolls of toilet paper, environmentally friendly and in beautiful packaging!

Which, if it was gifted around March 2020, would have been brilliant, as one of the most sought-after items at the start of the first lockdown.

Then there are so many examples of gifts that are just blatant burns towards the teacher.

Anti-ageing night cream! I was in my twenties.

But that is what teaching does to you, ages you quicker than Robin Williams in the film *Jack*.

One year I received 15 tubes of hand cream from a class of 32 children. I don't think I have particularly dry hands!

Something like that would surely make you paranoid, just constantly staring at your hands wondering why half your class felt compelled to buy you hand cream.

Not sure if it is the mug I received from a parent with their child's face on or the mug with my face on that was taken from the school website. Both a little creepy, if I am honest, but both gratefully received.

First of all, every teacher knows that the mug shot taken for your teacher lanyard or website is the worst picture of you in existence. I regularly get asked by the children who the person is on my ID badge, and when I tell them it is me, they look confused, fully believing it is a different person. This in itself doesn't make any sense; like I would be walking around school with a picture of a different person on my lanyard? Secondly, if we are ever given a gift that features a picture of a child from the class we can never use it as we know we would then be accused of favouritism – and everyone knows teachers never have favourites 😊.

A car stereo with the wires hanging out of the back. Although I was very touched, I handed it straight over to the head. Turns out the stereo belonged to one of the kitchen staff who had their car broken into the week before.

A box full of condoms and sex toys for the whole staff. Wow. One can only imagine what the staff meetings must be like at this school!

I think one of the most disgusting gifts that was ever given to a teacher was this one:

I worked abroad at an international school. Most of the pupils were local but were sent to the private school to be taught the English curriculum. I for one wouldn't encourage this – who in their right mind would want a curriculum designed by Michael Gove? Anyway, I am detracting from this horrific and truly scarring gift I received. I was once gifted a bar of soap. I did what anyone would do and gratefully accepted the gift and put it to good use, as did my partner for a good few months. At the next parents' evening, which were more regular as it was a private school, the parent asked if I'd enjoyed the gift I had received. Of course I answered, 'Yes,' to which they replied in broken English with 'Good, it was made from my own breast milk.' I assumed that had been lost in translation and asked her to repeat what she had just said, to which she reiterated the soap was created from her own breast milk. I had been washing myself in one of my parents' tit milk for months. I couldn't believe it; there was no apology or even admission from the parent that it was slightly weird, and I had the most awkward moment of just staring before thanking them once again and moving on to their child's maths target.

Some teachers love show and tell as it's an easy way to kill time, but plenty of them dread the mundane conversations initiated by a rosette for horse riding or another bloody LEGO model. If you're a parent reading this book and want to send something in that will REALLY liven up your child's show and tell session, we wholeheartedly suggest that you do.

Hopefully your inappropriate item will cause a bit of chaos, and you may even end up hearing us sharing it on the podcast!

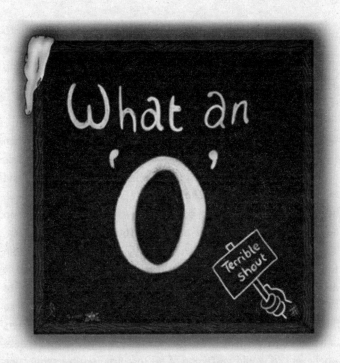

Adam, you're definitely the man to explain this chapter.

Glad to. Have you ever done something really, really ridiculous?

Regularly.

But an error of judgement so embarrassing that everyone is questioning how you manage to put your underpants on in the morning?

Not quite as regularly.

  I mean, these are world-beating-level public mistakes that as soon as the words have left your mouth, you know you've screwed up ... BIG TIME! A great example would be your trip to the cinema to see Sam Mendes's World War I epic, *1917*.

That was a brain fart and a half! I'd gone to the cinema to see the 8:15 showing of this film and as I was waiting outside the screen to be let in after the last showing, a friendly chap asked me, 'Is this *1917*?' I said, 'Sorry pal, this is the 8:15 showing.' What an 'O'!

What an 'O', indeed! Let's start at the origin of this expression. When I was growing up, there was a lad my age who lived in the house opposite, and his name was Simon O'Brien. He has been my friend for over 25 years, but it probably wasn't until we were eventually heading to the same high school that a few of us noticed that Simon had a gift. Now it wasn't like a gift you would want to brag about, like amazing football skills or an outstanding knowledge in a certain subject. Unfortunately for Simon, his gift is opening his mouth or doing something, which results in him making a complete fool of himself or a 'terrible shout', as I like to call it; all harmless but oh so hilarious. By this time, we had nicknamed him O'B (first two letters of his surname O'Brien). The reason why this is important is because whenever O'B would make one of his famously terrible shouts, we would call it an 'O', and this quickly caught on. Every person from every walk of life can make an 'O' – highly embarrassing moments where you want nothing more than the ground to eat you alive.

Before we share some of the absolutely amazing 'O's we have been sent, let's take a moment to hail the Godfather of the 'O', Mr Simon O'Brien himself. Back in 2010, we were sitting around shooting the breeze and talking about our favourite action movie stars. Being a big wrestling fan, we ended up talking about the movies of Dwayne Johnson (aka The Rock, for anyone who has been living under a Dwayne Johnson). O'B then mentioned to me that he had recently watched a cracking film starring The Rock called *The Pacifier*. Being a huge movie buff, I said to good old O'B that I had seen *The Pacifier*, but it was Vin Diesel who was the main star. He said 'Yes I know', so, confused, I replied with, 'But you said it starred The Rock?' To my utter astonishment, he said 'Yes, I know, Vin Diesel is The Rock.' I took a moment to compose myself, before bursting out laughing while trying to explain to O'B the size of the howler he had just made. The best thing about this was, roughly a year later, *Fast and Furious 5* was released in which both Vin Diesel and The Rock starred and they were front and centre of the poster. Safe to say, I ordered that poster for my good friend to adorn his wall, as a reminder.

An 'O' can not only be something painfully stupid that you say, but terrifically bad actions can qualify as well. Let me tell you about O'B's first day in his new job. This basically sums up the man and seals his place in history as one of, if not THE *most* legendary creators of blunders (well, at least in my circle of friends). Now, my good friend O'B currently resides in the land down under (although knowing him he thinks he lives in the land up over). He moved to Australia for a change of scenery and a new job. (I think he was trying to do what the guy did in *Love Actually*, when he went abroad to get lucky with the ladies, and he thought this would happen in Oz.) He was slightly nervous the night before his first day in a new office job and he treated himself to a few cold brewskis. Later on that same evening, he thought he'd best make himself a lunch for his first day, so he popped some eggs in a pan of water and thought he'd go healthy with a couple of your finest boiled eggs. Then he went to bed for some rest before his big first day in a new job in a new country. He woke up, popped the eggs in a Tupperware box, sorted himself out and set off for work. His day was going swimmingly, meeting new colleagues, learning the ropes of a new environment and new culture. The clock hit 12 and O'B saw all his new work crew eating and chatting at their own desks. He thought it was strange they didn't have a staffroom, but no drama, O'B was ready for his lunch. He got out his lunchbox at his desk, pulled out one of his 'boiled' eggs and cracked it with a knife over his brand-new work laptop. Unfortunately for O'B, the night before the few beers had turned into a few more and he had attempted to boil eggs in freezing cold water (lo and beyond, apparently heat was a cooking requirement). Egg on his face and now the inside of an egg slowly integrating itself with the internal workings of his new laptop keyboard.

The food-related shenanigans don't stop there either; he recently told me a tale of when he decided to mix up his dinners after 'boiled-egg gate'. He went to a supermarket to buy something quick and easy so decided on ham sandwiches. How wrong can you possibly go with a ham sandwich? Well ... he saw a family pack of bacon rashers, which looked suspiciously like ham. He had been told that bacon doesn't look the same in Australia as it's cured differently, so he bought the pack and presumed they called their ham bacon! A full week went by and O'B continued making himself ham sandwiches for work. He thought nothing of it until the final day arrived, he used his last few rashers of 'ham' and before he threw the packaging away he noticed, upon closer inspection, the back of the package said 'Ensure thoroughly cooked through before consuming.' So there you have it, the godfather of the bad shout ate raw bacon sandwiches for a whole week ... Oh what an 'O'!

My ultimate favourite 'O' that isn't school-related happened to our mum and dad early on in their relationship. They are still going strong and will be close to their fortieth wedding anniversary when this book is released. They had a fairly short courtship before they got engaged and were enjoying their first holiday away together alongside our grandma and grandad. They ventured to Malta and from the stories they tell it was a lovely holiday. There were a couple of minor 'O's taking place that trip involving my grandad's sunburnt legs, due to forgetting to put on suncream, which were made even worse by my grandma spilling hot soup on those same legs. This resulted in a sweary outcry that could have been heard back in England. But these minute 'O's pale into insignificance compared to this infamous cringey moment from my mum during a horse-riding excursion during that same holiday.

At the stable, they all got the gear on, sat through the safety talk and were ready to go on their hour-long ride. Under the blazing heat, they all enjoyed a lovely trot on the horses, taking in the picturesque local landscape. For one reason or the other, the group got separated but the route was clear enough, so there was no worry about being lost or losing one of the group. My mum was the first back to the ranch and dismounted, thanking and patting her new-found hoofed friend. Soon, my grandad appeared, shortly followed by my grandma, but there was no sign of Big Mike, our dad.

Not too concerned, my mum and grandparents got themselves a drink, expecting my dad to appear at any moment – but that moment didn't come. Now at this point of the story, it might be worth explaining that our dad is quite a tall man. At 6 foot 4, his size could have been a factor in why his trusty steed was not performing at its usual best, coupled with dad having longer than average lower limbs that he'd managed to use to inadvertently excite the horse, making it bare its rather large horse member. That's right, a giant horsey wang on display for all to see.

The next session, which turned out to be a stag do, was waiting impatiently for the final arrival, and as stag dos tend to be, they were being rather raucous and noisy. Worried that her betrothed had not returned yet, my mum alerted the staff and one of them mounted a horse and headed into the woods on the hunt for my dad. After what seemed like an eternity, my mum started to hear loud and erratic clip-clop, clip-clops; Big Mike had returned! From behind my mum, and staring at the rather aroused horsey schlong, one of the stag party shouted, 'Oh my, look at the dick on that horse.' Without thinking, my mum turned round and instinctively barked back, 'Excuse me! That dick happens to be my fiancé.'

In my mother's haste to defend my dad she had admitted to the whole of the stag party that she was in fact engaged to the huge horse penis. It was an 'O' of epic proportions – and the photographic evidence backs up the story.

Good old Mum! Since we started the podcast and explained what a traditional 'O' is, the amazing listeners have provided us with some of the most hilarious tales ever, some of these even O'B, all the way in Australia, would be proud of.

An 'O' can come in all different shapes and sizes. Some of the best 'O's happen in schools and we're amazed just how many aspiring O'B wannabes have taken his work and applied it to the primary school setting. Take, for example, one of my favourites involving a TA in my school. For some reason, this particular TA had a rather irrational fear of our headteacher. It's not that he is necessarily an intimidating fella, because I have always found him to be fair, and as long as you are working hard he would always be accommodating if you ever needed something in return. One of my all-time favourite quotes about leadership is that 'A person who feels appreciated will always do more than is expected.' I couldn't agree more; I have always been willing to go above and beyond my job description at my school as I know I am valued and that works both ways. That is not to say there aren't staff members who take liberties, but creating the right culture in a school goes such a long way.

Anyway, for some reason, this TA always felt intimidated and awkward in the presence of the head. On one particular day she had received a phone call to say that her son, who was now in secondary school after being a pupil at our school, had been sick and needed to be picked up. The TA informed her classroom teacher, who told her to go and pick him up but to just mention it to the head on the way out. As luck would have it, the head was walking down the corridor as the TA was on her way out. She explained what had happened, saying, 'I am really sorry, but I am going to have to pick my son up. The school has just phoned to say he is not well, and it is apparently coming out of both ends ...' at which point the head held his hand out in front of her. Now to any normal person of sound mind this was a signal to simply stay 'stop', I don't need the rather graphic details of both vomit and diarrhoea coming out of your son's orifices. But this TA, who would have felt a level of anxiety having to speak to the head and also the worry about her son, decided to place her hand in his. Yes, she randomly and rather embarrassingly clasped the headteacher's hand after explaining her son's illness. WHAT AN 'O'! I often think what she must have thought once she realised the gaffe, but more importantly what the head must have thought after she had nestled her fingers in his. She never lived it down and we would regularly take the mick by pretending to high-five every time someone shared something similar to being ill.

Don't forget this classic 'O' shared with us recently, a story about a nervous supply teacher and how a simple message mix-up can provide one hell of a hilarious tale:

This happened a few years ago, but I still often think about it and laugh to this day. It was a typical crazy school day. I was, at the time, a Year 5 teacher in a two-form-entry primary school. On this day of days, my TA and year-group partner teacher were off poorly. Obviously it was hectic to try to get everything sorted. We had a supply teacher come in for the day; she seemed quite young and quiet, she also mentioned she had never really worked with older children and she was mainly based in lower Key Stage 1, so I thought the best thing to do was to try to make it as simple as possible for both the staff and children. I was going to do the input in one class, then swap over with the young, nervous supply teacher, meaning all she had to do was oversee the work and monitor how the children were getting on.

The morning session went without a hitch, the work was being done, the children were engaged and the supply teacher seemed relieved she didn't have to improvise on the spot, something she wasn't prepared for. Fast-forward to after lunch, I was running late, and as I made my way to class one I quickly ushered over the supply teacher and said, 'While I'm giving the input to the first class, could you just have a quick class discussion and create some mind maps about what they know about gravity? I will be in shortly,' to which she nodded as if it was no problem and she was all good with the instruction. Once I had done the input with class one, I swapped with the young supply teacher and she came in to oversee the gravity work I had started with class one. When I walked into class two, I was extremely confused. On the tables they had large pieces of A3 paper with things such as 'pie, Sunday dinner, Christmas dinner and chips' written on it. In a heap of confusion I said to the class, 'What exactly are you doing?' at which one confident lad responded, 'The teacher that was just here told us to talk about and write down everything we knew about gravy, so we're writing what goes well with it, Miss.' Clearly the supply teacher in a fit of nerves had misheard gravity and thought I'd instructed her to begin the lesson sharing knowledge of gravy. Funniest thing is, when the supply teacher went into class one, they were all working on gravity worksheets after my input, and the penny must have dropped. When my headteacher approached me at the end of the day, and said, 'Did everything go OK in Year 5 with the supply today?' I simply replied, 'Yes, Miss, all gravy!'

Onto another truly cringey 'O' that happened during the most stressful experiences of any school staff member.

Yes, if you ask any teacher or school staff member to tell you the most stressful period of their teaching career, pandemic aside, it will be an Ofsted inspection. Now, I have no issue with the concept of Ofsted, a body of inspectors whose job it is to ensure schools are performing to the best of their ability. A level of accountability is important, but there are many, many flaws in Ofsted's approach to school inspection. Firstly, their logo has to be one of the biggest lies in education. If you visit Ofsted's website you will see their motto/tagline that reads, 'Ofsted, raising standards, improving lives.' Which is a crock of crap. Let's be honest, Ofsted don't 'raise' standards. Just look at the role they played in helping schools during the pandemic. What role? I hear you cry. Exactly, they did nothing. Ask most teachers if they've ever been told anything by an Ofsted inspector that has made them better teachers and tumbleweeds will suddenly appear. Ofsted don't raise standards, they check standards, which is absolutely fine, but don't make it out like you do something you don't. I have said before that my biggest issue with Ofsted has nothing to do with Ofsted itself, it is to do with schools and their approaches. I understand why schools do it but what I can't stand is when Ofsted are used as an excuse for bad practice. Leaders who want to micromanage staff will blame Ofsted to justify why they are overworking staff and making them do unnecessary and pointless tasks. There's a huge amount of unnecessary pressure on staff, and the teacher in this next story sounds like they were completely on edge during their Ofsted visit before they made their epic 'O'!

During the inspection, this teacher was due to be observed straight after the lunch break. Almost the entirety of their lunchtime was spent organising the classroom to every inch – sharpening every pencil, cleaning every whiteboard, stapling any display that had peeled away. If you had a minute to eat, that would be a luxury, but this teacher managed mere minutes at the end to shove a sandwich in her gob before the bell signified the start of the afternoon session. The teacher in question did not reveal their sandwich filling, but going off what happened after, I am assuming it would have been a chicken and mayo combo, possibly with sweetcorn or bacon. The only guarantee was that there was a comprehensive helping of mayonnaise.

Straight after lunch, the teacher had collected their class and settled them in. The deputy immediately brought in the inspector, who came over and shook the teacher's hand. He then proceeded to point to his cheek, which confused the teacher slightly and in her nervous state she leaned forward and kissed the inspector on the cheek!

Holy crap! No way!

He said, 'Thanks for that, but you have some mayonnaise on your cheek.' One can only imagine the size of the hole the teacher wanted to dig and jump into.

Now this really does epitomise the definition of an 'O', misreading the situation so that it led to an embarrassing action that will surely still stick with that teacher to the day they die. At the most random of times – in the shower, just before going to bed – that moment when she leaned in and pecked an Ofsted inspector on the cheek will make them wince and cringe over and over again. I have nothing but respect for the teacher who then had to teach a full lesson to her class in front of the inspector. Although I am taking a stab in the dark, I suspect the teacher was KS1, as if that happened in front of a Year 5 or 6 class the rest of the lesson would be a write-off – at every opportunity the students would ask or remind you of the embarrassing situation that had just unfolded. 'Is that your boyfriend?' 'Why did you just kiss that man?' 'Are you marrying them?' 'You didn't mean to do that, did you, Miss?'

I would also have been disappointed in my class if they'd failed to tell me about the dollop of mayo on my face. The teacher had ventured out into the playground to collect them, walked them to the classroom and not a single one had said anything. Primary school children are renowned for picking you up on anything. Ask any primary school teacher what happens if you forget to change the date on your board: the children relish the opportunity to tell you that today is a different date. But in this situation they failed to notice the mayo painted over the teacher's face. Unless, of course, she is a person who always ends up with food all over their face. 'Are you saving that for later?' You know the type of person I am talking about here. It could be the case here that the children noticed it and just thought, 'Here she is again, obviously devoured her lunch in seconds and it's now plastered all over her face. I suppose it's better than spinach being stuck in her teeth all afternoon.' Whatever the reason, this will always go down as one of, if not the cringiest interaction with an Ofsted inspector. Outstanding, indeed.

From mistaken body language to a bad case of mistaken identity.

I once walked back into my classroom after dismissing my class to their parents to find our cleaner, Sue, doubled over in fits of laughter.

One of our HLTAs (High-level teaching assistant) could be politely described as a hippie-dippie meditating type and she'd started growing her own fruit plants. Sue, who worked part-time as a cleaner and part-time in the kitchen, had asked Wendy (the HTLA) if she could buy a tomato plant, and Wendy said she'd bring it in the next day. Just before I'd walked into the classroom, Sue crossed Wendy in the corridor walking in the opposite direction to the canteen and said, 'Ooh, is that for me?' and went to take the plant, only for Wendy to move the plant back, clearly embarrassed. 'Oh, I'm very sorry, this is for Sue the cook! I can bring you one tomorrow if you'd like?' Sue thought she must have been joking, so replied, 'I am Sue!!' And Wendy (no personality) said, 'I know love, but this is for the other Sue – the cook!'

So she thought she'd try something – she went into her locker in the staffroom, got changed into her cook uniform and went back out into the corridor. Unbelievably, Wendy proceeded to tell her the whole story, slagging off 'Sue the cleaner' for being so presumptuous and not putting in an order, and finished it with 'You're bloody lucky, she nearly had your plant!' We asked the kids the next day; they had no idea she was the same person either! Sue now always buys me two cards on my birthday, or Christmas, and signs one from the cook and one from the cleaner!

There is nothing more embarrassing in day-to-day life than when you are convinced someone is waving at you, so you wave back, only to realise they were in fact waving at someone behind you. Imagine the cringe-induced coma you may fall into when the headteacher walks past you in the morning and says, 'Hello, dear.' For you to reply, 'Good morning,' only to realise they were in fact talking to the child walking behind you.

For anyone who works in school, sending texts or letters home is extremely important. You have to make sure that everything is checked twice – or if it's me, three times, because unfortunately there is always a chance of a mistake, as this story painfully confirms!

*This is a mistake no one would want to make. A member of staff from a school was sent a reminder to all staff and parents about a welly-wanging competition taking place during an upcoming lunchtime. To the despair of the staff member, they sent a reminder to all staff and parents about a '**willy wanking**' competition. She attempted to recover it, but the damage was done! Luckily the staff and parents all saw the funny side.*

I wonder how the competition went? Who came first?

Gross, Adam! Although a technological faux pas is perfectly normal, it can also be your downfall, like in the next story.

I was having dinner and drinks with some colleagues and we were joking around with that popular app that was viral at the time – FaceApp.

(For those of you who are not familiar, FaceApp allows you to upload selfies of yourself or each other and apply a range of different filters that can change your age or gender. The results are often hilarious, especially when you use the age filter over and over and over, making you look like you've just survived your first week-long class residential trip.)

Several glasses of wine later, I went home and the FaceApp pics continued to be shared in our WhatsApp group. I decided it would be a good idea to download our headteacher's photo off the school website and put it through the app, in this instance the gender swap!

(Risky business, even though I am sure the portrait of the headteacher that is usually on the welcome page to the school website will have been downloaded and used in a variety of ways. I am sure some tech-savvy pupils will have done all sorts and some parents have it printed on a dartboard.)

Sometimes these results come out looking like a real person, but this was not one of those times, this was

definitely an older gentleman in a wig and bad makeup –
it looked so funny! I shared it with the group, had a giggle
and went to bed.

The next week in school, I was in the head's office, talking
about some possible new furniture for my classroom. Forgetting everything, I took out my phone to show him some
samples I had found online when the FaceApp image inexplicably flashed up on my screen!

I get on well with the head, he's a nice guy but can sometimes be unpredictable and definitely does not like to be
perceived as the butt of a joke. Luckily, he isn't the best with
technology but this picture was so obvious – I was petrified.

He looked at me and said, 'What's that?' In my absolute
panic, I said the first thing that came into my mind. It was
so, so stupid, I can't believe I said it! 'Oh, it's my dad!' My
head is now looking at me incredibly concerned ... 'Your
dad?' Now realising my head thinks my dad is some
amateur drag queen, I mumbled 'Err yeah' and tried to
change the subject back to furniture. Five excruciating
minutes later, with a bright-red face, the meeting was over, I
stood up and the head reached into his desk and handed
me a chocolate bar with a sympathetic look on his face – I
guess to help me with my family's journey! I ran back to my
classroom, shut the door and lay on the carpet for ten
minutes to calm down.

It's been months now and he's never mentioned anything
about it. Hopefully I won't have to pretend my dad is audi-
tioning for RuPaul any time soon!

Let this be a lesson: if you find yourself changing the
gender of your Senior Leadership Team for some strange
reason, either hide the evidence or delete the pictures when
you are once again sober. If you are a headteacher reading

this, download the FaceApp and face the music yourself. To be honest, it is great fun and in my humble opinion I reckon I look well fit as a female.

A few general quick ones for you now, and this proves it does not matter how clever you are (or think you are), an 'O' is never too far away:

- *Walking out of the cinema after watching the movie Titanic, I asked my friend what she thought of it. They said, 'Bit too far-fetched for me. No way an iceberg would have sunk a ship that size in real life.'*
- *One of my mum's friends once said, 'It's truly amazing how they got the dinosaurs to do what they wanted in Jurassic Park.'*
- *My sister-in-law once asked my brother how often they painted the white cliffs of Dover.*
- *My sister once asked aloud which part of the cow the cheese came from. She was in her thirties.*
- *I was talking to my old neighbour a few years ago. She was telling me how her husband was having terrible trouble with his vagina. She meant angina!*

Back to school again, and you can imagine these bright school staff regretting these 'O's, after reading these beauties:

- *When planning history with my year group partner, she asked, 'We're doing the ancient Greeks from Rome?'*
- *In my first year of university (BA Hons in primary education) during a lecture on the literacy hour, I accused David Blunkett of reading from an autocue (yep, not the best thing to accuse a visually impaired person of doing).*
- *My lovely, brilliant and intelligent mum, who taught secondary*

French for the best part of 35 years and was on her school's Senior Leadership Team, genuinely thought that the £1 coin you put in the trolley at the supermarket travelled through the chain to the trolley behind!

'O's can hurt; they can obviously hurt your pride (and make you feel like a complete jackass), but they can also hurt you physically. Working in a school is the same as any job, in the respect that you need to have a laugh and need colleagues who are able to have banter with you on a daily basis, but as the next tale will show, sometimes it can go pear-shaped …

A few of us KS2 teachers are constantly pranking each other, and this includes writing funny things on each other's whiteboards, or hiding each other's chairs. The main one, which usually happens when kids are not around, is hiding and jumping out to scare the bejeezus out of each other. Unfortunately, my co-worker, who was trying to get me back from a few weeks prior, made an 'O' that will be heard about for years. They waited in my classroom after I had been downstairs speaking to a parent at the end of the day, and when they heard footsteps coming down the corridor, as soon as they were in earshot, they jumped out with a huge 'rahhhhhhhhh'. Unfortunately I was still downstairs with the parent, and the person nearly scared to death was the headteacher, who was also carrying two mugs of coffee. This caused some nasty burns to her hands, but fortunately the prankster crew were let off with only a stern warning and she didn't make as big of a deal about it as she could have. I wanted to give her a high five, but it was probably not a good idea due to the bandaging!

Ouch!

Ouch indeed, and that now explains why we all have to consume hot drinks from a mug with a lid on. I always thought it was health and safety gone mad, but something must've gone wrong in a number of schools for the rules to change and for lids to become commonplace. Whether they involve teacher-on-teacher pranks is a different conversation altogether.

I often think about the stories that cause a rule change. Something so significant that a school or educational organisation has to implement a serious policy amendment. A good example of this was on my first residential as a teacher. If you have ever been to a place like Robinwood (my school's regular residential trip provider), you know the best part is the teachers' lounge. Yes indeed, these places have a place for teachers to take a break from the little cherubs and, amazingly, there's a fridge containing beer, wine and confectionery!

Most teachers will usually join in the activities with their class but you can, if you want, stay in the teachers' lounge and relax. When I went to get a soft drink from the fridge, there was a printed piece of A4 with a message along the lines of:

Feel free to take a
drink and relax,
however, please
remember your role as
a responsible teacher
still working as a
member of staff for
your school.

All I could think about was what must have happened to cause the venue to make a point of reminding staff to not go turbo with the free booze? Seriously! I bet it was some of the teachers I know. There's a story there that we can only imagine but I suspect it was followed by some sort of disciplinary action when the staff got back to school.

Don't forget this absolute classic sent by an unfortunate gentleman, which proves, even if you're 99 per cent sure that your intuition is correct, never abandon the 1 per cent, as you will see with this following 'O'. A lad reached out to tell us this …

I work in a great school that has quite a few male staff members, so there's always banter around the corner (WHEYYY, LADS LADS LADS). One morning, I was engrossed in writing my date and learning objective on the board. One of the other lads came into my room and slapped my arse. The slap hurt, but it didn't come close to the pain of having to redo my long date on the whiteboard. I just about clocked who it was as they legged it out of my room, so after school that day revenge was in the air; I went on the hunt to find the mystery arse-slapper. After a quick glance into the photocopier room, I was certain that I had located my target. There he was, sporting skinny-fit, grey trousers with no socks (I really don't understand this trend; one day without socks and my shoes smell like a wheelie-bin). Anyway, my colleague was bent over, looking like he was restocking the paper trays, perfect opportunity for sweet, sweet revenge. I tiptoed into the room and struck his arse with the force of a Beckham free-kick. Unfortunately for me, the photocopier was in fact broken (no shock there) and the recipient of smacked bottom was …

… the photocopier repair man! Yep, I viciously assaulted the posterior of a total stranger who was trying to innocently go about his day job of fixing a problematic A3 drawer.

What an 'O'!

Now we'll go from checking the potential person you're going to slap, which I'm sure isn't a daily occurrence for most staff, to checking what exactly you are showing your children when it comes to online resources. Now, as my brother ICT with Mr P (aka Lee) preaches quite regularly, technology has enabled lessons and learning that we could have never thought possible years ago, and while most of the stuff is child-friendly, you cannot cut any corners when it comes to checking the content you are going to share. A classic example of this was from a good friend of mine who I worked with many years ago. He was ex-army and he was in school doing workshops about resilience and teamwork, and was asked if he could run an assembly for the whole school to discuss his experiences in the army. Now, my friend won't have any issue with me saying that he was fantastic with a class of children but as I'm sure school staff everywhere will vouch for, full-school assemblies can be quite nervy. He had planned on starting with a discussion, followed by a Q and A, finishing with a video of an activity he had taken part in, where the group of soldiers jumped into icy waters.

I placed myself at the back of the hall, excited as I knew how nervous he would be, but also excited by the fact I'd never actually seen him public speaking. The assembly was going well and I was actually impressed; I could see the relief as it surprisingly passed by without a hitch. When he had reached the finale, the children were engrossed as he was describing the feeling of jumping into these icy waters and the painfully low temperatures he dealt with alongside his army comrades. The video was playing, of all these men jumping into these ice-cold lakes, screaming like babies due to the shock, and the children were laughing. I looked at my pal and he gave me a big thumbs up, as if to say, 'I've just smashed this out of the park.' However, in life you learn not to celebrate early; with about 30 seconds to go of the short clip, a soldier who had just climbed out of the sub-zero ice chasm went up to the camera and screamed 'IT'S

F**KING FREEZING'. The children's reaction was priceless. The Year 5s and 6s were making the 'oooh' noise like when you know someone is about to get in trouble, the Year 3s and 4s were repeating what was said to anyone who didn't catch it first time. I mean, the two F-words were an acceptable example of alliteration but not the ones we wanted the kids to go home and share with younger siblings. Our poor guest presenter had gone from strutting around like John Travolta in *Saturday Night Fever* to looking as embarrassed as Judy Finnigan when she flashed her bra at that awards ceremony. Once I was out of the children's earshot, I cried with laughter. I bet my mate wished he'd stayed in the freezing ice after that débâcle.

Don't worry, though, he's not the only person that has suffered a technological school mishap.

In my previous school, I was in charge of the end of year production for our Year 6 children. One year, myself and another teacher decided we would get a little bit more adventurous and use GIFs on our interactive whiteboard as our backgrounds, to add a bit of excitement since we didn't have any budget to create amazing scenery. We decided on the day of the show to end with some moving fireworks exploding into the sky, so we searched on a site and added the first one we found to our PowerPoint. During the first dress rehearsal to all the staff and lower year groups, all went well until our last slide of fireworks. As the rockets on the GIF started to explode, they formed a shape ... which would usually be quite impressive, but the shape on this occasion was of ... A HUGE PENIS! I've never seen anyone run so fast to end the PowerPoint! Word of advice: always watch things to the end before adding them!

What a cock-up! Despite being someone who loves technology, it can certainly backfire, as in the time one teacher tried to communicate with parents using Google Translate:

We had a child who came over to our school from South America and his parents only spoke Spanish. One playtime this child accidentally hit his head and needed slight medical attention. Rather than phone the parents, who, if you remember, couldn't speak English, we decided to email them and use Google Translate. All was going well, translating the phrases from English into Spanish. The intended wording was something like: 'Dear ... We are sorry to inform you that your child has had a slight injury and needed first aid. We administered an ice-pack, etc.' and we sent the email off. In literally a few moments, we got a reply back from mum, literally full of exclamation marks and clearly not happy, asking what on earth was going on. We were a little confused, as it was only a bumped head and it wasn't a big injury. Then I decided to check exactly what we had sent in our original email and translated the Spanish we had sent back into English. We immediately saw why the mum was so upset. 'Dear ... We are sorry to inform you that your child has drowned. We have given him an ice-pack.'

¡Santa mierda! It's not just head-bumps and drowning that get lost in translation, though; there are plenty of times when homophones (words that sound the same but have different meanings) can create a misunderstanding that can lead to a brilliantly awkward moment of cringe.

I had landed a new job and finished at my previous school for the summer. I loved the kids and staff, however, some of the SLT were a nightmare, in particular the deputy. She was a b*tch, a horrible woman who just treated everyone like crap but thought she was amazing. Anyway, during the summer holiday I was at a really busy pub and coming out of the loo there was a huge queue for the ladies. At the back of the queue was none other than the deputy.

There was no way around it, I had to give her a heads up that the toilet cubicles to the number of people needing to pee ratio wasn't in her favour. After some really awkward small talk, I left with 'Have a good break, good luck with the wait.' However, the deputy heard it as 'Good luck with the weight.' Which was something she was sensitive about. She gave me the dirtiest look and said, 'You what?' To which I said, good luck with the wait, you know, for the loo and pointed at the queue. I could see another lady behind her pissing herself laughing at how awkward the situation was. I made my escape and thankfully have never seen her since.

Or a misunderstanding of the pronunciation of different words.

When I was younger, I thought the car, Audi, was pronounced 'Awdy' and not 'Owdy'. So during a staffroom discussion, a member of staff says, 'Yeah, me and my brother both have Audis.' This other teacher then said, 'Yeah, my mum has an Audi.' I seriously thought they were talking about belly buttons and said, 'I have an innie.'

And a lesson in making sure you understand that a pyjama day does not necessarily mean you wear exactly what you would do for bed.

My friend and I both worked in a Church of England school at the time and were having a whole-school pyjama day. As all the children filed into worship (what we call assembly in our school), the hall was buzzing with excitement. I settled my class and took my seat next to my colleague, who grinned and said (just as the head addressed the school by lighting the candle and silence fell, the children took their daily worship very seriously), 'This is incredibly liberating, isn't it?'

'What do you mean?' I whispered. 'Not having to wear knickers to school,' she replied, as serious as anything. Not quite believing what I heard, I couldn't quite contain my laughter! After seeing my reaction, the colour on her face drained as she realised her massive 'O'.

Yes, she had come to school in her pyjamas with no underwear on! Luckily, she lives just a few minutes from school so she shot up from her seat, leaving me with instructions to give to her TA to cover the class while she ran home to put on her underwear. We still crack up to this day 10 years on!

Was the school called St 'Knicker-Less' (you know, Nicholas)?

Very good, Adam, although talking of feeling loose and breezy down there, this story is a stark warning of making sure everything is in its right place.

I was doing supply a few years back and got some regular work at a lovely little church school. I'd worked there for pretty much the term when it came to sports day. It was a glorious day and we were allowed to come in sports gear. I decided on the textbook T-shirt and shorts. The day coincided with my PPA, so my morning was spent in the staffroom marking away. During the last minute of lunch, a member of staff rushed into the room to fill up her water bottle when she turned to me, spat out a mouthful of water and said, 'You've got a bol**ck out!' Unbeknown to me, one of my testicles was hanging out of my shorts. I quickly readjusted myself. I then spent the whole sports day wondering how long one of my balls had been on display to the whole staff during that day.

There are also the 'O's that leave you cringing to your core. We are talking about a moment of utter regret that leaves you thinking about it for years to come. Lying awake in the middle of the night or while standing in the shower, this moment will repeat over and over.

This didn't happen to me but a friend's dad, who was a headteacher. A few years ago, he went to a wine festival and on his way home (slightly drunk) on the train, he ran into the parents of a boy he used to teach. They got to talking and that's when the dad asked how the boy was ... The parents just looked shocked and said, 'He passed away last year ... you were at the funeral ... you spoke.'

I'm in the last year of my BEd (Batchelor of Education) and on my final placement. I have one lesson observation a week to check how I'm getting on. I was having my observation and I'd just finished an input and asked if they had any questions (on it, aiming for a high grade, me). A child asked me something and I answered, addressing the whole class. Kids went off to do their learning and one child came up to me straight away and asked the same question I had literally just answered five seconds before. It's my time to shine, get a big old tick in that behaviour management box, setting those expectations.

Now at this point, I would just like to interject to defend the teacher here by saying that any teacher will tell you that repeating instructions literally seconds after explaining them happens more often than anyone could imagine. However, in this instance it soon backfired massively.

I came out with the old 'I have just answered that question, I'm not going to repeat myself, you will have to ask a friend. Next time you need to do good listening, [child's name]'. As soon as I said their name my heart dropped, just remembering that this kid has a bad hearing impairment, as if the two hearing aids they were wearing weren't a big-enough reminder.

Those last few ones will haunt the people committing each 'O' for years; the levels of guilt mixed with cringe must still send shivers down their spines.

I think we need to end this chapter on one final school-related 'O' that has everything:

A terrible shout	✓	Yep!
School children	✓	Of course.
A massive cringe moment	✓	As standard.
An embarrassing consequence	✓	Yes please!

We've used a little bit of artistic licence for comedy purposes, but this 'O' actually happened to a podcast listener:

About 25 years ago, I booked my infant class to go on a train journey, and as you can imagine, the children were absolutely buzzing with excitement. For some of the class, this would be their first experience in taking the train and for many, the only things they knew about the railway probably came from watching the beloved Thomas the Tank Engine series. One of the parent volunteers kept talking to the children about which of the engines they may meet at the station. Would it be Thomas? Could it be Percy? James would be acceptable but nobody wanted to see Diesel. Poor old Diesel, although his behaviour in many of the episodes warranted a bad reputation. Ringo Starr definitely put on a nasty voice whenever Diesel spoke.

We walked to the train station with the children holding hands and, seeing as this was the mid-90s, there amazingly weren't any teachers wearing bright pink or yellow safety vests. Can you believe that? As we approached the station, we were greeted by one of the lovely volunteers that helped to run the place and she informed us that we were just in time for the next train ride. I think she was the lady that took the booking and her husband was the steam enthusiast driving the train. The children were starting to get even more excited as we made our way onto the platform, but with a group of 30 children we needed to be very careful that none of them came too close to the edge. Most teachers would have to do the classic teacher callbacks such as '1,2,3 ... look at me!' or something else to grab little Johnny's attention so that he doesn't end up falling into the gap between the train and the platform. Problem is, shouting 'Pop, pop, pop ... everybody stop!' back then wouldn't have worked as successfully because that sort of stuff wasn't commonplace. This needed something far louder and far more effective ... my trusty whistle! Much like Arnold Schwarzenegger in Kindergarten Cop, my class were fairly well drilled and knew to stand to attention if they heard my whistle. Clever me!

Well, not so clever as it happens. Before the children had a chance to get on the train, I blew my whistle in a way that was remarkably similar to the whistle to tell the driver that they could leave the station. That's right, instead of catching the attention of sweet little Grace holding hands with her best friend, Rebecca, I had inadvertently given the signal for the driver to start moving.

With no mobile phones available, it wasn't until the train was halfway towards Evesham before the driver was informed by an out-of-breath volunteer in his 70s that the children were still at the station. Fortunately, he returned in time for us to still have an enjoyable day out but I'm not so sure the Fat Controller/Sir Topham Hat (or whatever we're supposed to call him nowadays) would be impressed that I used my whistle to cause both confusion and delay!

What a chuffing 'O'!

So now you know what an 'O' is. Next time you make a mistake that you know is a terrible shout, you can mutter to yourself, 'What an 'O'!' Most people will wonder what the hell you are talking about, but at least you know that you've joined an impressive club of legends that make life fun. Just try not to refer to our dad (Big Mike) as a 'd*ck on a horse'. Mummy Parkinson won't approve!

Out of the
Mouths of
Babes

Ask any teacher or school staff member what the best part about their job is and I guarantee they will almost always reply: **the children**. Any teacher worth their salt will genuinely want all the children in their care to achieve their best and go on to great things. They are hard work a lot of the time, but seeing them do well in all aspects of life is a genuine privilege. That said ... they don't half talk and write a load of boll**ks sometimes! I've said it before and I'll say it again, some kids are accidental comedy geniuses.

Every teacher will have so many stories of things children have said or done that have left them in stitches. The majority of the time the children themselves have no clue about how hilarious they are. They sometimes reveal too much about their loved ones, sometimes they comment about things in a way that can leave you trying to contain your laughter or on the verge of tears because it was so eloquent and inspiring. Some kids can absolutely 'burn' you (as the cool kids call it nowadays) as well, where they humiliatingly diss a member of staff intentionally or unintentionally and jaws immediately drop in response to the ahem ... 'sick burn'.

Best put a wet paper towel on it! Seriously, though, I've been burned so many times by kids and also had myself stifling giggles at some of the hilarious things children write.

I love the random things I see in pupils' exercise books. One of my favourite examples of this is a lesson I always love to do that is based around proverbs; it is the perfect way to explore the wonderful, innocent and sometimes odd inner workings of your little cherubs. The idea is this: you introduce the concept of proverbs, explaining that these are well-known sayings that go beyond the literal to teach us a lesson or guide us on how to live a happy and fulfilled life. You then share a few examples, such as, 'Don't count your chickens until they hatch.' To which you can explain that we are not talking about literal chickens but the message is don't assume everything will always go to plan.

Once the children have grasped the concept, or in my case you think they have grasped it, you challenge them by giving them a list of well-known proverbs but just the first few words.

For example:

Too many cooks ...

Fortune favours ...

It is all fun and games until ...

You can lead a horse to water ...

The idea is for the children to then complete the sentence, creating their own proverbs. There is no wrong answer (actually, there are quite a few) as long as their finished sentence has a meaning. It can be both hilarious and beautiful. I have had really inspiring responses, such as:

People who live in glass houses ... must be boiling.

Unless you live in Manchester, of course, where that might only happen one day a year.

When in Rome ... eat pizza.

Solid advice, try the pasta too.

When the going gets tough ... watch a YouTube video.

Genuinely, exactly what I do if I ever need to do any DIY around my house. 'I'll do it when I get some time,' was the excuse that got me out of every request my wife had about work around the house until, of course, lockdown hit and suddenly I had that time. Fixing the boiler, mending the cupboard, sorting out the plants – straight onto YouTube. Don't get me wrong, there is such an abundance of horse poo content on there (mostly the stuff binged on by my own kids) but when it comes to 'how-to' videos, it is a goldmine.

People who live in glass houses ... have wooden windows.
Moving swiftly on ...
It is all fun and games ... until Darth Vader comes.

He's not wrong.
There's no place like ... McDonald's.
Copyright Mr P's Year 2 class. I tell you what, forget 'I'm loving it', this is begging for Maccy Ds to use this for their next advertising campaign.
A picture is worth ... a lot of money.
I wish that was true given the amount of pictures I am given – especially during wet play – but I have yet to make a penny!
No man is ... smart.

Not going to lie, the girl who wrote this was not going for the inspirational but more the straight-up burn towards the smelly, horrible boys.

Hope for the best ... but then get an axe.

Michael, Michael Myers? See me after the lesson.

And now for the utterly inspiring:

You can lead a horse to water ... with a carrot.

Meaning, sometimes you need to give somebody something to help them get somewhere.

No man is ... unloved.

Doesn't need any explanation.

Don't bite the hand ... that hurts.

If someone feels down, don't make it worse.

Don't judge a book ... by someone's opinion.

Just because someone doesn't like it, it doesn't mean you won't like it too.

Too many cooks ... will make a mess!

This one hits deep, especially for all those teachers working in Multi Academy Trusts where there seem to be more managers than teachers. SLTs may consist of a teacher with a TLR (teacher and learning responsibility), which effectively is the teacher getting a tiny increase in pay to take on huge responsibilities within the school. Middle managers, phase leaders, assistant headteachers, deputy headteachers, headteachers, executive headteachers. You can ask me to explain the difference between some of these roles, but to be fair, I don't really know with some; over the past few years it seems you have to be everything other than an actual teacher. Some teachers love the labels and roles they have and think, the more the merrier. In fact, they start to sound like Daenerys from *Game of Thrones*.

Who am I?

I am Lee of House Parkinson, executive practitioner of the classroom, associate coordinator of history and English, director of curriculum design and analytics, chief organiser of staff parties, the implementer, the breaker of photocopiers.

What's wrong with just being a teacher? As stated in the proverb, with all these people making decisions it tends to end up a mess.

But my ultimate favourite from the proverb lesson was: 'Beauty is in the eye of death!', which at first caught me off guard. I replied, 'Damien, you can't say things like that!' Only joking, but when I asked the child to explain what she meant she stated, 'Well, you know when someone passes away, you tend to only remember the beautiful things about them.' I am not going to lie, my eyes filled up in an instant at the sheer beauty of the way some children view the world. The children asked whether I was crying, to which I replied, 'No it is just my hay fever' (it wasn't, I was close to full on blubbing in front of those Year 2s and none of them would have a Scooby Doo as to why).

Another time when I have instantly welled up after something a child said was with my own son Harry. I have ten-year-old triplets at the time of writing this and they are my world. Two identical boys and a girl, who, despite having the exact same home life and being in the same class at school, couldn't be more different as people. All three have amazing individual qualities that I adore, but Harry's – I want to say unique – outlook on life sometimes leaves me speechless. He struggles quite a bit with school as he is severely dyslexic, but his emotional intelligence must be up there. We were having a conversation one mealtime where I asked the three of them what they would like to be when they are older. 'An actress,' my daughter shouted, which if you have seen her epic TikTok lip-syncs you'd know the potential. 'A builder,' replied Charlie, who has discovered this career path after being introduced to Minecraft during lockdown one. I thought, of all the video games, Minecraft is a good one as they can build anything. If they can think of it, they can build it, almost like virtual Lego – and a lot cheaper than real Lego. What I did not envisage is that soon my boys would discover that they can jump onto YouTube and watch videos of fully grown American men playing Minecraft. How in the hell is that entertainment? I couldn't think of anything worse. It was one of the first experiences where I realised I'd turned into my dad. Back when I was a kid, we were lucky to have Sky or cable, as it was called back then, giving us access to Nickelodeon. We were obsessed with shows such as *Kenan & Kel*, *Sister, Sister* and *Boy Meets World*. My dad would slag them off something rotten. 'How you can watch this over and over? Every episode is the same, it is a load of rubbish.' These are now the exact words I express to my children about YouTube. But I will argue till the cows come home that *Kenan & Kel* is elite-level entertainment compared to American geeky men screaming about spawning and zombies. Anyway, I could see Charlie being very happy with a career in construction. Especially if he can sort me out with a cut-price extension down the line.

I finally turned to Harry and asked him the question, 'What do you want to be when you're older, mate?'

He looked up at me and without skipping a beat he just said, 'Happy,' and went back to tucking into his spag Bol. I was left speechless. What an answer! If I could have given him a star of the week certificate I would have done. 'Don't ever lose that outlook on life,' I eventually said once I had got over the emotional slap he had just delivered to me.

As teachers, we all know that sometimes children will say things that leave you speechless out of shock, laughter or utter bewilderment. My favourite example of this was when I was given a reply that left me so flummoxed that to this day I still don't know whether it was an act of genius or not.

It was the first day in September. There is an unwritten rule in teaching, it is one that I am not a fan of and wouldn't ever encourage anyone to follow literally.

'Don't smile until Christmas.'

Seriously, some teachers (usually seasoned, old sages that take themselves way too seriously) say this to NQTs – or ECTs as they are now known (Early Career Teachers) implying that in order to keep their class under control and behaving properly, the teacher should stay sour-faced to send the children a message that they are not to be trifled with. I'll expand a little further on why I have a huge issue with this particular line later in the book, but for now let's just say that the class I was going to be working with was rather renowned throughout the school to be challenging. Smiles or not, I wanted to set out my expectations, early doors, be consistent and establish the boundaries so the learning could follow. I introduced myself to the children, explained how excited I was to work with them and how I had planned some really special lessons, some of which would be using some new apps to enhance our learning ... and then I was interrupted by a grumble. One child had mumbled something. I thought, here we go, here's my chance to set my stall out, nip it in the bud and let this class know that Mr P is firm but fair. Unfortunately, I couldn't quite make out what was said and couldn't 100 per cent say who it was.

Now, faced with potential mutiny amongst the children, I didn't want to accuse anyone unless I was 100 per cent sure it was them who had been muttering. Instead, I addressed the whole class, a little bit like if you hear a child swear but you haven't got the time to go through the whole rigmarole, so instead you say, 'I REALLY hope I didn't hear what I think I heard, because if I heard what I think I have just heard someone would be in a LOT of trouble!'

This time I said, 'OK class, if someone has something to say, you need to put your hand up.' Textbook line but no hand went up. Back to the lesson we go. I set the children off with the task and all was looking promising – the children were all getting on and I was questioning the reputation this class had. Then I spotted a child who was yet to pick up his pencil. I walked over to him. Now to give you a bit of context, this child is Liam Gallagher in child form. When *Saturday Night Takeaway* had the feature of Little Ant and Dec, this child would be a shoe-in for Little Liam Gallagher. He is the most Manc (Mancunian) child you have ever met. He doesn't walk, he bowls wearing a Parka coat. There are certain children in a school whose reputation precedes them, and he is one. But I pride myself on always giving children a completely new slate when it comes to being in my classroom, so I strolled over and said to the child, 'Is everything OK? You don't seem to be getting on with the task. We want to get this task finished and produce some work we are really proud of. That's what you want to do, so we can do that, can't we, get this work finished?'

He looked up at me through his long fringe and said in the most Mancunian way, 'DOUBT IT!'

I was taken aback; in all my years of teaching I had never had such a response. 'Pardon?' I mustered.

'DOUBT IT,' he stated once more, sounding increasingly like Bez from the Happy Mondays.

I was flummoxed. He had well and truly stumped me. In the response he had given, he had not said no to me but at the same time was making it rather clear that the task would indeed not be finished and if (and it's a big if) it was finished it most certainly wouldn't be something he would be proud of.

'Well, let's give it our best shot, shall we?' I said as I walked back to the front of class, realising that Manc Kid had just trolled me in a way no child had ever trolled me before. I've had children call me 'd**khead', 'wannabe Joey Essex' and 'pregnant', but nothing had bewildered me like this. The closest had been when a child had punched another child on the school field and when confronted by the teacher on duty he answered back, so I intervened, throwing a classic teacher line in the mix, 'Err, who do you think you are talking to?'

The child looked at me and yelled, 'YOU!'

Rhetorical question, mate. He was caught up in the adrenaline of the situation and so I calmly asked him to count to five and I would ask again. He soon realised and apologised. But when asked why he punched the child, it became clear that, sadly, the child throwing the punches was told by his idiot father to do so if he was called a name by another child. For any parent reading this, tell your children to tell a teacher and we will sort it; any act of violence will always be punished as it is never acceptable. I almost wish Manc Kid had done something properly wrong so I could dish out a consequence, but technically he'd not refused to complete his work and he hadn't actually been rude to me.

After taking a moment to think about Manc Kid's epic reply, I suddenly realised he may well be a genius! I mean, he's clearly not, but maybe he is the superhero we all need. There are so many situations where Manc Kid could come flying in with his Parka as a cape to save the day with a resounding 'DOUBT IT!'

Imagine in the climax of the biggest-grossing film *Avengers Endgame* (spoilers ahead) when Thanos puts the glove on and utters the words, 'I AM INEVITABLE' – forget Iron Man, it should have been Manc Kid who turned round with the glove and stones with the immortal line, 'DOUBT IT!'

Or during the most memorable scenes from *Star Wars*:

Darth Vader: 'Obi-Wan never told you what happened to your father.'

'He told me you killed him.'

'No, I AM your father!'

Enter Manc Kid, 'DOUBT IT!'

But more importantly, where was Manc Kid during Brexit? Imagine every time one of the lying politicians came out with a statement, 'We will have more money for the NHS,' followed by Manc Kid, 'DOUBT IT!' Stick him in Parliament so every time someone like BoJo and his ilk waffle on with some untruths it can be challenged with a resounding 'DOUBT IT!' from our superhero.

I just feel sorry for his partner when they get married.

'Do you take Shelley as your lawful wedded wife? To have and to hold? For richer? For poorer? In sickness and in health? Till death do you part?'

'DOUBT IT!'

Manc Kid was also part of the 'Great Escape', which turned out not to be so great. Alongside a few fellow wannabe escapees, he seemed to have had enough and wanted to make an escape from the school. They hatched a plan where one of them managed to get their hands on a key that they were convinced could unlock the gate. They even drew a map detailing the plan. The escape was foiled, however, when the teacher got wind of it and made them hand over the evidence. Manc Kid was not happy. Hilariously, the key was actually a shiny, plastic toy key from what looked like a lockable diary.

I am sure most teachers know a child like Manc Kid, who provides so many stories from tripe they spout in class. Here are some of my favourite stories of things children have said.

When we were learning about **Hindus** *in RE, a child said to me, 'Me Mum went on a* **hen do** *at the weekend.'*

A great line, for sure, but something that would need to be addressed straight away; you wouldn't want children confusing Hinduism, the faith, with the antics of a traditional British hen do. The misconceptions would be downright offensive!

'OK class, can anyone share what a Hindu might wear?'

'A pink sash, a T-shirt with the name of the bride, the town they are visiting and the year they went, penis straws and pink cowboy hats.'

'Does anyone know who Hindus worship?'

'Is it the fireman from Blackpool who isn't actually a fireman but talks about the big hose in his pants and then dances while taking his clothes off to music, then puts whipped cream on his hose before getting the lady with the white veil to lick it off while all the other girls scream, laugh and drink Smirnoff Ice?'

Wow, that is WAY too specific, Lee.

Erm, that's what I have heard about hen dos anyway. Moving swiftly on ...

Teaching RE comes with plenty of specific vocabulary and plenty of new words for the children to learn, and ultimately recall very differently.

Working at a Catholic school:

Me: 'Can anyone tell me which special church season lasts for 24 days in December?'

Student: *answering with the supreme confidence* 'It's Adverb, Sir.'

It's not just religious festivals that children mispronounce.

Reception child: 'I know what the seats in church are called, they're pubes!'

Another cracker:

Me: 'What does BC stand for?'

*Child 1: 'Before Christ.'

Me: 'Good! What about AD?'

Child 2: 'After ... dinosaurs?!'

*Yes we know some refer to it as BCE (Before Common Era).

In answer to who can name the four gospels who wrote about the life of Jesus: Matthew, Mark, Luke and ... said with great confidence ... Steve.

We had 'gold, frankincense and custard' once in KS1 Nativity rehearsal. I wanted to keep it in, but I was overruled!

To be fair, if I was Jesus, I would have definitely taken custard over myrrh (not just because it's easier to spell).

Moving away from religion:

We had Ofsted in the room, parent helpers, too. I'm an NQT. Getting kids ready to walk to the park to explore pushes and pulls. (Reception.) Suddenly, child starts to cry. I asked, 'What's up?' Reply was, 'I've got an erection and it hurts.' Parent helpers burst out laughing and have to leave the room, Ofsted inspector makes a note and looks at me over her glasses. I gulp and say with dread, 'Show me where it hurts.' Child points to his ear. 'Oh,' I reply ... then at the top of my voice, 'You mean an ear infection.' Inspector bursts out laughing and has to leave the room.

'Miss, I'm getting really good at wanking ...' proceeds to show me by closing one eye ...

The relief that teacher must have felt when they realised he had been practising his winking.

'The pool formed at the base of a waterfall is called a "clunge pool".'

'Don't talk to me, I'm on my period.' Eight-year-old boy in a bad mood.

Observing Year 6, discussing extinction. A boy in the back turns and says to the TA, 'Miss, isn't the Dildo an extinct bird?'

'I like your new testicles, Miss.'

'You mean spectacles? Glasses? You like my new glasses.'

'What is your daddy called?'

'Daddy.'

'But what does Mummy call him?'

'An arsehole.'

'My dad's job is looking after people's plums.'

His dad is a plumber ...

When asking a pupil why we are doing this fundraiser, she said we were raising money for someone who went bowling in Africa ... Maybe because they need new bowling shoes?

It was for Ebola (not a bowler).

A parent emailed me because his daughter had announced at the dinner table she was going to be a virgin 'like her teacher'. After he had spat his dinner out and questioned further, he realised she meant vegan.

Sometimes what children say can be pure poetry.

A few weeks ago my students were writing Shakespearean-style insults. They picked words out of three lists and put them together to make their best insult: 'You spotted, belching toad.' Their task as they left the room was to give me their best insult. One girl said, 'Miss, please can I go first, I have a great one?'

'OK Emily, up you come.'

Emily: 'YOU BELL END.'

Clearly the task was lost on her. I know old Billy Shakespeare did indeed invent a wealth of words that make up our wonderful English language, but I am not sure bell end was one of them.

The honesty and abruptness of children can often catch you off guard, but at other times they just say what everyone is thinking.

One of my slightly irritating co-workers was leading a carpet session with a group of three- to four-year-olds. She took the opportunity to have a slight rant at the children about the state of the classroom that morning, when out of nowhere a little boy says: 'STOP YOUR F**CKING MOANING!' I had to go into the store cupboard to stop myself from laughing as she told him off!

I like the way she said 'slightly irritating'. That's a lie. Everyone has a colleague who is properly irritating. The child has simply articulated what most of us think when that colleague asks another question at the end of another staff meeting that has already run over time.

Honesty is always the best policy, is what they say, but often that honesty can catch you off guard, and you struggle to articulate a response. If you are a teacher reading this, I would love to know how you would respond to these admissions from students. I will share my imaginary responses, which would not be what I would actually say. Isn't it weird that we live in a world where I have to give that warning, but if I didn't it is likely this page would be shared on Twitter with someone being offended that I would actually speak to children like this:

Year 10 who was wearing golf gloves in class.

Me, 'So do you play golf?'

Year 10, 'Nah Miss, it's so when I go robbing they can't get my fingerprints.'

My response: What do you rob? WHSmith, by any chance? I only ask as I am running low on Pritt Sticks and highlighter pens. Only joking, I admire the ingenuity, but casual pursuit of five-fingered discounts is not the after-school hobby he should be pursuing.

Six-year-old boy after coming out of the toilet:

'I wouldn't go in there yet, I just did a massive sh*t.' Said with the straightest face.

My response: I appreciate your concern for other people. Let's make sure there are no naked flames within the vicinity, too.

A boy messing around with his trousers. I asked him to take his hands out of his pockets and stop messing. He said, 'I'm just playing with my snake.'

I've never been so relieved when he brought a plastic snake out of his pocket!

Me: Even though I am so relieved, I am going to ask you to put your snake on my desk as this is something you shouldn't be bringing into the classroom.

One of my five-year-olds was having a bad day and was obviously feeling a bit hard done by. He got angry and shouted out, 'I'm going to kill my teacher!' The death threat didn't bother me as much as the other child who turned round and asked with genuine interest, 'How are you going to do it?'

My response: Don't you worry, this job has already killed me years ago. I am but a moving skeleton, trying to get to each weekend in one piece.

To be fair, I am surprised the teacher didn't listen to the rest of the conversation and make notes to show evidence towards the early learning goals that they showed great initiative and imagination.

'Me dad wears me mum's undies sometimes.'

Me: Good for him, I can only wish my wife's silky numbers would fit.

The head caught a student drawing a penis on his work. She asked, 'What is it with boys drawing penises in their books?' The student's immediate response was 'Coz fannies are too hard to draw, Miss.'

My response: While true, why not get some tracing paper and give it a go? And if you are going to graffiti another phallus, can we include veins, hair and shading in the right places?

Again, I jest, but it is certainly one of life's unanswered questions: why do teenage boys love drawing penises everywhere?

Talking of life's unanswered questions, how's this:

When explaining in an English class that my dad had lived in his house for over 35 years, one GCSE-aged boy mused, 'Wow ... I wonder how many times he's opened his front door.'

Ever wondered how Rudolph got his red nose? As one child proudly announced, 'His mum got busy with a clown.'

'Miss, you know when a pregnant woman goes swimming? Does that make her a submarine?'

'Sir, if plastic takes thousands of years to decompose, does that mean Kim Kardashian is immortal?'

We all know swearing is unacceptable in the classroom, even though a teacher's inner voice probably drops around 250 a minute, but I have to finish this chapter with some stories where students drop a swear and, despite the inappropriateness, they aren't half hilarious.

During my NQT year, I was reading The Gruffalo to my Nursery class while being observed by an LA assessor. The kids were so engaged, then I asked, 'How would you have felt if you were the Mouse?' One child said, 'I'd have sh*t myself!'

To be fair, they aren't wrong.

TA: 'Fill in the missing space with an adjective – The _____ neighbour is looking over the fence.' (TA thinking maybe curious, nosy, etc.)

Child: 'The f***ing neighbour is looking over the fence.'

Again, it is a fair description of those pesky, nosy neighbours.

Yorkshire Nursery child: 'Please can I go t'toilet?'

Me: 'Of course.'

Yorkshire Nursery child: 'Good, 'cos if I don't go soon I'm gon' sh*t meself!'

(The inclusion of the region where the child is from is crucial in this story as it makes you read it in the accent, which makes the story even better.)

OK, not funny at the time (well, one of those moments where I was more in shock) but a Year 1 turned round in Literacy and said, 'Well, this is f*cking sh*t!' to their friend.

Brutal feedback, to say the least.

A Reception pupil didn't answer the register so I repeated their name ... to be answered from the class toilet cubicles with a slightly echoed 'I'M HAVING A SH*T!'

'Oh, shh children, can you hear the birds singing! Isn't it a beautiful sound?'

A child replied, 'I will tell you what that bloody bird did! It sh*t all over the floor!'

Reception child looking out of the window at the pouring rain: 'Bugger me, it's pissing down out there!'

Was discussing that the word 'b*tch' in a book was refer-ring to a female dog and a wee boy put up his hand inno-cently and said, 'What's a male dog called?' And another girl, quick as a flash, said, 'Oh oh oh ... I know ... SON OF A B*TCH!'

As embarrassing as it is when children swear in front of a member of staff, and however funny it may be, you still have to tell them off for using bad language. The most important thing when doing this, however, is to make sure you don't accuse the wrong child. I'm sure you've already guessed by now that this has happened to me. On a residential with Year 6 to Robinwood, my group was doing the big swing activity. This consisted of two children being harnessed to a huge swing that would be pulled by the rest of the group to an impressive height and when the children on the swing were ready they would pull a lever, then drop and swing through. I had positioned myself a little bit further away to photograph them when two boys, including one of the ones that didn't always make the right choices, went up to the top, ready to pull the lever. The rest of the group gave them a countdown to build the anticipation and ... snap! They dropped. I managed to capture a picture as one of them shouted, no, screamed, 'SH*T!'

Everybody heard it and I immediately burst into laughter. Luckily I was far enough away so no one could see me creasing up. I managed to compose myself by the time the boys had been unharnessed and pulled them to one side. I didn't go in too harshly as I am also terrified of heights and so could relate to the shock; however, I had to address the language and how disappointed I was to hear it. I looked my suspected culprit in the eye and asked him to apologise. Problem was, it wasn't that lad, and the sweet, angelic lad by his side that wouldn't say boo to a goose politely interrupted me to admit that it was him. Dammit! This led me to having to apologise to the boy I assumed it was. Luckily, the photo I had taken was a live photo which meant I could turn it into a video, which had the child screaming, 'SH*T!' It provided plenty of laughs in the teachers' room later that night, I can tell you.

We now move on from accidental swearing to a few examples where children say things that may be well-intentioned but actually leave you devastated. This next section features plenty of the aforementioned 'teacher burns'.

Sometimes young children say something to you that they intend to be very innocent or even sweet, but in reality it embarrasses you beyond belief. When you get burned in front of a class of 30, you have one option: try not to cry and brush it under the carpet. Even if you try your best to forget about it, you will be having your tea that night – let's say Turkey Twizzlers, potato smiles and spaghetti hoops (yes, that's still a mainstay tea in my household) – and you will remember the line that completely ended you that day in school and somehow your Michelin-star meal doesn't taste the same.

One of my most embarrassing burns was back in 2013, while working in my old school. My friend the Geordie PE teacher (not his real name, obviously) had come into the class to do a theory intro-duction to his upcoming gymnastics lesson. I was sitting at the teacher's table, sorting out the class reading books. Geordie PE teacher began speaking to the class about why it is important for you to warm up with stretches before any physical activity, I mean, this is textbook PE chat, but unfortunately Geordie PE teacher wasn't getting the desired response when briefing the children on the importance of stretching. He said, 'Come on, guys, it's really impor-tant to warm up with some stretches because of what?'

This was met with the classic apathy from a group clearly wondering why they were spending their PE session indoors talking about their lesson when they would rather be outside (which I completely understand, I hate theory stuff). Trying to coax the answer from the class, he said, 'Well, when Mr P does exercise, he will have to do a lot of stretches, this is because he has a lot of what?'

Immediately a boy's hand shot up, being a nice, quiet, knowledgeable boy. Geordie PE teacher pointed in excitement and said, 'Yes, shoot,' and the boy shouted very animatedly: 'FAT!'

The class burst out laughing. I mean, being over 18 stone he wasn't wrong. The funniest bit was when Geordie PE teacher walked over to me, as my face looked like I'd been in 40-degree heat without any cream as I was so embarrassed, and said to me, 'Howay pet [yes, he really speaks like this], I thought he was gonna say muscle!'

The funny thing is, a burn about your weight, even if you aren't big in the slightest, is that it is a regular occurrence in every classroom across the land. No decent teacher would ever dream of making fun of a child's physical insecurities, but funnily enough the children have zero issue in doing this to their unsuspecting grown-ups as you will be able to tell from some of these:

I was doing supply and a child asked when my baby was due, turns out, about 8 years later!! He was mortified when I told him I wasn't pregnant, I just really liked cake! It was a shame – really liked that dress!

When I was covering a different class, the desk chair I was sitting on kept very slowly getting lower and I was obviously looking confused because one of the kids tried to reassure me by saying, 'It's all right, Mrs M, it always does that when something heavy is on it!' The look on their face was a picture when they realised what they'd said – I couldn't stop laughing!

I was invited to try on a firefighter's outfit when we had the Year 5 fire talk. I happened to mention that the trousers were a bit tight to get on, and one girl shouts out, 'You've only got yourself to blame!'

Another time I was working in Year 1 and wearing a short-sleeved top. I suddenly became aware of a child playing with my upper arm. I tried to ignore it but had to ask him why he was doing it. 'Because it's squishy,' came the reply.

Many years ago, teaching Year 3, a child said they liked my trousers. I replied that I liked them as they made me feel skinny. One child piped up with, 'What? Skinny in a fat way?' I laughed and laughed. Then, when she returned for a placement 15 years later, I reminded her. Every. Single. Day.

A small child looked at me carefully before starting to draw me. I was flattered when he said that I had a skinny face. Then it became clear that what he meant was that it was covered in skin!

A high school pupil said to me, 'I've had my Covid vaccine. You might get called for yours soon, because, well, because you're massive. I just wanted you to know.'

My husband has just been on a residential trip with his Year 6 class. Seeing him in a wetsuit, one boy said, 'Sir, you've got a dad bod!'

Only yesterday I weighed myself and I'm a new low! Feeling on top of the moon as my diet is working, I walk into Nursery and one of the lovely angels said 'SARAH!' So I turned around thinking I'll see a new first or something they found on the floor; the angel then said, 'You have a really fat belly,' and then let out a giggle. I'm nearly a size 10 ...

I know what you're thinking: how do you put up with these brutal burns on a daily basis? It's quite simple, really. Ninety per cent of the time they are said with such innocence and are side-splittingly funny, so you can't stay mad. But like most things while working in a school, it can age you, and nothing ages you more than when a child comments on how old you are or look. My first day as a teaching assistant in 2012, I walked into school as a fresh-faced 23-year-old, hair was looking on fleek and confidence was relatively high. I was told to make my way to the bottom class-room as I was assisting with Year 6. When I made my way down the corridor, butterflies began to fly in my gut as I sheepishly knocked on the door and the teacher invited me in. Upon introducing myself, a child began to laugh and proceeded to say, 'Haha, we ain't getting taught by a 40-year-old One Direction wannabe, are we?' Wow, first things first, which 1D member was he referring to? I mean Harry Styles I would take but my hair looked nothing like his. Liam? I digress. Forty years of age, though, what?! I still had spots on my face! Well, I am clearly not the only one to get burnt by cheeky cherubs abusing your age – check these out:

- *A child asked me once if I was alive when pavements were invented ... I was about 22 at the time.*
- *'Were you in the Navy when World War II happened, Miss?' I was 39!*
- *A child told me and the headteacher last week that we wouldn't be at school if he came back as a grown up because once you are 40 you stay home and wait to die alone.*
- *I was once asked by a Year 1 pupil if I had electricity in the olden days, when I was little?*
- *History lesson on old toys ... I got asked if I had a penny farthing when I was a child!*
- *A boy drew a picture of me (a 35-year-old woman). I said, 'Wow! That's really good, you have even got my wrinkles.' He then looked at me and said, 'That's your beard!!' I stopped and shopped at Boots on the way home!*
- *Mrs S, when you and Jesus were alive, were the dinosaurs there?*

Children are innocent souls, and whenever they blurt out an absolute burn it can truly make your day, even if your confidence is ever so slightly hit. It was only recently that a lovely girl walked over to me in the playground and tapped me on my back. During this lunchtime the weather was truly horrendous – it was cold, it was miserable, I was freezing and feeling sorry for myself, although unfortunately it was not wet enough to blow the whistle and shatter the dreams of the innocent cherubs by calling wet play. There is something about a cold strong wind: it sends the children completely cuckoo! Surely everyone has experienced this?! Something about when children are in gale-force winds, they suddenly all become possessed.

After the girl tapped me on the back, I turned around, probably looking miffed as I could no longer feel my face. I was 100 per cent expecting a classic telltale about another child, but I was wrong. This lovely girl said, 'Do you want to hear a joke?' I thought, wow, clearly this child has seen I'm a bit miffed with the weather and she had come over to warm my heart. I replied, 'Thank you, I'd love to hear your joke.' She smiled and waved me towards her. In a very excited voice she screamed, 'YOU!' then walked off like an absolute boss. I was left standing in the middle of the playground, with nowhere to turn or look (this was half to do with being absolutely burned by a six-year-old and half the fact I was frozen all over). I had to hold my hands up, what a joke, one that must have slipped past me in my youth, as I would have definitely said that one!

World Book Day in school is always brilliant, a chance for children and staff to dress up, to embrace and celebrate the fantastic world of books and reading. The majority of children and staff really go for it, with amazing outfits and hairstyles. I remember many years ago, a girl came to school dressed as Cindy-Lou Who from Dr Seuss's classic *The Grinch*, with a plastic bottle placed on her head. Her parents were able to use a few tins of hairspray to make the most amazing hairstyle and she absolutely stole the show!

From the same year, a member of staff I worked with, a truly memorable individual, with one of the coolest teacher names I've ever heard – Mr Edge (if ever a child was pushing their luck, you could always remind them that they were getting close to the edge). He was a slick, smart and stern teacher, who demanded the respect of the children and staff alike. It was rare that he dropped his strict persona; however, fortunately on World Book Day he decided to join in and have some fun. The day arrived and he came in dressed in a full tuxedo, hair combed back, and announced to the staff, 'The name's Edge ... Mr Edge.' He'd gone all out as James Bond and I was very impressed. As the children filtered into the class, Mr Edge was stood outside waiting to make a star entrance. Once all the children were sat down, he swung the door open, acting very much like 007 while singing the Bond theme, then reached the front of the class and did the classic Bond shooting down the lens pose. It was at this point that Mr Edge was very much shaken and stirred as a child put their hand up and said, 'Sir, why have you come dressed at Mickey Mouse?' Mr Edge went from having a goldeneye to a very red face. I'm not quite sure if Mr Edge participated in the madness of World Book Day again, but as I reminded him, 'You only live twice.'

Mr Edge isn't the only person to feel the burn on a World Book Day. There is the story of the lady who was eight months pregnant on World Book Day. She decided to just go in her own clothes. She decided to not even attempt to dress up. A lad in Year 3 asked her why she hadn't dressed as a character; the teacher simply replied, 'No stores seem to stock a World Book Day maternity range so I'd not been able to find anything to wear.' He said, 'I know who you could have come as! Him who was in charge of all the engines on *Thomas the Tank Engine*! What was his name? Oh yeah, that's it ... the Fat Controller!'

Playgrounds are a great place for a burn; they show the children in the wild, so who knows what they could come out with. Reminds me of this classic tale from a retired teacher who was returning to her old stomping ground after she had left for retirement bliss. She had a short pixie cut when she left and had more of a cropped bob on her visit. In early autumn she walked across the playground at play-time after coming to watch the harvest assembly. Seeing staff friends in the playground, one spoke to her, saying, 'I haven't seen your hair that long for ages, I love it.'

'But does it make me look older?' she replied.

'No,' she said, alongside several children agreeing with her.

Feeling good, the retiree began to move away. The bell went and the children passed by her. One boy stopped, looked at her and said,

'Oh it's you. I thought it was just some random old woman on the playground!'

Before this chapter finishes, I have to throw this final one in there. A colleague of mine had the funniest little tale about a boy in her class. I guess you can call this a teacher burn, or at least you can use the item to calm a burn. One morning, a little boy ran into Year 1 all excited and up to Mrs G. All thrilled, he handed her a sheet of folded-up paper and said, 'I saw this and thought of you.' Every school staff will be given lovely notes and pictures across the year, they may not all survive the recycling bin, but the thought and effort always holds a place in your heart. Mrs G thanked the child and thought it was a lovely gesture to start her week. She opened the note, assuming it was going to be a drawing of her. Now, we always know that a child-drawn portrait can go two ways: you can have a child be very generous and knock some serious weight off you, or you can be drawn as a human elephant. It could be a lovely note to say how appreciated you are, no doubt spelt wrong, but as always, it's the thought that counts. To Mrs G's shock, it was none of the above. It was, in fact (and I guarantee anyone reading this is not going to guess the correct item Mrs G was given), to her shock, an information booklet for ...

VAGISIL CREAM!! Yes, that's right, the itch-relief ointment for soothing sore lady parts. I guess it's a welcome change to the normal drawings and letters that school staff receive, but what exactly was the child trying to say?!

No matter how high you're riding, if you work with children, a fall back to earth is only around the corner.

Kids are gross. They are. No ifs or buts about it, they are a big pile of yuck. Yes, there are some beautifully behaved, immaculately presented and hygiene-conscious young people, but sadly they are the complete outliers, because KIDS ARE DISGUSTING!

One of our favourite podcast features that usually gets us giggling uncontrollably is the one we call 'Disgustin', based on the video of the two Scottish kids performing a Cher Lloyd (don't bother googling her) song before their mum bursts into the room and interrupts:

'Why does somebody not know how to flush a toilet when they've had a SH*T?!?'

Youngest child replies, 'It was'nae me!'

Mum declares, 'Well it was f**king one of yuz! DISGUS-TANG!!'

If you haven't seen it yet, go find it on YouTube. It's hilarious and tragic in equal measure but it inspired us to create a section of our podcast where readers share their revoltingly hilarious stories about poo, bogies, farts, burps, wee, sick and, if we're really lucky, ear wax!

It tends to be less terrible higher up the school, so if you teach at the top of Key Stage 2, then it's fair to say you will usually have a lot more marking to do but, fortunately, a hell of a lot less faecal matter to deal with.

Swings and roundabouts really, although I think we may have already been sent stories where there's been mystery brown stuff on swings and, indeed, roundabouts! There is something about the word disgusting; personally, I like it, because unlike some really annoying primary school words, it is pretty much spelled how it sounds. This word is used to describe many, and I mean many, occurrences during a school day. I must be clear: when we talk about the disgusting things that happen in schools, 95 per cent of the stories are about the children, and something unfortunate they have decided to do.

We should take a moment here, as it is so important in this chapter of all chapters to salute the Early Years staff again, because your days are filled with crap (that isn't a metaphor for a rubbish day, that means these heroic school staff members who work with the youngsters have days literally filled with crap). Yet somehow they find the funny side of it and, lucky enough for us, they send in their hilarious, disgusting tales so we can all have a laugh and appreciate the strong stomachs of the Early Years staff/legends.

One of my personal favourite disgusting stories comes from being on a residential. Taking groups of children away for a period of time to a place outside of their normal surroundings, what could possibly go wrong?

Walking through a lovely part of the Lake District, the group leader of our trip explained to the children that if they pick up certain rocks, check them properly as they could turn out to be limestone. As you can imagine, the children were very excited, me not so much, because on most residentials you have to try to last a full day of long excursions only eating a child's packed lunch, which potentially consists of a sandwich (cheese, ham or cheese and ham), a piece of fruit, a warm yoghurt and warm carton of orange juice. A man of my stature (ok, size) needs far more than this for sustenance so you can imagine me traipsing around with a rumbling tummy and dreaming of eating a Big Mac.

For one of the boys in my group, let's call him 'Andrew', I was really hoping this experience would open his eyes to the joy of being a decent team player (it didn't). I was also hoping his sand-wiches were up for grabs (they weren't). To describe Andrew is tricky, as he didn't really like school, the staff or his peers and had been quite open about the fact he had hated being away and didn't enjoy the activities. Luckily for us he was interested in rocks, fossils and dinosaurs so he was actually engaged in one particular task after a previous lecture on limestone. He was loving it. He was picking up rock after rock, getting close and finding out whether he had picked up the sought-after limestone he had been learning about. A few minutes later, a huge cheer went up just in front of me. Andrew leaped for joy and was telling everyone that he had a beautiful piece of limestone; he was polishing it, looking very closely and stroking it to try to see the formation and composition (yeah, I was listening to the instructor). Then he put it in the pocket of his new North Face climbing jacket, you know, the expensive coats you try to beg parents not to buy for these sorts of trips. At 10 years old and mostly working outdoors for a week, there is a huge possibility of those posh jackets getting ruined by the end of the trip.

Andrew's 'limestone' was stroked, polished, examined and played with for at least 45 minutes before being tucked away safely in his lovely expensive pockets. Once we had finished the walk, the instructor gathered us all in for a bit of show and tell. The children were getting their stones out, comparing them with each other's and asking the expert instructor if indeed they had picked up limestone. To many of the children's disappointment, none of the rocks they had picked up were in fact limestone, just normal rocks (including mine unfortunately – I think the snail trail on it made me think it was more than it was). Andrew waited patiently, before excitedly pulling out his rock for all to see. He shoved it right in the face of the instructor. The instructor pulled an awkward face and inspected it for a quick second before announcing to Andrew that his 'limestone' was actually a piece of 'doggy doo doo'. So for the past 45 minutes, poor old Andrew had been in possession of a beautifully hardened piece of dogsh*t. The best bit about this story is Andrew found it very, very funny, laughing with me and his peers about the disgusting piece of limestone that never was. It was really positive to see Andrew come out of himself and it's true that sometimes sh*t happens, but in this case, in a good way!

I think this is a good time to issue you with a warning: if you are reading this book accompanied by some nice food, I highly recommend you just pause, finish your food and then continue reading after. We are going to take you through some of the most disgusting tales but, I have to admit, some of these stories will give you that feeling in the pit of your stomach, like when you're on the top of a rollercoaster, or when you were younger and your parents would drive over a big hill. Prepare for a weird sensation in your tummy; not quite butterflies in this instance, more butterflies are covered in unpleasantness because, as we always like to say, primary school children are the weirdest, funniest and most disgusting creatures in the world!

It's time to embarrass one of my nearest and dearest friends now, and they won't mind as I'm not actually going to name them. And before anyone even thinks it, I did not commit this act and I'm not just covering for myself now ... I swear. When you were in Nursery or Reception (aged three to five), I'm sure if you try to remember things from your school days at this particular age, it's a struggle. It's like the amazing Pixar movie *Inside Out*. You make millions of memories but they fade and are replaced by new, stronger memories as you become older. But certain memories are core memories, and these are etched into your mind, never to be forgotten ... and this is the case for poo gate!

My friend in primary school went to the toilet while the teacher was reading everyone a story on the carpet; unfortunately he wasn't completely toilet-trained by this point and decided to go number two on his hand. Now, after doing this surely any normal person would then put the excrement inside the toilet bowl – actually, scrap that, any normal person would simply do their business straight in the loo and go about their day. However, in a mass panic, the boy decided to wipe the faeces all over the surrounding cubicle ... and himself. Just as the teacher was about to finish the *Very Hungry Caterpillar*, the boy appeared, looking like he'd been on the children's classic game show *Get your own back*, but instead of being doused in green slime, he'd unfortunately been covered in his own dung! He was eventually toilet-trained and the story would only be mentioned to him by his mates once or twice ... a day. He sees the funny side, and having children himself now, he knows the struggle to try to contain a child's instinct to turn themself into a human (or indeed poo-man) Jackson Pollock creation.

In and around June of 2020, there was an announcement from the UK government saying that three year groups within primary school would be able to safely return to classrooms, as long as they abided by the social distancing rules (keep 2 metres away from each other). I'm sure you don't need me to go over the meaning, as after the last few years these are core memories for all of us. The three year groups to return to school were Year 6 – understandable, they are 10 to 11 years of age and have the maturity and knowhow to stay distanced from their friends (well, we could hope) – and the other two year groups chosen to return were Reception and Year 1. Now, it does not take a rocket scientist to figure out that children aged four and five would not be able to stay away from each other. There is more chance of me going to KFC and turning down the 'go large' option on a Zinger Tower Meal than the youngest children in schools maintaining any measure of hygiene or social distancing. Speaking to any member of school staff from the Early Years would have highlighted the impossibility of such a task with youngsters. Taken aback by the ridiculous suggestion that little ones would be able to maintain the required space, to have some fun we appealed to our Facebook and Instagram followers and simply asked them to complete the following sentence: **'I don't think Reception children can social distance because I once saw ...'**

The responses (as I'm sure you can imagine) were absolutely outrageous. Prepare to laugh, and potentially lose your lunch (we did warn you).

Let's start with the discussion you are probably expecting: POO, otherwise known as poop, doodoo, slop or crap (did anyone's parents ever view this as a swear word?). A nice, simple one to ease us in gently: one teacher found two children rolling a piece of poo to each other in the kitchen area of a Reception class!

Moving on to a similar idea, I always remember a classic tale from the first school I worked at, involving my friend who is a Nursery teacher. She chose a boy to go round the class giving out fruit, then the teacher noticed something drop to the floor, so she scurried over and picked up the item that had dropped, thinking it was a piece of fruit with a mind of its own. Upon quick inspection, though, she realised it was in fact a piece of poo. She turned to the boy who was still handing fruit out, like everything was normal, and simply asked, 'Is this poo?' The boy replied instantly, 'Yeah, it fell out of my leg!' Lesson to everyone: don't use your bare hands to pick up anything suspicious – you won't just have egg on your face, you will have crap in your hands, too.

Talking about crap in your hands, a child announced to a teacher that they thought they may have diarrhoea by holding up his poop-covered finger in her face. Not all heroes wear capes, but any brave soul putting up with that sort of stuff on a daily basis deserves all the respect in the world.

If you work in an Early Years setting, or you have young children yourself, you know that children soiling themselves is a stage of life. Nine times out of 10, by schooltime this is a stage of life that may be in most parents' rear-view mirrors, but in some cases – as for my friend at primary school – it can take longer. Luckily, school staff are prepared for this; there is always a box of spare uniform or underwear on hand if anyone makes a mess. One child who often soiled himself had an agreement with his teacher that, if it was to happen, the teacher would put the soiled, messy clothes in a bag and place them in the classroom cupboard for the child to take home at the end of the day. This was going swimmingly (wish I hadn't used that word now) until the day the child forgot to take the bag of mucky uniform home; this unfortunately coincided with the teacher going on maternity leave. Unbelievably, when returning to the school a year later, the bag was still in the cupboard! Imagine the stench! I mean, if you were a fly on the wall in that cupboard, you'd probably be a dead fly from breathing in the horrendous odour that built up over a year.

A teacher once saw a child pick a scab from another child's knee and eat it. Now I'm sorry, it does not matter how hungry you are, or even if it was a quiche day in the school dinner hall, there is never an excuse for that (even if they had permission from the scab owner). Maybe the child was looking to expand their taste palette or potentially improve their immune system. Whatever it was, it was yuck!

One child decided to lick another child's eyeball. I mean, it's all well and good wanting to be the star pupil, but licking an actual pupil will not help your cause. In another experiment to broaden the taste buds, two children licked all the carpet spaces to see if they tasted the same. Now we are talking about roughly 20 carpet spaces, each sat on by pupils who probably are yet to be able to wipe their backsides properly, so yeah, make of that what you will.

When a class was getting changed for PE, a teacher came in and saw one Reception child licking another classmate's toes. When the teacher said, 'Stop that right away!' the child replied, 'Why?! He likes it!' The last thing you expect to see in a five-year-old is an early foot fetish! These stories clearly show that children do not care about germs or hygiene, they just want to taste different things, like the child who was seen deepthroating a door handle! Children experiment, and sooner or later they will realise it's probably not the best thing to do (or lick, or eat).

Children will often use their hands to feel different things and experience different textures and surfaces, but unfortunately this can also lead to some disgusting tales.

I always remember my friend from secondary school, he used to do a thing called the 'credit card' – whenever one of his mates bent over he would swipe his hand up the arse crack of the school pants and yell 'CREDIT CARD!' Looking back on your school days as an adult, you realise that some crazy stuff happened that at the time was just everyday life.

Back to Reception now. While sitting on a carpet, one child put his finger in another child's bum crack. On a different occasion, one boy was trying to stick USB leads up his friend's arse cavern! I bet the USB lead was upside down, not that it is important, but whenever you plug in a USB lead, even though there's a 50 per cent chance you will put it in correctly, you always do it the wrong way, but I'm sure it made no difference when two children were putting them down each other's back passages.

Enough of what comes from the botty; it's time for some tales that are snotty. Everyone can trace their mind back to when they were in school, there were always one or two children who had out-of-control mucus – I'm talking noses constantly stuffed, certain days it looked like the Grinch was popping out to say hello, jumpers reflecting the light like solar panels on a summer day from all the snail trails on them, and if you can't think of that child in your school, well, I'm sorry to say, it was probably you, you snotty bugger!

In one school, two children picking each other's noses in sync. As school staff we are all up for teamwork and helping each other, but when it comes to mining for nose gold, it really should be a solo mission with a tissue.

A child sneezed into the palm of her hand, on which ended up a generous quantity of runny, bright green snot. The child looked at the mess in her hand and decided on her next move. A tissue maybe? Run it under the tap? A wipe on the jumper/cardigan? Unfortunately, none of these were the options taken; instead, she put her mouth over the mess and slurped it back up. Scientifically, we are aware that this actually may help the child to build up her immune system, but surely a mouthful of grollies is a bit too far. What should they call it? Green cuisine? Cordon bleuargh? Still with us? These next teachers wish they weren't anywhere near their children's nasal mucus deposits.

One child gave a staff member a rolled-up bogey and convinced them it was Blu Tack. Now I'm not the sharpest knife in the toolshed, but surely the fact the Blu Tack was green was a slight giveaway. Lower down in a school, you will always see children picking their noses, choosing a winner, having a snoot root, but here is a word of advice: always make the children clean or wipe their hands immediately if you witness them in the act. We were told about one child who ran across the classroom and fell onto the teacher in the class, with the bogey they had on their finger landing in the teacher's mouth. I mean, what can we say to that? Absolutely heartbreaking scenes for the teacher involved, my thoughts and prayers go out to them.

Now that you're all feeling quite nauseous, I think it's only fair we stick with that theme as we approach some delightful tales involving vomit. Rarely a day goes by that a little cherub isn't green around the gills, feeling a little bit under the weather. Upsettingly, the forecast will be less like cats and dogs and more like carrots and sweetcorn. Sorry, couldn't resist. In preparation for this next section, a mere wet paper towel may not suffice. You'd best grab that sick bag, just in case!

I have a personal tale of woe. On the way to a school trip, we warned the children to not eat too many sweets or treats before the 90-minute coach ride to the museum. Initially, my fellow staff members and I felt like our words of warning had been listened to, but yes, you guessed it, one child thought they were the exception to the rule. To my horror this child had decided to have a healthy breakfast of a Haribo cocktail made up of three small bags of Tangfastics, three small bags of Starmix and three small bags of Supermix (balanced, I suppose). The fizzy, jelly sweet concoction combined with whatever she had consumed before the trip was a disaster waiting to happen. Unsurprisingly, this resulted in projectile vomiting, two rows in front of me, and because we were driving at a pace, the sick was flowing like a lumpy moat right to the back of the coach. It felt like slow motion; I picked up my bag and asked all the children to lift their feet and belongings. It was a trying time and unfortunately there were a few good water bottles that were lost to the spew river. It didn't really feel like the right time to give it the old 'I told you so' to the sugar-filled child, as rings, eggs and bears were floating towards the back of the coach. The most awkward conversation was with the driver: 'Really sorry, mate, but your drive back is going to be one to forget. Maybe put some earplugs up your nostrils, pal!' Strangely, I never saw that particular bus driver again.

At high school my friend O'B (yes, the one who makes shocking shouts) hasn't always had the best diet. I mean, I'm hardly one to talk, but one morning before we caught the 723 bus to school, O'B decided to eat six packs of Wotsits – a whole multipack to himself. I don't know what offended me more, his carrot-tinged fingers or his tango-looking teeth. We were on the school bus, bear in mind we attended an all-boys' school but we shared the 723 bus with the local all-girls' school, so you were always on guard to look and smell your best. Due to his horrendous choice of breakfast cuisine, O'B suddenly turned white in the middle of the journey and it was inevitable what was going to happen, so everyone around him started to scramble to move out of the firing line. With girls all around, too, O'B tried his best to cover what was going to be a highly embarrassing situation for him. He ended up opening his school bag and throwing up inside it! He had to zip it back up and carry it off the bus at the end of the journey. Truly disgusting scenes! His classic secondary school French textbook *Encore Tricolore* was never the same, and the bag and all the contents ended up in a bin, alongside O'B's chances with any of the girls on that bus on that really cheesy Wotsit morning. I'm sure our teacher had heard some homework excuses in his time, but 'Sorry sir, I ate six packs of Wotsits for breakfast and threw up in my bag and binned the whole lot' surely was a first!

Ever wonder what children are given for breakfast? A child was sick on the first day back of term. When they were picked up, their parents said, 'I knew she shouldn't have had biryani for breakfast.' The staff thought this could be the case as she had remnants of rice on her lips after she was sick.

You have to feel for any member of school staff that gets covered in sick. It's slightly different to if you're out on a drinking session and you either have too many yourself and end up chucking up, or your friend goes too far and you're either holding hair back or rubbing the back of someone who is heaving. But this is happening during work, the profession that you've trained for. You don't expect to be covered in sick at 10am on a Tuesday. I'd say the difficulty as well is the fact that children rarely give you warning if they are going to throw up, like this unfortunate Nursery teacher ...

A Nursery child was sobbing. She sat on the teacher's knee and said she didn't feel well. Out of nowhere a warm, damp patch crept across the teacher's knee ... then suddenly the child threw up all over her!

Now you can almost forgive a Nursery-aged child for not being able to verbally communicate the feeling they are experiencing just before they are sick, but by the time they reach Year 6 they know the golden rule - get out of the classroom ... Just go! Not this particular child, though. During a guided reading session, without a single word of warning, the child who looked as green as a Teenage Mutant Ninja Turtle blew chunks on the table and the unbelievable force directed the sea of sick straight into the face of the teacher!

Always check that children are well enough before any sort of school performance. During a festive performance, a child was sick down his recorder in church. Now I think we can all agree that the noise a primary school recorder makes can make anyone feel queasy, but this was another level. In another performance-based barf, you have to respect the absolute commitment by one member of staff who, while watching a school choir performance, saw a child throw up a whole portion of spaghetti and heroically leapt down to grab it before it reached the floor. That's not all; this legendary teaching assistant knelt there holding it till the four verses of 'Away in a Manger' had finished. You might think this is a Christmas miracle, but no, this is classic school staff dedication!

When tidying up sick at school, you usually have a designated member of staff who will clear up with no complaining or any reaction to the potential stench. When applying your clean-up tool of choice, whether you put a paper towel on it, sawdust or powder, always make sure children are away from the affected area or you may have more children struggling like a weird vomit domino effect. One staff member cleared up some sick and went to put the cleaning products away, when a child announced, 'Look, it's been snowing,' while playing with the 'vomit powder' that had been placed over the sick that his classmate had just produced! He wasn't too happy once he realised that his 'snow' wasn't quite what he thought it was. I've never thought a pile of vomit with sawdust or powder covering it looked like snow. I just hope that the child didn't try to make a snowman, even though they may have been able to locate a nose ...

A child in a different school saw a pile of sick on the floor covered in 'vomit powder' and told everyone who would listen that there was a huge apple crumble on the carpet. I am keeping everything crossed that the child wasn't tempted to bring some custard to the party. Imagine explaining that to the parents!

To end this chapter, I think it's important that we go all 'Mythbusters' on a certain urban classroom legend.

Which one?

Do teachers fart in class and blame the kids?

Oh, that one.

I'm able to reveal (potentially) for the first time in print ...

Shall I do a drum-roll?

Save that for the audiobook.

Good plan.

So ... Do teachers fart in class and blame the children?

Go on then ...

Well ... it depends on which teacher.

Cop-out!

Well, some excellent classroom practitioners are the epitome of professionalism and would never pass wind and blame a poor child.

Most teachers ...

Most teachers, however, have definitely let off a nervous toot mid-lesson and decided that the class trump machine should take the hit for their pungent air biscuit. Better that than Miss Francis be forever known as 'Fart-Pants Francis'.

If you are asking me and Adam, however ...

OF COURSE WE BLOODY DO!

Adam, would you like to share the time when Cockney John grassed you up in front of the kids?

That was a bad one. Egg City!

So, I dropped me guts at the back of the room and slowly made my way to the front of the class. I saw the kids getting a little disturbed by the pong I had emitted so I did what any bright spark would do, ask the rhetorical fart question:

'Oh dear, children, there's a bit of a funny smell. If you need to pop to the toilet, just go. Don't be embarrassed!'

And I would've gotten away with it, if it wasn't for that meddling Cockney John!

Ruh-roh! (Scooby-Doo voice)

Just as my disgraceful whiff made it to CJ's desk, his face changed. It was like he'd been smashed in the face with a 'poo-bat' (Kenny 2006).

'Bruv! Oh my days! What the ...'

'One of the kids needs the toilet, I think.'

'No way, bruv, that's from an adult. Dat was you!'

I whistled and continued to deny it, but they all knew it was me.

Ploppy-Pants Parky?

I dunno. I'm just glad they were Year 6 and leaving soon. The last thing I needed was a guff-based nickname being spread around the school.

And there you have it, folks; children are definitely disgusting creatures but the gross shenanigans aren't limited to just the younglings.

Ah ... and one piece of advice.

Go on.

Much like the class phantom farter, make sure you don't let rip on a plastic school chair; it acts like an amplifier and denying the supplying is near impossible!

Did you learn that the hard way?

Of course!

Zoinks!

Injuries at School

If I were to ask you which jobs you think come with a higher risk of danger and could lead to a career-threatening injury, the first few that come to mind may well be: soldiers, fire-fighters, police officers or people working with heavy machinery (before you say it, a jammed photocopier is not heavy machinery). Believe it or not, being a teacher comes with a high risk of injury, and before anyone says, 'Oh yeah, a paper cut!' try this one for size:

This is an injury that haunts me to this day. It didn't happen to me, instead I was the one who caused the injury. Back in Year 1, the teacher had handed out worksheets, and being the polite and happy-to-help pupil, I started handing them out to others on my table. I took one piece and turned to pass it when the child behind me put his head forward and, yes, you probably guessed it, he got a paper cut in his eye. He ended up having an eye patch for a while. I was mortified and remember crying for hours about how I had blinded a fellow classmate. I often stare at my ceiling while in bed, reliving the moment I almost blinded another child.

Granted, this happened between two pupils, but that could have easily been a staff member. Teaching isn't really a role that you necessarily associate with bad injuries, but in this chapter we are going to run through some tales to prove to you that working in a school can be one of the most injury-filled jobs in the world, and we're not even talking about swinging back on your chair – although that is incredibly dangerous and no child should ever do it. Remember, four legs, two feet on the floor if you want to stay out of hospital.

One of the worst classroom injuries I have witnessed as a teacher happened a few years back. There was a teacher who decided to invite a visitor into my classroom without even asking or checking with me. She just rocked up into my classroom and quickly introduced this student who was developing something tech-based at a university and wanted to see how technology was used in the classroom. I was a little pissed off as I had just been completely blindsided. But I decided to crack on, and asked a pupil to grab a chair from the school hall and tried to ask a little more about why this young man had come to visit. However, I quickly realised the gentleman spoke little to no English, which was going to make the lesson even more interesting as I couldn't work out what he wanted to know or see and he couldn't explain either. The pupil brought back the chair and as I started the lesson the gentleman decided to unfold the chair but didn't do it fully, and for some strange reason unbeknown to any of us to this day, he put his hands under the chair as he sat down and trapped his hand. I heard a yelp and assumed it was one of the usual odd noises my class made. I continued with my input for possibly 15 minutes while this young man sat there clutching his hand in agony, but he didn't make a sound or draw attention to himself. He was too polite to interrupt and it was only once I had set the children off with some work and he came over with his hand wrapped in a blood-stained handkerchief that I saw what had happened: his finger was almost ripped off. My stomach churned as the colour drained from the visitor's face. He was trying to tell me in very limited English that he was in a lot of pain while I was trying not to draw the student's attention to the fact that the unexpected guest had nearly chopped his own hand off. I immediately sent for the school office manager while trying to keep the gentleman from not fainting as blood poured from his hand. I gave him a constant feed of paper towels and tried to keep my class on task with the work I had set. The office manager came and escorted the guy back to the office. I wish I could now explain what happened after, and whether the severed finger was stitched back on, but truth be told I have no idea. I never spoke to or heard from him ever again. It was one of the most surreal experiences of my teaching career, but it taught me a valuable lesson I sort of already knew: don't put your hands under a foldable chair when you sit down.

Every teacher will probably pick up an injury or two when joining in with their class PE sessions over the years. A tennis ball to the head, a hamstring strain and maybe a bit of writers' cramp when jotting down the number of rounders in a game. Nothing that requires hospitalisation, hopefully. Not Mr Barry, though. Mr Barry, my high-school PE teacher, was not only injury prone, he could almost be considered as slapstick personified. Poor Mr Barry was a typical PE teacher; he loved getting involved in the sessions and had clearly been a great athlete in his formative years, but like all of us, time catches up, and unfortunately for Mr Barry he was at loggerheads with Old Father Time and constantly trying to prove to the whole school that he still 'had it'. This is what led to some painful, embarrassing moments that have not just left scars on Mr Barry's body, but also in the minds of all the pupils 'lucky' enough to witness these fails. In hindsight, we should have changed Mr Barry's name to Lemony Snicket, as his lessons were usually a series of unfortunate events!

Let's kick things off with a famous Mr Barry warm-up. Now, for anyone who remembers PE in school, or teaches PE in schools currently, warm-ups are crucial to begin every session, not just to start up your cardiovascular system by raising your body temperature and increasing blood flow to your muscles (can you tell I did A-Level physical education?).

I think most of our readers are shocked you made it to A-levels, mate!

However, when you are teaching, the warm-up is always a good time to ask questions or introduce what the lesson is going to involve. Also, while the class are stretching, you can try to set up the equipment because you had bugger-all time to do it beforehand. During Mr Barry's warm-up this day, he asked the class to step on and off the 'classic' brown school benches, you know the ones – the benches that Year 6 get to finally sit on in their final year of primary school (although they don't just have those in primary schools, secondary schools also have the same ones!). I feel we have to take a moment to appreciate the durability of these bad boys: even if they are on the cusp of breaking, they seem to last year after year, decade after decade (and century after century, with any luck, considering the current budget crisis!). Anyway, back to Calamity Barry. As the class were stepping on and off the benches, Mr Barry was not very happy with the effort being displayed – I mean, you can't really step on and off a bench incorrectly, but Mr Barry took exception and started shouting at them, questioning the technique on show. He blew his whistle and said, 'Right, everyone cast your eyes this way. This is how I want each and every one of you to be doing this!' As Mr Barry stepped on the bench with intent, he stepped off and fell over like a pile of aggressive PE-teacher spuds. The class burst out laughing, thinking it was nothing more than a slip, and he shouted out, 'Go and get Mr Jones.' Mr Jones was a small scouse man who taught PE and economics, if I remember rightly, but he definitely was not a first-aider. When we finally located Mr Jones, he instructed a few of the stronger lads to lift Mr Barry into a wheelbarrow. Yes, a wheelbarrow! Where this wheelbarrow came from is still a mystery to me (and the more I write 'wheelbarrow', the more it's turning into one of those words that doesn't seem to be a real word and now I'm questioning what a 'barrow' even is, so I'll move on). Obviously with risk-assessments nowadays I'm not sure this would be allowed, but back then he was wheeled off to the medical room like it was normal procedure, an ambulance ended up being called and, to the shock of the class, it was revealed days later that Mr Barry had suffered a broken ankle! Let this be a lesson: warm-ups do prevent injuries, but in Mr Barry's case they caused a momentous one. We had to make a substitution in the middle of the lesson – subbing Mr Jones in for Mr Barry – and hope that Mr Barry could take his place on the bench better than he could step off it!

The ankle injury to Mr Barry clearly affected him, not from a confidence standpoint because as soon as his ankle was healed he was back thinking he was still the young whipper-snapper he once was in his youth, but, as you will grasp from this next tale, the bench injury affected him as it surely weakened his ankle resistance.

Fast-forward now to the summer term. It was athletics season, a time in school that I loved as a child, with throwing, running and jumping events. It was like the Olympics, but I can't imagine an Olympics where the athletes were drinking pop, eating sweets and some performing events like the 100m sprint and the high jump in a pair of thick, black, leather Kickers shoes as they had forgotten their trainers. The day had finally arrived for our class to perform the triple jump. If you're not familiar with this event, it's similar to the long jump but involves a hop, skip and jump. We were all running down the track, one by one, attempting this hop, skip and jump with limited success. I could tell Mr Barry was becoming frustrated with the performances he was witnessing; it looked more like a class sprinting well towards the sandbox then doing a Village People-esque YMCA dance and landing in the sand, hoping to be measured the furthest. Mr Barry did what you have probably already guessed he was going to do – yes, you're correct, he channelled his inner Jonathan Edwards and took to the track with supreme confidence. To my shock, he didn't even do a warm-up (this may have had something to do with the warm-up that cost him four months of injury). He stood at the start of the track, commanding everyone to 'turn, watch and learn', then set off like Usain Bolt, about to reach the point when he transitioned into the hop, skip and jump. The class waited with bated breath as Mr Barry did a huge HOP, a gigantic SKIP and a monumental ARGHHHHHHH (SNAP)!

If you haven't already worked it out, Mr Barry did not manage to land his jump, and came crashing down to reality, merely touching the sandbox with the top half of his body. He was crying out in pain;

it was clearly the ankle again. My heart went out to him, but I had to laugh as a classmate came over and said, 'I measured, sir. You only got 0.8m.' Not what Mr Barry needed to hear when he was writhing in pain. With no wheelbarrows available at the time, Mr Barry had an ambulance come out again. It's a shame they didn't have an ambulance clubcard, because he would have collected some serious points. Unfortunately, the ankle was indeed broken ... again. I think this event did change Mr Barry, as I think he realised the Olympic dream at 55 years of age was truly gone. He never really tried to demonstrate anything as strenuous as this again (I presume the school was getting tired of constantly employing a supply teacher to cover Mr Barry's absences) so he was much more careful. The story, however, of Mr Barry's cavalcade of calamitous consequences is not over, my friends ...

Before I left the school, the last few PE lessons were made up of fun games, which all our year group loved – a game of football here (Mr Barry refereed), a game of rugby there (Mr Barry watched from the sidelines) and then right towards the end we had a huge game of softball. Now if you're not familiar with softball, it's like a mix of baseball and rounders, played with a large white ball and a bat. We were playing a game roughly 10 against 10 with everyone enjoying it and Mr Barry staying out the way, keeping score. Everyone was having a turn with the bat and anyone who wanted to could have a crack at bowling. At one stage in the game, one lad stepped up to the bowling mound and began to bowl, but clear inexperience of the technique caused him to throw what we like to call 'daisy cutters' (ones that annoyingly end up rolling along the floor). Bowling like this was incredibly frustrating for the batsmen as we only had a specified time to finish the game.

Mr Barry had seen enough. He hobbled over (there was definitely no hopping, skipping or jumping) and I'm sure he thought to himself, 'I'm just bowling a softball. What's the worst that could happen?'

(Yes, that's from the throwback Dr Pepper advert.) He asked the bowler for the ball and the next batsman stepped up. He wound his arm up and delivered a lovely, accurate ball which the batter completely misread, swung for and missed. Mr Barry was BACK, confidence was high and he was on top of the world. The next batter came into the firing line. Mr Barry was so pumped up he was throwing shade at the new batsmen, daring them to hit his 'curveball'. Again, Mr Barry pulled his arm back and released a ferocious-looking ball. The batter positioned himself and smashed the ball as sweet as a nut, straight back in the direction it came from. That direction was Mr Barry's and the ball smashed him in the face, knocking him unconscious and breaking his nose! The lad who delivered the knock-out strike made sure he checked on Mr Barry ... but only after he'd made it round all four bases to claim his home run. Ouch!

Sadly, this was the last time Mr Barry inspired us during a PE session. He recovered quickly and carried on teaching for years beyond. I doubt he participated quite as regularly during future PE sessions, but with a competitive fire always burning deep inside I couldn't rule it out. I guess the best way of finding out would be checking his ambulance reward card and seeing how many points he has accumulated ...

I mean, I can't really talk, I am a walking disaster, or should I say, limping disaster. I can't tell you how many times I have twisted an ankle in the playground trying to show off to the kids that I can still do things like I used to be able to – I must get that from good old Mr Barry. My most embarrassing injury came while out of school, though, when I broke my ankle, which forced me to be off work for two months. Now, I have had a history of ankle and foot injuries (which is the main reason I never trained to be a WWE wrestler), but up until this point I had never broken any bones. Upon sustaining such an injury, I wish I had a heroic tale to go hand in hand with the injury. Unfortunately, I broke my ankle playing golf ... yes, you heard it right, golf. Arguably one of the safer sports around. I had been playing quite regularly, I had bought some clubs and on the morning of that heartbreaking day I had gone to SportsDirect and purchased a large 16-pack of new golf balls. The only thing I didn't purchase was a safe pair of spiked golf shoes. I mean, I wasn't trying to make the PGA tour here, so I never saw the need to fork out for a pair of shoes I would rarely wear. If Primark doesn't do them, I probably don't need them! Anyway, it was a wet and slippery day; I made my way to the clubhouse with the Geordie PE teacher to play 18 holes on a full course. I was actually wearing a pair of K-Swiss trainers that were very old and had a serious lack of grip, because I was slipping and sliding throughout the opening nine holes. I blame that for my score being truly astronomical. Once we were on the back nine I realised taking small, shuffled steps would help me with my balance – so far so good, I had just smashed a beautiful drive on the 14th tee. Seriously, it was a monster. I was like a giddy schoolboy. I grabbed my golf trolley (which was rented; that was another piece of equipment I could not afford to purchase) and started marching down the fairway, slightly downhill, while boasting to Geordie PE teacher about how much closer to the green I was than him. It was at that moment that I lost my footing and I felt my ankle snap. I crumbled to the ground in the middle of the 14th fairway and, to add insult to injury, my golf bag was open and as I fell the trolley tipped over and the box of 16 balls (now down to roughly 13 due to stray play during the opening nine) rolled down the hill past my lifeless, whale-like physique. Geordie PE teacher didn't know what to do. Once he had stopped laughing he said, 'Howay man! Can you not finish the last five holes? I'm on for a record score!' I began to crawl as I was in excruciating pain, then saw two lads behind us arrive at the 14th tee. I thought, brilliant, these lads will help a golfer in need. They peered down and saw me sprawled out in a sea of cheap Dunlop golf balls and in clear need of assistance. Instead of helping me up, these two lads began to place their balls and pick which club to attack the 14th hole with. Once I finally crawled into the rough, Geordie PE teacher packed my bag and wheeled my trolley off before walking back to reception to get some help. The manager came in a golf buggy to pick me up. I felt like I was back at school and I didn't have the right PE kit, because while I was in the worst pain I'd ever felt he was lecturing me on how I should never play without the correct footwear and how I had let myself down. I honestly thought he was going to give me old-school punishment lines of 'I will never play golf in old K-Swiss shoes again' one hundred times.

So that's an injury tale that I am not proud of in the slightest. It ended my aspiring golf career and when I returned to my school and walked back into my Year 6 class they all shouted 'FOREEEEE' under Geordie PE teacher's instructions.

School injuries can happen anywhere, any time and any place, but they seem to be so much more brutal when they involve school equipment. Who knew child-size chairs and tables were so dangerous? You have to feel for this student on her first day at a placement while at uni …

A child swung back on their chair and landed it with its full weight onto the student's foot. However, she was so intimidated by the teacher she was working with that she didn't want to say anything, and instead hobbled through the rest of her placement day before finally seeking medical attention in A&E, where she was told that she had broken every bone in her foot! (I mean, is it even possible to break every bone in your foot? You have five metatarsals; how thick was that chair leg?!). The only positive to come from this painful experience was the lump on the side of the future teacher's foot that she was able to use to prove the urban legend was true – you must keep four legs on the floor or you could break a bone. Or 26, in this case!

I remember an absolute classic from my old school, during an assembly. I'm sure we can all agree that the chairs the staff have to sit on in a school hall assembly are at the top of the uncomfortable chain. My former colleague, Mr Woolley, to whom I am still close to this day, brought me one of my funniest assembly moments. With 180 children sitting in neat rows in the hall, all the staff were tactic- ally positioned down the sides of the room, confined to the old, brown wooden chairs. Now, as an 18-stone unit I was always worried about sitting on the chairs – a creak here, a squeak there – I had an irrational fear that at any point in front of the whole of the juniors my chair could give way. Mr Woolley, on the other hand, was a maximum 13 stone (he will appreciate me saying this, as he's been working abroad for a few years now, so chances are this number will have grown), but at the time he cycled to work every day and was fit as a fiddle. One Friday afternoon, Mr Woolley had just finished handing out his star of the week certificate at the front of the hall, and as he strolled back to his seat he spotted a child in his class not making the right choices. With a click of the fingers he ordered them to come and sit beside him at the end of the row, so he could make sure he was giving the children who won the awards in assembly the respect they deserved. Once the child had reluctantly moved to where he was directed, Mr Woolley sat down on his chair with authority. It was at this point that each leg of his chair collapsed and spread in four different directions with the seat crashing to the floor, leaving Mr Woolley lying on a pile of wood in the middle of the hall during a full assembly. The best bit about this was there was a serious lack of concern on anyone's part, but the child who had just been moved to sit next to him had front-row tickets to his teacher's most embarrassing moment. He was the happiest I'd ever seen him! Mr Woolley hopped to his feet and slid all the excess pieces of wood to the side of the hall. He immediately darted to the science cupboard that resided in the hall and remained there for the rest of the assem- bly. Everyone (staff, parents and children) did their best to show their respect to the award winners, but every few minutes the boy who had been moved to sit next to him would glance over to the cupboard and try his best to hold back his laughter. He wasn't on his own, though; all the staff were in stitches for the rest of the assembly!

A chair-related injury is a common feature of working in a primary school; breaking your finger on a photocopier … well, that's slightly more of a rarity. A female teacher went to put paper in one of the trays (because the last person who used the photocopier – definitely Year 6 – would never dream of replenishing it before walking away!), but unfortunately for this unlucky soul the tray flew back, taking her hand with it. She broke her finger clean across the knuckle of her ring finger. A TA drove her to the local hospital where she spent four hours in minor injuries, eight weeks in a splint and then had to have physio to regain movement in her finger. All at a time when her boyfriend was intending to propose! If this teaches you anything (and this will p*ss off a lot of school staff), you should always wait for someone else to replenish the paper!

One thing that probably deserves a place in the Random Things chapter is the trusty guillotine. If you are lucky enough to find one that actually works around the school, please be VERY careful. There can't be many pieces of school equipment that are named after a decapitation device made famous in the eighteenth century by French people. The school-based version is also a dangerous creation, whose job it is to trim up to 10 sheets of paper at a time (15 if I'm in a rush, but there's no guarantee on the quality of the slicing). If you're not careful, you may end up like one poor teacher, who rested her hand on a paper cutter, slicing the knuckle of her middle finger. The head-teacher had to drive her to the hospital to have the knuckle stitched and fixed with a wooden splint. Apparently, the poor teacher was not allowed to return to school until she could stop flipping the children the bird – something many a teacher would in fact like to be able to do!

Teachers and school staff throughout the country LOVE laminating and so did this eager teacher who was quickly tidying her classroom on the last day of term because she was trying to catch a flight to go and see her parents. While she was collating her latest laminated creations to cut out over half term, she scratched her eyeball with a laminated sheet by accidentally swiping it across her eye! In a mad dash to the airport, there was no time for A&E and during take-off and landing the pain in her eye was excruciatingly painful due to the pressure. Thankfully she arrived safe and sound with no permanent damage, but that's a red-eye flight she will always remember.

Chairs, guillotines, photocopiers and laminators – four clearly dangerous pieces of school equipment, but beware, injuries in school can be caused by small humans and come about when you least expect it. Take, for example, an excitable child who knew the answer in class and stuck his hand up enthusiastically to answer a question. Unfortunately, at the time, his teacher was leaning over him, and his attempt at answering the question resulted in scratching the teacher's cornea with his fingernail. The amazing thing about this was the teacher carried on teaching for the remainder of the lesson, then took herself to hospital at the end of the day.

I wonder if the child who shot his hand up gave the correct answer? How gutting for the teacher if the child raised his hand and asked to use the toilet. The teacher may have resented spending three weeks in an eye patch and looking like Captain Jack Sparrow's mate for a piddle request!

Being able to go to the toilet in school is a rarity, so teachers and school staff have mastered the silent art of bladder control (well, most of us). If you're in class with 30-plus children, it's doubtful that you're going to be able to slope off and use the loo, but be warned, toilets can be a dangerous place, too. Just ask the teacher who was sitting on the toilet, and after having finished her business she realised her sock had fallen down. Bending down to pull it up, she stood up and sliced her head open on the metal toilet-roll holder. Her headteacher ended up driving her to A&E to get it glued. Ouch! This resulted in all metal toilet-roll holders being changed to plastic ones in that teacher's school.

From bathroom brain-bashing to another place with plenty of hazards. The lunch hall is an absolute wacky warehouse at times, where you can injure yourself so easily. Now, I love the lunch hall, obviously, as that's where I was introduced to my first love, Bernard Matthews' Turkey Twizzlers, but it can be a near death trap for school staff everywhere. Spilt food, excitable children, kitchen staff on their last nerve with hot gravy, the chances for injuries are endless.

In a packed lunch hall, one unfortunate teacher slipped on some spaghetti Bolognese and launched herself halfway across the hall. Her colleagues witnessing the event had their hearts in their mouths as this happened only twelve weeks after the poor teacher had a C-section. To the relief of everyone, she escaped serious injury, unlike this next poor soul.

This next story involves another incident in the school hall but with painful consequences on a wet floor. Surely, at this time, we have to question the clean-up process in that school dinner hall? Where are the plastic yellow wet floor signs when you need them? This was a scene where a staff member slipped. Let's hope they didn't slip on the quiche, because if I was injured by a horrible quiche I don't know what would hurt more, my limbs or my pride! Anyway, after slipping on a wet surface, the poor teacher came a cropper and hit the unforgiving wooden floor … hard! Adding insult to (literal) injury, lunch carried on being served, but they had to do it around the teacher as she lay waiting for an ambulance. The teacher ended up with a broken arm, and with metal plates and eight bolts holding it together! I have to say, I'm not sure how much of an appetite I would have after witnessing such a horrific injury, but I guess the more important question would be, what was on the menu that day?!

Hungry or, even worse, HANGRY kids can be a nightmare when they finally get to their dinner time. If a scuffle in the lunch queue happens, there'll always be some wrong choices made, and if it escalates to fisticuffs then grown-ups need to step in. Children of certain ages don't always show the necessary respect to their lunchtime supervisors, so a teacher may need to get involved and act like Lieutenant Colombo to work out what went down. Annoyingly, it is very rare to get the *true* retelling of the story – and unless you have that child who is as honest as the day is long, you then have to hunt for witnesses. Children love nothing more than retelling a scenario to which they were an eye-witness. It's like they're in a courtroom drama, where every detail is not only explained clearly, examined beyond belief and as drawn out as possible, but the information changes regularly when the story is shared again, or if they are potentially providing evidence against one of their mates.

It's a tough spot, but like a courtroom drama, the cross-examination of those present would be essential. Asking children to recall what they saw is a helpful process but school staff may wish to avoid carrying out a full reconstruction of the events as it can land you straight into the teacher injuries column. This chap found out the hard way.

A new EAL (English as Additional Language) boy recently joined my Year 4 class. He's quite a big lad but seems nice and friendly, very broken English but hopefully he can pick it up quickly. In his first week he was witness to an incident in the hall between two of his peers (wrong-choice-makers). As part of my investigations, I was asking the new boy what happened but he didn't understand and couldn't reply. I naturally started playing charades with him, but still, nothing was landing. It was only when I presented my hands forward and said 'Show me' that we made any progress. He wound back dramatically and threw a straight right arm ... straight into my meat and two veg! It was so painfully accurate and – wow – did it hurt, and I'm a 25-year-old man. By the end of this, I was less bothered about what had taken place and more worried about my high-pitched voice and swollen testicles! Ouchie!

The thing I love about school staff injuries is the reactions. It's like live television; keep your cool, act like nothing has happened and draw no attention to the fact there is a major problem. Case in point the teacher who was showing a class of secondary students how to safely use sewing machines. She looked away (after repeatedly telling the children not to) and the needle went straight through her finger. The teacher then had to manually unwind it out of her finger and ended the demonstration by announcing, 'That's what happens if you don't follow safety instructions!'

Huge round of applause for the bravery there and level of professionalism. That story sounds painful enough in front of a class of 30 students (and if, like me at school, quite a few wouldn't be paying attention), but now imagine an injury in front of the whole school. This one required a professional reaction and a half from this teacher taking part in a dance-off during a whole-school pantomime (as you do). Whilst busting some considerable moves this teacher felt sharp pain shoot up her leg and felt a crack, not once, but twice! She had managed to break her ankle in two places, falling backwards and taking out half the set as she tumbled off the back of the stage. For the first few seconds the children thought it was part of the show and greeted the act with a mixture of cheers and laughter. It wasn't until the music stopped and the other adults looked very worried that the audience knew something was up. A hush fell over the crowd as they learned that this was not a pratfall performed for their entertainment. A TA rushed over to help her fallen comrade up and as soon as the children saw their teacher was able to stand on one leg they clapped and cheered to show their love and appreciation. Showing true grit and determination, she left the hall hopping, smiling and waving to the children, so no one was upset, to rapturous applause. Imagine being a child in the audience, watching this lovely pantomime, then witnessing one of your teachers breaking it down during a dance-off, only to snap their ankle and fall into the back of the stage. OH NO SHE DIDN'T ... Oh yes she did! Now that is bravery at its finest.

As we reach the end of this chapter containing school-based injuries, there is only one more thing we can really add to these painful tales ...

PLEASE DON'T TRY THIS AT HOME OR AT SCHOOL!

Teacher Confessions

TOP SECRET

Oooh, confessions time!

This has to be my all-time favourite feature from our podcast. When we first had the idea to ask for confessions from school staff, I don't think we had the faintest idea of the Pandora's box of juicy secrets we would open up. If I can pinch a lyric from Elvis, prepare to be all shook up, because some of the tales here are out of this world.

It is important at this point to make it clear that, as teachers, we are all human. School staff are incredibly hardworking, they go above and beyond to help and support their pupils in every way, but at the same time we are human beings with human emotions and feelings. While 99.9 per cent of teachers are able to stay professional at all times, there are the ultra-rare occasions when teachers make the mistake of acting on these feelings. If they aren't acted upon, they will definitely be thought about. A simple way to prove this is, at the next staff do – whether it is the Christmas party or the end of year knees-up – play a simple game of 'I've Never'. I am sure most people reading this book are aware of this game, but just in case you aren't, everyone playing needs to have an alcoholic drink and they take turns listing potential experiences they've never had. If someone has done the action in question, they take a shot or a sip (or whatever other consequence you dream up). If no one has done the action in question, the person who posed the query takes a drink. Here are a few potential questions you can use to get the party started:

I've never ...

- Caught sick in your bare hands
- Slept through alarms and been late to school
- Been hungover at school
- Cried at school
- Taught a whole lesson from your desk
- Necked with a colleague
- Accidentally sworn in class
- Stolen glue sticks / stationery from another class
- Not chosen a child for something because the parent has complained and made your life a living hell
- Fancied a parent
- Cheated on SATs
  and Adam's personal favourite ...
- Farted in class and blamed a child

Well, while we're on the subject and before we share some of the juiciest, sauciest confessions we've ever heard from school staff, I feel it is only right that we share some ourselves. After establishing once and for all in printed text that teachers DO indeed fart in class and blame the children (and yes, I, Adam Parkinson, am a repeat offender), it feels only fair to acknowledge and disclose a similar, equally shameful act that involves classroom flatulence. One I am not proud of but one I am willing to admit to, in order to heal my sin.

Now let's discuss the different terms you may use for breaking wind. I most certainly do not call it breaking wind, I usually say trump or ask the question to my kids, 'Right, who has done a Donald?' The most common term in school is still a fart (actually considered swearing where I come from, but it seems to be acceptable now), although there are plenty of other ways of expressing the act, including: guffs, bottom burps, backdrafts, trouser-coughs, a loose deuce, gas deposits and the classic: letting rip.

You will remember from your personal school days that every class had unique odours; 99 per cent of the time they were not very enjoyable, not even someone who had made dandelion perfume on the playground or another person who doused themselves in their dad's Brut could save the situation. A mixture of different gases from the four corners of a classroom can be really off-putting. It takes a while as a school staff member to pin down the culprits, but once you do, it's all about tactical seating – either far away from you, near a window, next to a child who doesn't make the right choices (they probably deserve it) or towards the door so you can give them a quick wink and nudge and they can head to the toilet to make sure they haven't followed through.

Back to my personal confession … While working a day in Year 1 a few years ago, one boy had openly admitted to letting rip early in the morning and it was a real eye-watering stench. The children were laughing while pinching their noses, and the boy who had released Polly from prison ...

'Release Polly from prison'? I've never heard that one!

You do at my school. Anyway, the trumping culprit was loving life and, of course, the attention. As the day moved on, the classroom pong had eased up, windows were open and fresh air was finally in regular circulation. After lunch, I returned to class; at this point I started with a tiny bit of a stomach ache, but it began to worsen and the feeling was building. I knew I had to release Polly from my own prison, as soon as possible, or I could be in a real mess (literally and figuratively). Sweat began to build on my brow; I was supervising the class on my own. With no other adults available, there was no way I could leave the children unattended. To my shame I casually walked round to check the work of the boy who had proudly released some food ghosts earlier in the day, and as I peered over his shoulder and congratulated him on his task, I subtly released an SBD (Silent But Deadly). Walking away, I knew I didn't have long before the nostrils of the class would begin to tingle. I decided to get ahead of the heat by putting my hand over my nose and enquiring which child needed to go for a number two, despite knowing it was me that desperately needed it. Yes, I'm probably going to hell for this, but what on earth was I supposed to do?

With no Cockney John at the front of the class to call me out, I chose to blame an innocent five-year-old for a fart he did not commit. It's a good job he was so young, otherwise he could've turned the tables with the ever-popular 'whoever smelt it, dealt it' line. Fortunately, he didn't have the rhyming vocabulary as we could have gone back and forth with plenty of the following:

'Whoever said the rhyme, did the crime!'

'He who denied it, supplied it!'

'He who sensed it, dispensed it!' etc.

You get the idea, but I was really grateful he was only five! As you can probably tell, I had those lines locked and loaded in my mind if the occasion was to arise. Back to the stinky classroom, the class began to react, including a few looks in the direction of the usual suspect. I began to feel real guilt and I thought to myself, I can't let this kid go down for something I did ... but just as I was about to come clean, something my boxers were not at this point, the boy in question burst out laughing. He apologised to the class and admitted that he had let one go and didn't think it was going to be that bad. Amazingly I was in the clear.

The best bit about this story is that many years later I fessed up at his Year 6 end of year leavers' disco. Fortunately he forgave me and thought it was a legendary prank. Imagine if he'd called me out in front of all his pals; it could've been cringeworthy!

Speaking of things that may make you cringe, some folks may need to cover their eyes at the pure horror of this next tale.

Is that possible when reading? Still wouldn't work with the audiobook. Have you thought this through, bro?

Fair point, but just a quick warning that there's every chance our next confession will give you a feeling of immense relief in the pit of your stomach that this hasn't happened to you! Time to find out (I'll do an evil laugh on the audiobook).

In this day and age, everyone has a mobile phone, and a popular trend that I only remember becoming the norm in recent years is to have a work messaging group. To be honest it makes sense; emails are tricky to keep up with (usually because when you have finished work, the last thing you want to do is check your email) and you always have your mobile phone on you. The most popular is a WhatsApp group, a really easy way to send quick messages, videos, images and whatever else you need to, but the problem is that on your WhatsApp you have a lot of groups on the go. There's a few friendship groups always popping off, you may have a parents' group if your children are at school, you have your family group, and, if you're unlucky like me, you have your partners' family group (this is the one where you can mute the messages, and when you do you get three options, eight hours, one week or always – for my in-laws chat group, always). It can be quite difficult to keep up with all the messages vibrating and beeping, but I'm always conscious about making sure I never send anything into my work WhatsApp group, as every single member of staff is in there. Now on this point, I was told this story from a woman, let's call her Sally, which will long live in my memory and I would like to thank Sally as it has made me double/triple check every time I am sending a message on my phone. Here is Sally's story:

I didn't think I would ever share this tale, but I felt I had to. In 2019 (before the craziness of 2020) our work set up a WhatsApp group. Every staff member was part of it and I felt like it was a nice way of sharing and catching up with the members of staff you may not see regularly, this was until ...

I am a young woman, recently single, in my early twenties at the time. I started seeing a lovely chap through a dating app, the chat moved from the dating app chatroom to WhatsApp – this is when you know you're getting serious. One drunken weekend we were sending flirty messages all night and this led on to sending flirty images. As the wine flowed, more skin flowed. I was very drunk by the end of the night and passed out. It was only when I was awoken to a mountain of missed calls from numerous staff members that I realised something was clearly amiss. I opened my messages and, to my horror, the final picture (of my chest with no bra – if you get my drift) that I meant to send my squeeze had actually been sent into my work WhatsApp group. I was horrified! Monday came and it was all a blur, I felt like I locked myself away. It took until the Christmas party for people to bring it up and have a laugh about it.

Fun fact, as I write this I am currently moved in with said squeeze, so it had a nice ending. I just hope no one from my work saved the picture to their camera roll.

Oh my goodness, that story made me feel slightly queasy, just the thought of it. I mean, I guess it wouldn't be too bad for you, Lee, as people probably wouldn't be bothered trying to zoom in on your picture ... WHEYHEYYY.

Thanks for that, Adam; this coming from officially the third best-looking Parkinson brother.

School residentials are probably the most tiring expedition known to a human; I mean, I know probably climbing Everest is hard, but taking 60-plus children away to an activity centre for up to five nights – give me a freezing cold summit any day. On a serious note, they are also fantastic. As I touched upon in the disgusting chapter, it gives the children a chance to be out of their comfort zones and really able to develop their character away from a classroom, but on these trips it's not necessarily the children or the school staff you should worry about. This next confession will alert you to always check your bed before you sleep on a school residential.

Many years ago, I worked for a residential holiday company (a huge activity centre). During my time there we had many fun and interesting interactions with teachers. They used to come and get extremely merry in the onsite bar while the children were in bed being overseen by the evening activity centre staff. Now, we sometimes made our own fun, so basically, staff at the activity centre had a points system for any shenanigans that happened with school staff or coach drivers. For example, a kiss would be one point for another staff member, five for a teacher and ten for a coach driver (they were always the toughest, so you'd need a lot of points to go there). The points were higher for more, how do you say, intimate goings on, and it was always the talk of the site when anyone managed to pull a teacher. By the way, it happened quite a lot! Personally, I managed it twice, which I don't think is a lot but I ended up being known at one point as 'head of teacher liaison'.

Another confession about my time there is that whenever a school group left, we had to change the beds. One time (or more), after a drunk last night with the teachers in the bar and then some after-hours liaising, I was so hungover and tired that I didn't change the teacher bed, instead I just remade it and left it for the next school group. Now every time I go to a residential area, I am so paranoid about the bed sheets being clean!

There is definitely something about residentials. I think being away from the stress of school life and being at one with nature can allow anyone to forget their troubles and relax. Unfortunately, sometimes you might relax too much, so here's a quick tip for anyone reading this who is going on a school residen   n fact going away at all: always take your own toiletries (esp   hower puffs). If you're thinking that a shower puff is a random sh   , you're about to find out why with this confession:

It was my first year at my school and we were on a residential trip. The staff were all sharing a small dorm and private bathroom. I got up early and showered, ready for the day. While in the shower I let a massive fart rip. I didn't think much of it and carried on showering. I realised I didn't bring a shower puff with me so just grabbed one I found hanging in the shower. It was only when I was washing my skin and my bottom that I realised the fart was more of a shart than I had first thought.

Needless to say, I rinsed the shower puff as best as I could before putting it back. All fine, or so I thought. It was only when one of the teachers was doing a shop run in the evening and asked if anyone needed anything. The deputy piped up, saying, 'See if they have any shower puffs. When I washed my face this morning, mine smelt like arse so I think it's time for a new one.'

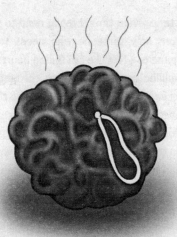

One last thing about residentials: it's a perfect time to play some pranks. I went on two of these trips in my first school and the pranks used to be my favourite bit. I remember one year, a group of Year 6 boys had started to spread rumours that the house we were staying in was haunted. This freaked out a few of the other children and it came to a head on the first night when we had a lot of disturbed nights' sleep. The next day, myself and my colleagues hatched a plan to try to get our own back on the rumour-starting crew. The night activity was a fire in a teepee, and we tasked them with taking some wood down the path to help the staff prepare for the flames. All the while myself and the infamous Cockney John (more on his residential tradition soon) waited behind a big tree for the boys, who were strutting because they thought they had been chosen as they were the 'strongest' children in the year. I mean, that is such a primary school flex, getting chosen to carry some-thing heavy. I used to think I was a young Hulk Hogan when it happened to me. I don't want to brag, but I used to be chosen 80 per cent of the time, every time. I really need to stop reliving my glory years, I am now someone who needs to choose strong students to help me as I feel like I'm falling apart! Anyway, about six lads were walking down a dark path carrying some firewood towards the teepee. After finally arriving at the big tree, Cockney John and I jumped out and screamed the old classic: 'BOO!' The reaction of the lads was one of the funniest things I have ever seen; the language, on the other hand, was not what I would expect from our children. I did not know at the time that ten-year-olds knew such bad language. Safe to say they didn't scare or wind up anyone else on that residential, as our part of the deal is that we did not share their reaction with the class, or share the language blurted out to their parents. I'd say a fair deal!

One of my most memorable experiences came on a residential trip with the one and only Cockney John! There were four staff members – two women and two men – with roughly 40 children in their care for a three-night stay. Cockney John had the dubious pleasure of checking the boys' rooms, with obviously the women checking the girls'. I remember hearing how immaculate the girls' rooms were and how lovely it all sounded. Cockney John had the look in his eye, there was no way we were being outdone by the ladies. We went into the first group's room and went full drill-sergeant. We knocked on the door and made it very clear that military-style inspections were imminent. When we entered, the lads were actually standing and saluting. Cockney John had a look around the room and saw a tube of toothpaste and enquired,

'Right, who's toofpaste is dis?' (sic)

A child trying to contain his laughter raised his hand and said it was his. Cockney John went on to open the tube of toothpaste and squirt some into his mouth from above. He then declared,

'Well done, bruv, it's extremely MINTY!!!!'

As you can imagine, the boys were chuckling away.

After that, we went into the next room. You could see the children trying to remain in role and calm. Cockney John peered around the room and saw a near-empty bag of crisps, and he went on to pour them towards his mouth. The crispy shards missed his chops and landed on the floor. The lads knew this was sabotage but they did their best to stand to attention. John declared:

'Well done, lads, the room looks good, but I said COMPLETELY CLEAN! Get them crumbs gone!'

The boys did well to salute and stifle their giggles. We continued our inspection and when we got to the final rooms Cockney John decided that he wanted to end strong. Upon entry, the children were standing straight but not as straight as the previous rooms/regiments, so he made them do a number of press-ups as a comedy punishment for their indiscretion. Cockney John looked around the room, and on the side was one of the children's thick coats. He said, 'Tell you what, boys, I'm feeling pretty chilly - gonna need to borrow a jacket!' He picked up what was clearly a small boy's coat, and proceeded to try to put it on. With half an arm in he stripped it off and threw it on the floor shouting, 'IT DOESN'T FIT!' The kids absolutely lost it.

I wish I'd had a Cockney John on my school trips as a child. Amazingly, at the end of the residential many of the children's highlights were the room inspections!

One word of advice, though, would be to make sure when playing any sort of prank you are always careful, because sometimes a prank misfire can easily happen, especially if you're sharing your residential with another school:

On a school residential, our staff thought they would play a trick on our children. While the children were having tea they went to their log cabin accommodation and moved their sleeping bags around so when they got back they would be confused. This operation took time, carefully removing the sleeping bags from the bunk beds and swapping them around. After tea the children returned to their cabins to get ready for the campfire. All was quiet in the cabins, no noise, no fuss.

Another school came down and entered their cabins next to our row in the woods. From the other school came cries of WHAT! and NO! and SIR!

After a lengthy telling off by their teachers attempting to find the silly person who thought it would be funny to mix up everyone's belongings, our school and its staff sheepishly took our responsible and sensible children to the campfire and let the whodunnit saga continue!

Residentials aside, we have been sent some other cracking confessions. Things that have happened to teachers that if they were to be named and shamed could end up with the staff in question no longer allowed to work in schools, or at the very least facing some sort of disciplinary action.

First of all, I will share this confession, which could have easily been placed in the chapter about the most disgusting things that happen in a primary school.

I have never told anyone this, but as I will remain anonymous I thought it might raise a few laughs. A few weeks into my NQT year, I was gearing up for my first observation by the local authority inspector.

It was my mate's birthday the night before and we had celebrated by having a curry at the local curry house and a couple of drinks. I didn't go overboard as I knew I had the observation the next day. I'd arrived nice and early in school ready to smash this lesson observation when, just as the bell went, my arse completely dropped. Welcoming my class in, I was desperately trying not to sh*t myself. I was sweating, panting, I was in excruciating pain. The inspector joined us soon after and I must have just looked like I was so nervous but I actually was about to unleash the biggest assplosion I had ever had. DAMN You Chicken Vindaloo!

Just as I started the lesson, a miracle happened. I felt my stomach ease and the urge to relieve myself subsided and I thanked the gods as I was able to continue my input with little to no distraction. That was until I set my class their work. A second wave came and I knew I was done for. I was wandering the classroom with a painful look on my face as I was desperately trying to keep my cheeks together. The inspector kept looking over as I nodded, assuring him I was on my A game – little did he know the A stood for arse-clenching like no tomorrow. I thought I had seen the light at the end of the tunnel with only 15 minutes left of the lesson, when disaster struck. A child asked a question, to which I replied with what could only be described as top-grade teacher banter, and in my relaxed chuckle I let out what I thought was a fart. Luckily, as my class were also giggling the noise went unnoticed. But I knew, it wasn't just a fart. The smell emanated through the class at a ridiculous rate. The children were all distracted by the pungent smell of post-curry poo. I was trying to contain the madness that ensued, with children gagging, hiding under their jumpers, knowing full well I had sh*t myself. The inspector came over to me and whispered into my ear that I might want to address this by asking the culprit to take themselves to the toilet. I nodded in agreement and went to get on my high horse and tell the class that whoever it was needs to go and relieve themselves. No one owned up, and I continued my line of enquiry, thanking god I hadn't decided to wear my beige chinos that day. The lesson ended and the inspector approached me to give his feedback. I asked him for two *minutes while I nipped to the toilet. I desperately dashed down the corridor like Finch in American Pie. I eventually made it to the toilet and unzipped my trousers to reveal what looked like a poonami, it was trickling down my thighs. I panicked and sat there for what felt like an eternity trying to rid myself of the rest of last night's feast and tried my best to clean myself. I had to ditch the underwear, luckily not my finest boxers, and decided to go commando as I strutted back to get my feedback. The inspector refused to do the feedback in my class because of the lingering smell. Feedback was all good and I am lucky to be the only bloke in the school as no one went to the male toilets to find my stained kecks.*

What a rollercoaster. Observations are bad at the best of times but the added stress of feeling like you are about to explode would take the anxiety to a new level. I feel if the teacher can make it through that he can make it through anything.

And now for a story that involved teachers getting high during the school day. For the record, not intentionally:

My year group partner and I were rehearsing the nativity with all of KS1 one year. As you know, this can be quite tedious and often needs a regular top-up of caffeine and sugar. So before we went into the hall, my colleague nipped into my classroom with a sweet treat to get us through the morning. I took a huge bite and quickly realised something was awry. Now, I've never actually smoked weed but it's safe to say it's very recognisable, especially when you've just eaten it! I quickly ran into my partner's classroom, who had consumed the whole 'sweet treat' and hadn't realised as it had been brought in for her by a child. I spent most of the nativity with my head down the toilet as it turns out I'm not that good with drugs and my partner had a major *headache afterwards! *Disclaimer: other non-stoned teachers were present to supervise children!*

I tell you one thing: watching a nativity while high on marijuana would make for one interesting afternoon. You would be tripping at some of the storylines of the traditional Nativity. 'Why are three kings coming to visit a baby in a shed?' 'You know you really have to question Joseph and how easily he accepted the fact his missus got knocked up by someone else.'

This story certainly benefits from the anonymity of the podcast:

I once left a kid on a bus. I worked at a school for children with SEMH (social, emotional, mental health) needs and we used to go swimming once a week. There weren't many staff and it was a busy public car park when we got there, so I'd get the kids to stand up in the mini bus, count them and move off, locking the door behind me (I also drove).

One day we got into the changing rooms and a few minutes in I realised we were a kid down! I ran back to the bus and he was waving at me through the bus door with a big smile on his face. I was totally panicking and he was so chilled.

When I asked what happened, he said, 'My legs got tired so I sat back down again' ... he'd simply got bored!

Luckily I had a good relationship with his carer and we laughed ... but it was still one of the scariest moments of my teaching career.

And it seems that isn't the only time when a child has been left behind:

It was the last week of the Christmas term and as you'll know, it's a busy, tiring term! One child in my Reception class was falling asleep in the afternoon so I put her in our reading area, which was a large basket with net drapes around it. It was later that afternoon that I was helping dress 56 four-year-olds into donkey costumes and headbands, so as you can imagine it was very chaotic. We walked down to our school church (which was a good few metres away from the school) to perform our nativity to the whole school and to the parents. Children were waving to their parents and then I spotted a parent coming towards me. It was the parent of the child who had fallen asleep ... and was still asleep in the classroom. My TA sprinted back to school to get her, and when the parent asked where her child was, I explained that the TA was bringing her down later as she was tired. The TA and child came back to church and to this day only myself and my TA know I left a child behind at school.

But if we are going to reveal true confessions with the help of anonymity, we have to share this one, which we came so close to telling on the podcast but decided to save for the book. Now we want to make it clear, we do not condone this sort of behaviour; however, there may be arguments that it was justified and, for any teacher who has had to endure working with a truly diabolical leader who has made you question your ability as a teacher or as a human, this might be something you can understand. But we will simply leave that up to you.

Before I get into the crux of the story, I need to give some context to explain the motivation behind why I did what I did. A couple of years ago, we had a moderation meeting to assess our Year 6 writing for the year. The moderation process, by the way, is a complete and utter crock of sh*t. I was all for moving away from the writing SATs paper, but to *then move towards a system that can be so subjective and actually be manipulated to benefit certain people? The lady who came to moderate turned out to be someone I knew very well – a member of the SLT at another school where my friend had worked. Although, my friend no longer worked there at that point, thanks to the nasty bullying at the hands of this member of the SLT. My friend was a brilliant teacher, we had trained together at university and she was a natural, but to see the way she had been treated by this knob of a deputy was disgusting. I had numerous phone calls with my friend where she was crying down the phone about things this boss had done and said to her. I know you have featured some terrible, diabolical leaders on the podcast, but this person would make them look like heroes. My friend finally made the decision to leave the school and it infuriated me that the leader in question was never punished. And now here was this former colleague of hers being the beacon of our local area when it came to moderation.*

That particular year group I had at the time were challenging to say the least. However, I had made real progress with them and despite the numerous issues I felt we had produced some incredible writing. In fact, we had used some of Mr P's Read Write Perform packs and the impact was phenomenal, the quality of writing was so good.

Hang on a minute, did the person actually say that or have you snuck that in for shameless promotion?

Hand on heart, the person submitting their story wrote that.

We had used the Battle Cry pack to get some of our independent writing to show at moderation. I knew alongside other examples that the quality of the work was more than good enough and should have improved the scores we had the previous year. However, when this b*tch of a moderator entered the school I knew straight away this was going to be a disaster. Some people have a mean resting b*tch face, but she wore the crown.

Before she had even seen any of the work, she had already made comments that gave the impression it was going to be a sh*t show. She took a few of our books and barely scanned them before judging that it wasn't good enough and started discussing levels lower than the year before. I was fuming and every time I tried to justify or argue against her thoughts she shut me down and wouldn't even entertain anything. She started suggesting we used resources her school used to support writing – and guess who sold these expensive resources? Yes, the moderator. She was going around schools and downgrading them so she could then suggest buying her resources as her school had the best results in the area.

I excused myself from the room as I couldn't contain my anger. I asked whether anyone wanted a drink and went to the staffroom and brewed up. I was so angry at the fact this woman was going to fail my class and me purely so she could profit from it. This was at the time of performance-related pay, too – not that that really mattered – but the fact I had worked my arse off with this class to have one person completely ruin it left me in a fit of rage. Plus everything she had done to my friend.

I suddenly had an idea to give this woman a taste of her own medicine. A real taste of karma. While making a brew, I decided to top it up with a little dash of laxative. Now, I don't need to explain why I had laxative, I will leave that to your imagination, but in that moment I was livid at what this woman had done to my friend and was now doing to my class all so she could make money. I gave her the brew and finished up the meeting.

I don't know what exactly happened after that, but one can hope that at her next school visit she ended up having sh*t coming out of the right end rather than speaking it all the time. Last I heard, the deputy was finally outed as a bully but was training to be an Ofsted inspector, which says a lot. As for my friend, she managed to find another school and is flourishing. Do I regret doing what I did? Not really. Given the amount of misery this person had caused to so many, having the Brad Pitts for the afternoon feels the least I could do.

Let that be a lesson to all toxic leaders out there: treat people nicely otherwise you could be spending a lengthy period on the porcelain throne.

And now for the juicy confessions:

At my old school, there was a married male deputy head whose wife came to school quite often and knew the staff quite well. One day she came to school at dinner time while we were in the staffroom, and she asked if we knew who 'Louisa' was. Everyone looked confused, the deputy walked in, got a slap. Turns out he was having an affair with a parent.

And that is just the beginning of the extra-marital affairs that seem to occur within the staffrooms of different primary schools.

OK. Here goes, this is something I've never told anyone, not even my closest friends. I had been working at a school that I hated, I was on the brink of leaving the profession and even reached out to Mr P for his advice, who explained that I should try another school before leaving altogether as there is always the right school out there. I acted on his advice and managed to get a job in a different school. I was on a night out in town celebrating the new job and ended up chatting to this guy who was a little bit older than me but really fit. I have a thing for older, more sophisticated men. Imagine George Clooney with a mix of Matthew McConaughey, a dreamboat, if I remember, but I was a fair few drinks in so that could have been the alcohol talking. We were flirting all night. I'm a young single girl so I did what any young single girl would do and invited him back to mine and we had a rather enjoyable night and morning. We swapped numbers but nothing really happened and it petered out.

Fast-forward a couple of months. I had settled into my new school and I was getting on really well with my new head teacher.

The Christmas do came and we were all out in town having a few drinks and a dance and enjoying the night. At closing time, the head decided to invite us all back to hers for more drinks and so a few of us jumped in a taxi and carried on knocking back the gins at the head's house. As we're laughing and joking away, the head's husband enters the kitchen and, to my surprise, is only the guy I'd had the one-night stand with in the summer. I froze on the spot, feeling unbelievable guilt as the head started hugging and kissing her husband, gushing over their long and amazing relationship as I wanted the ground to eat me up right there and then. Awkward is an understatement. Safe to say, I've kept this to myself as I quite like my head teacher and I quite like my job!

This final confession has a similar vibe but we think this is a belter. Definitely some creative embellishment applied to this story to protect the innocence of the teacher that sent it in, but I think it is my favourite confession we have ever shared. Enjoy ...

When I was in my first year as a qualified teacher, I went on a night out. While teachers may strive to be dedicated, approachable and professional, we are still allowed to let our hair down from time to time. Maintaining a professional image is incredibly important and it's drummed into us during our initial teacher training that we should be role-models inside and outside of the classroom. In fact, we must meet a specific set of standards in order to qualify. That said, teaching in your first year is a complete rollercoaster so every time there's an opportunity to let off some steam and have some fun it's essential that we do, and that's exactly what I did.

At the end of a busy week, I donned my gladrags, had a couple of cocktails, then danced on a table to some Vengaboys! A great night, made even better when I locked eyes with a handsome young lad who seemed to be very interested in me too. We had a few drinks, a few laughs, plenty more drinks and by the end of the evening I was in a taxi going back to his place. I want to make it very clear I do not make a habit of this.

We arrived at his place and one thing led to another, as they say (wink wink). Shortly after we had done the deed, I stumbled out of his room half-naked to try to find the bathroom. Still full of cocktails and tipsy as hell, I was tiptoeing across the landing but managed to reach the toilet in time. After emptying my bladder, I stepped out of the loo and I bumped into a figure. Initially, I thought it was that evening's dance partner but I was actually greeted by his slightly angry looking father. Even worse, when I took another look I realised it was none other than ...

THE HEADTEACHER FROM MY SCHOOL!

Yep, I had basically just had a one-night stand with his son! Talk about embarrassment. Safe to say I finished my NQT year and moved to a different school that summer.

Wow! Now *that* is a teacher confession. You can just imagine the embarrassment of waltzing out of the bathroom to be greeted by your boss in just your undies ... Yikes! It's no secret that my favourite part of our podcast is when we get to read out amazing confessions like this. We are incredibly grateful to hear from so many school staff that are happy to tell us their juicy shenanigans, ill-judged hijinx and bad behaviour.

You are all a bunch of legends and, by the sounds of it, a bunch of very naughty boys and girls!

Parents ... they can make or break your job as a teacher. Some of the funniest times yet also the scariest times as a member of school staff come from the interactions we have with parents. As we established in book one, most parents are normal humans that just so happen to have brought other human beings into the world. But one of the stark lessons you learn as a teacher from very early on is the vast range of different types of people that exist within your local community.

Up until the point you become a teacher, you have only lived within your own echo chamber, whether that is online or in the real world. You are surrounded by people who are similar to you, have the same likes, dislikes and interests as you. Of course, if this is true, why in the world would you be friends with someone who is the complete opposite to you? That's why when you listen to the radio, hear stories on the news or even see certain viewpoints expressed online, you are often shocked at how some people can think or act like this. But when you become a teacher and start interacting with parents, it broadens your horizons and you soon appreciate why some children are the way they are.

There are plenty of interesting characters, and that makes working in a school so much more interesting ... but not always for the better. There are some parents that are rude, some that are inappropriate and some that are accidentally hilarious.

I feel that when we compare teaching now to what teaching was like generations ago, one of the biggest changes is the attitude towards teachers from parents. This reflects the view towards teachers generally in day-to-day society. There has definitely been a shift so that teachers have become undervalued and treated less as professionals and more like glorified babysitters. This has been beautifully illustrated in the meme that was doing the rounds online recently. It showed two pictures of a classroom with a teacher sitting at the desk and on the other side there was a student holding a sheet of paper that showed the low test scores and his parents. In one picture, titled 'Then', the parents are focusing their attention on the child for the low test scores, whereas the other picture, titled 'now', showed the parents berating and blaming the teacher. I am sure there are plenty of teachers who can relate to this and it can certainly feel like teachers are expected to do so much more than just teach. The fact that some parents are quite happy to believe their six-year-old child, who we have already established through this book are the most unreliable sources of information, over a trained professional blows my mind.

I often try to comprehend why this is the case and I think it is combination of things: the constant bashing of teachers in the mainstream media and the fact that in the extremely polarising society we live in most teachers tend to sit on the left side of the political scale can lead to being blamed for 'indoctrinating' children into a viewpoint that is different to the viewpoint of some. I always think about the parents who were completely against schools educating children about same-sex relationships; while the curriculum encouraged reading stories that included same-sex couples, some parents believed this was going to make their children 'gay'. This led to some teachers receiving a torrent of abuse, with protests held to try to sack teachers who were leading this aspect of the curriculum.

Firstly, who in their right mind thinks that if children are taught that same-sex relationships are a completely normal type of relationship this is suddenly going to make them turn gay? I mean, I learnt about the Tudors when I was at school but I don't now go around my day wearing a ruffle and chopping people's heads off. Secondly, who doesn't see this as just a simple way of teaching empathy and acceptance? Thirdly, who has the time to be so consumed with an issue so trivial? These parents are also putting a lot of faith in the fact that children actually listen and retain what they are taught. Think about all the content you learnt at school; I wonder whether you can still remember it precisely? Honestly, can you still remember Pythagoras' theorem? I only remember the fact that since I've left school I have never needed to use it in everyday life. The point I am trying to make here is that parents can sometimes get a bee in their bonnet about something and take it out on the teacher when all the teacher is doing is their job.

Obviously, teachers will always take parents' concerns seriously and investigate any issues that put children at risk – both physically and emotionally. But until you actually hear the complaints you don't know the severity and whether it is something that you will need to act upon. There will always be some parents who get a reputation for being someone who will complain about absolutely everything. We want to share some of the more ludicrous complaints and the worrying excuses parents have made to teachers. I hope this further proves the point that teaching is so much more than a simple job starting at nine and finishing at three. The amount of time wasted having to find time to hear these complaints, then discuss how they will be solved, when actually it could be so much easier if you could simply tell parents to – how can I put this politely and in a politically correct way? – GET A GRIP!

One of the worst complaints I ever had was when a class I was working with had done some brilliant work and so I treated them to some extra play. I took a picture of them playing outside and shared it with the parents through the app Seesaw. It was immediately acknowledged by a parent who was irate at the fact I had allowed their child to go outside without wearing their jumper. They said they had specifically told me the child had the sniffles and therefore I was going to make the child even more ill. The fact that it was during the mini heatwave we were having in May that year and if I'd have made the child wear their jumper they would have passed out through heat exhaustion told me I hadn't actually done anything wrong. But the parent wanted to discuss this further with me after school. This is where school office staff can be worth their weight in gold. Having a good relationship with the legends who work at the front of the school is imperative: they are well aware of which parents need to be avoided and therefore will make excuses or take the brunt of the complaint and relay it to you in a much more mellow tone. But my story pales into insignificance compared to some of the other complaints teachers have received.

Two weeks ago we received a call from a parent saying that she has been homeschooling her Year 3 child since March and not once had the school phoned up to thank her. They had called to speak to her child but never thanked her specifically for all the hard work she had done.

I mean, where do you start with this one? The fact that the parent felt that doing the basic job of supporting their child during lockdown was something that needed to be commended and celebrated when every other parent was in the exact same position is one thing, but to then expect teachers to be using their precious time phoning all the parents to thank them shows a real lack of understanding about the job we do.

At a welcome meeting for both Year 4 classes, I had a parent ask loudly, and in a very accusing tone, why my class were losing out because the other Year 4 class had a male teacher. She didn't think it was fair on her son that he had to have a female teacher. She said that the male teacher would be super sporty and her son needed that. My colleague pointed out that I was the school rugby coach, but it didn't make much difference.

Nothing beats a reminder of how far away we still are from the gender equality and lack of stereotyping we want our children to have.

I had a complaint that I hadn't changed a child's spellings. Also in the complaint was the fact that the child was an IVF baby and they had invested a lot of money in him for me to go ruining his education.

I was informed by one parent that their child was not given adequate time in my class to grieve the departure of their wobbly tooth from their mouth.

In all my years on this planet, from being a child to spending most of my adult life working with children, I have never – and I mean never – known anyone grieve the loss of a baby tooth. If anything, there are only celebrations towards the impending visit from the tooth fairy.

We didn't brush the children's teeth after lunch. Because we are apparently dentists as well as teachers.

A parent from another class decided that I was 'too close' to another teacher and she thought we were having an affair. I was with the partner that I am still with now, and my colleague and I are just friends. She tried to get me fired as she was into him herself. Luckily my work saw right through her lies.

I would have been very worried if any school entertained the thoughts of this next parent.

We did a Christmas play where the children were either birds or sheep ... a dad said how dare I cast his son as a sheep ... he's not a sheep (follower), he's a leader. I simply said it's not a metaphor, he's literally a sheep. 🐑

Apparently I gave a rude word as a weekly spelling. The actual word was 'aerosol' but the child copied it down incorrectly.

Nothing beats the feeling of smugness when a parent complains only for them to then be embarrassed by the truth. Like this one:

I got a complaint about the terrible standard of homework and proofreading, complete with homework corrected by the parent for 'very basic punctuation and spelling mistakes'. The homework was to correct the very basic punctuation and spelling mistakes.

I had a parent burst in after school one day clutching three or four jumpers. Shouted at me saying he's sick of his child bringing home the wrong jumper and me just writing his name in them. I explained that I hadn't written his name in. He argued I must have, because the sewn in label said GEORGE! I tried to explain that it was the name of the brand from Asda and in fact it definitely looked to be his son's top. He was having none of it.

A parent wrote a very aggressive note in a reading record accusing me of testing the children without giving notice and threatening to report me to the governors. She was furious her child had been given a mark of 1/10 in the reading record. I simply replied, 'It's the date. The 1st of October.'

I used to work in an independent school and a parent asked who she should send an invoice to to get paid. She said she billed £25 an email and had sent me four emails, which I had not responded to. I must add here that I was teaching all day, had no PPA time that day and so hadn't seen these emails until lunchtime. Anyway, the bursar was absolutely amazing at the school. She rang the mum up and said, given that the school was providing the service and the mum was the client, that maybe we should bill her £25 an email. Needless to say, the emails stopped ... for a bit!

I once had a complaint that I told a Year 6 that an angel was not a source of light when doing SATs revision.

'You moved my son when he hadn't done anything.' Parent went away suitably ashamed when I explained her son was correct, he was moved for doing no work for 40 minutes.

A colleague was doing a toast investigation to see which setting children preferred. A parent complained that she had given her child 'raw toast'. Erm, that would be bread?

On a report acceptance slip 'it was a shame Mrs W felt the need to have so much time off this year, it really spoilt it.' I was off for a term and a half with viral liver failure (in hospital for six weeks).

As a young teacher, I was trying to encourage the mums to run in the 'mums' race' on sports day. I was just over six months pregnant at the time but said I would join in. Several mums did then agree to run. Prior to becoming pregnant I was a fairly decent club athlete, and when the whistle blew I ran as a 'sprinter' would, and actually won the race. There were complaints that I shouldn't have been allowed to race as I hadn't given birth so couldn't actually be classed as a mum yet.

Sore losers, anyone?

A child broke their glasses when they fell off the slide in the foundation area. He told his parents another boy pushed him. This caused a meeting with the head! I said I was watching him and no boy pushed him, he just tripped *at the end of the slide. The parents were very angry and accusingly asked, 'Why were you watching our child?!'*

You just can't win with some.

I received a letter of complaint because when working in a church school I taught the Easter story to Year 6s (who, surprisingly, had no idea of the true events of Easter). This included mentioning that Jesus was crucified on the cross. The irate parent in question was furious that I 'couldn't have told them that Jesus died in a different, less brutal way'.

I mean, how does one then demonstrate the sacrifice Jesus had to make to save us all? Dying of natural causes surrounded by his close family just doesn't quite show the same level of sacrifice.

I am solely responsible for increasing teenage pregnancies because I teach about conception in Year 6.

Which either proves the teacher isn't doing a very good job of teaching this topic or the parent could do with sitting in on this particular lesson.

I think the most ridiculous complaint I have ever had was when a parent took time out of their day to complain to me that their child had been splashed with water and was upset. When I tried to narrow down when this happened it turned out that it was during a swimming lesson. In the pool! I was so glad I had used a good chunk of my valuable time after school listening to this parent's concerns.

I had a parent come in and complain one day that her daughter had come to school with her eyebrows and had gone home without them. So someone must have taken them at school! My colleague and I were struggling to hold it together, so to take a moment out and compose myself, I said, 'I'll go and see if she's left them in her tray!' As if her mum really thought they'd been 'stolen' at school. Turns out, her sister had shaved them off the night before and the child wore her hood up that morning so her mum didn't notice.

I am sure you will agree that these complaints are nothing short of absurd, but this request one parent expected from a teacher left me completely speechless.

I was teaching an afternoon class, where this parent's child was in the class. Midway through our carpet session, my email pings. I'm teaching so it would have to wait. Two minutes later, another ping. I am still teaching. It's an hour until the end of the day. It would have to wait until tidy up time.

Five minutes later, our office secretary walks in my room saying a parent has rung in saying they emailed me twice and I have not responded to the emails they have sent. My reply, 'I'm in the middle of teaching a class at the moment. Can you let them know that I will get back to them as soon as I can.' I'm thinking it must be something urgent at this point.

Anyway, it came to tidy up time. I read the emails, expecting to see some change to a pick-up plan or a family emergency or something.

Nope. The parent was chasing me down to ask if I would mind running some errands for their business during the weekend. Apparently I lived closer and they didn't have the time. They knew I lived closer because their partner was a school governor and had told them where I lived! I politely informed said parent that I was sorry I could not get back to them sooner but I cannot respond to emails mid-lesson and that unfortunately I had plans to visit family so I would not be able to run errands for them. I'd have said no anyway *but I tried to be nice about it. Their response? 'It's OK, you can do it on Bank Holiday Monday instead.' As generous as giving me a bank holiday to do your errands is, I'm still saying no. Said parent would not speak to me for the rest of the year.*

Dealing with complaints can be a draining and time-consuming element of the job as a primary school teacher. There are times when you have to interact with parents and this not only explains a lot about your class, it can also create some awkward and very cringey moments in a teacher's career.

As a nursery teacher in a small primary school, we see trends of illnesses and infections that spread around the children and staff year upon year. It was the turn of the chicken pox. The little red spots were popping up left, right and centre. A couple of days passed and a parent approached me for a chat. She started the conversation, looked at my face, stopped speaking and then said, 'Oh no, I didn't realise you'd had chicken pox too!' The thing is I hadn't, well not since I was about seven anyway! I awkwardly replied, 'That's just unfortunately my acne ...' She arrived the next day with an apology card and a Terry's chocolate orange!

Fair play to the parent for realising that catastrophic error and trying to make up for it with chocolate orange.

I organised a school trip to the zoo in the summer for my Year 3s. The new school push was to try to get dads to come and help to show males as more positive role models. I managed to get one of the dads to agree! I was chuffed when he actually turned up on the morning, as our parents had a habit of not doing so. Well, it was a lovely summer day, and Mr X, the dad, was wearing his usual beanie knitted cap – he was trying to be trendy! We all got on the coach, and Mr X sat near the front. About ten minutes into the journey, Mr X took off his cap, as it was super hot. To my horror, Mr X revealed a bald head with a tattoo that read 'f*ck you all' on the back of his head! He was asked to keep the cap on in the sweltering heat and we added tattoos to our school trip forms!

The worst ever interaction I had with a parent was when a mum told me her son had forgotten his dinner money. She reached down her cleavage, into her bra, furtled a moment and then handed me warm coins. This gay man is still traumatised nearly 20 years later!

I'd just got a new Year 1 in my class and his parents were cool, slightly intimidating but friendly people. One morning, on the door as I greeted the pupils the dad held out his fist. I glanced down and thought he must want me to fist-bump him. I felt awkward but thought, 'Why not? Don't want to leave him hanging.' As soon as I fist-bumped him he laughed and turned his hand over. He had a tightly bundled pair of pants the boy had borrowed the day before. The dad explained he was just trying to be discreet when returning them. I fist-bumped a dad! Cringe!

Cringe indeed, but a fist-bump is nothing compared to this fantastic gaffe.

I was the Year 6 teacher and it was the last day of school before the summer holidays. We had just finished the leavers' assembly and the parents and children were saying their emotional goodbyes with lots of hugs and thank yous. One of the pupils' dads came over to me to say thanks and that he enjoyed the performance. He then put his arm out and said, 'Aww, come here, you,' for a hug. I, awkwardly, leant in and hugged him back (it would be rude not to, right?!). He then put his arms in the air, leaving me hugging him, and replied, 'Umm, I meant my daughter?' who I then realised was standing right behind me. Absolutely mortifying!

We've explored this sort of behaviour in the 'What an "O"' chapter. The fact this happened to a parent makes it even higher on the cringe-ometer chart. Top drawer. They say actions speak louder than words but ...

I accidently told a parent that I loved them. I was closing the gate behind him and said, 'OK, have a great day, love you, bye.' Whoops! The parent gave me such a bewildered look before walking away. Parents' evening was never the same again.

Ah, parents' evenings, a night that many teachers and parents dread. A full-on evening of speaking non-stop about the lovely characters in your class. While I have always enjoyed parents' evenings – mainly due to the fact they have always been relatively straightforward – that opinion would be vastly different if I'd have experienced what some teachers have had to endure. Some of the things shared or revealed by parents during a parent/teacher conference would leave teachers scarred for life! I always commend how teachers can stay so professional when faced with such crazy incidents.

I once had a parent tell me she couldn't make parents' evening as she had a date. I replied politely, 'How exciting.' To which she replied, 'If he plays his cards right I'll let him smash my back doors in!' As you can imagine, I really didn't know what to say to that so I just said, 'Erm, have fun,' and walked off.

I thought I'd burn a candle in my classroom for ambience before our parents' night started. A parent singed her hair while signing in. Now I'm the teacher who set a parent on fire at parents' night!

Four years ago I was a month into a new academic year when one of the children in my class was really sick (let's call him Fred). Fred's parents were called and the receptionist let me know that Dad was on the way. Up until this point I had only ever met Fred's mum at pick up. It was lunchtime so I waited with Fred at the office for Dad to arrive. A little while later, Fred's dad arrived. I said hello and started to explain about what had happened. Fred's dad looked at me and all the colour drained from his face. He literally looked like he had seen a ghost. He mumbled thank you, picked up Fred and ran out of the school. I was so shocked, the office staff even commented how weird it was. I went back to class and carried on with the day. After all the children had gone home for the day, I checked my phone to see a text from my sister, all caps, saying 'COME ROUND AFTER SCHOOL!' I should mention at this point that my sister is actually my identical twin. I quickly drove round for my sister to tell me that she had received loads of random panicked texts from a guy she had met on Tinder a couple of weeks before and been on four dates with. You guessed it, Fred's dad! The messages were asking why she had lied about being a teacher and begging her not to tell his wife. He had thought that my sister was me! My sister was fuming about him lying to her about pretty much everything and we decided that the best punishment would be to not do anything. She let him obsessively text and call for three weeks before blocking his number, and neither of us ever told him the truth. I do feel bad about this as

Fred is now in Year 5 and his dad has never come into school again, not for parent meetings, assemblies, plays, sports days, nothing! It's gone on for far too long for me to mention it to any other staff at school. I just have to get through one more school year until Fred moves to high school and I don't have to listen to any more speculation in the staffroom about whatever happened to Fred's dad!

I once told a mum her daughter was starting to be distracted by boys. The mother announces to her daughter (and the entire room) that vibrators are better than boys and men anyway. Understandably, this was met with horrified silence.

That would make for an awkward rest of the meeting. I can only imagine the teacher trying to move swiftly on to sharing the child's targets.

This happened to a friend of mine a few years ago. Picture the scene: it's parents' evening, it's dragging on a bit. The parents come in and sit across from her. Dad is in tracky bottoms, and sits, typical lad fashion, slouched in his seat, legs spread wide. Midway through the conversation, my teacher friend catches something out of the corner of her eye. She glances at Dad's trackies to see a hole. But not just any hole. This hole has a friend inside saying hello. That's right, on a parents' evening, my friend got a full show of one of her pupil's dad's testicles! Cue a quick wrap up of the conversation before dismissing the parents to go and throw up in the staff toilets.

We had a Year 5 child not wearing pants to school and it was causing issues, especially when he was getting changed for PE. The other children would react with half-amusement/half-disgust, but he just could not see what the problem was. Myself and my TA had two main problems with it. 1) He kept putting his hand down the back of his trousers to itch, then proceed to touch everything in sight. 2) He always needed to borrow a PE kit! His excuse was always that he forgot to put his pants on in the morning. Thinking Year 5 was too old to be forgetting, and the fact that we'd had enough of being grossed out, we called in his parents. Mum and Dad then said, 'Ah, yes, it's because we don't wear pants at home.' Surprised, but trying to remain professional, we pressed on, explaining to these people that it's actually hygienic to wear clean pants every day and that the other children are beginning to comment, which could risk his mental health – really laying it on thick because I didn't want free willies or more poo particles than usual in the classroom! Mum then replied, 'I wear pants sometimes so I'll try to remind him to put them on when I do, but my husband will never be able to remind him, because he never wears pants at home.' She then came out with the biggest overshare in my teaching career thus far. Tapping/rubbing far too high on her husband's thigh, she leaned in and said in a stage whisper, 'He finds them too restrictive, same with condoms, he's got a giant dong.' My TA and I looked at each other in horror, then looked at the dad. He sat back, manspreading so far his knees were sat in different counties, arms folded with the biggest grin on his face. He then nodded and winked at me! Shuddering and feeling nauseous, I promptly decided I would set up a sticker chart for the Year 5 child to help remind him to wear his pants and asked them to leave. I don't think I've ever been more scarred by a parent interaction in my life. I was never able to look either of them in the eye ever again and as I was unable to look down for the sake of remembering the conversation, most *of my discussions with them after that were conducted by telephone.*

While most of these awkward interactions with parents happen within school grounds, the most worrying interactions with parents have to be in the wild, and by in the wild I mean outside of school. There has been the odd occasion when I have been out on a night out, getting merry when a shout of, 'Y'alright, Mr P,' can be heard and you turn around to see a parent of one of the children you teach. Nothing sobers you up more. I'd love to say that was the worst experience I have had with a parent in the wild, but unfortunately it isn't. Now this story could be considered extremely embarrassing and many people wouldn't dream of sharing it in a book that will hopefully be read by thousands of people. However, when so many teachers have willingly shared their embarrassing experiences, I feel it is only fair I do the same. The only difference is that all the stories shared are anonymous, meaning no one can be identified, whereas this can. Maybe I should have just added this as one of the anonymous stories, but it is too late, I am committing to it.

A few years ago, I had been suffering terribly from a pain in my stomach, it had continuously worsened to the point where I was in excruciating pain. My wife suggested we go to the walk-in centre at the hospital. Now, usually I am not one for going to the doctors unless it is absolutely necessary, but in this case I was happy to do so as I was in severe pain. After a long wait in the walk-in, I was eventually seen by a doctor who, after examining my stomach, initially thought it could be an appendix issue until I explained I had my appendix removed when I was a child. I was then sent for an X-ray and sat in the hospital room waiting anxiously for the results. A long while later, the doctor came back into the room with the X-ray to explain that the pain I had in my stomach was due to a severe case of ... constipation. Yes, I was bunged up. To be fair, the doctor, while identifying all the backed-up faeces on the X-ray, commented that he had never seen someone full of so much excrement, which prompted my wife to comment, 'You must know him very well.' The prognosis was to either wait and let nature take its course or to speed up proceedings I could have an enema. This involved having some sort of laxative liquid injected into my rectum, try to hold it for around 20 minutes for it to have the maximum effect and then I should be good to go to the toilet and relieve myself. I decided to try to do what would bring me the quicker results and opted for the enema. 'Ok, I will fetch a nurse to sort it out for you.'

A few minutes later, a nurse enters my cubicle and as you can probably guess turns out to be a parent of a child from my class. 'Oh, Mr Parkinson, fancy seeing you here,' she commented. I then introduced the nurse to my wife, who was trying her hardest to hold back her giggles as the thought of a parent shoving something up my arse to relieve the extreme constipation I was dealing with was too much. You might think the act of sticking the enema up me was the most embarrassing part, but it was actually the 20 minutes where I had to lie there, trying to hold everything in so the laxative could have the most amount of impact. They were the longest 20 minutes of my life. The parent kept checking in every two minutes, so I was nonchalantly making conversation about anything to do with their child while I was fighting the growing urge to literally sh*t everywhere.

Luckily, patient confidentiality prevailed and the story never made it to the school gates; however, I just hope none of the parents of children I teach now end up reading this book.

You might think that is possibly the worst medical procedure you could have done by a parent. But I take my enema and raise you this one:

One of my friends, who happens to be a headteacher, had his vasectomy performed by a parent. Pretty sure that has to be the winner!

I have to agree. You would hope that this would be the only story involving weird interactions with parents in a medical setting, but it seems to be more common than you would like.

When going into hospital for a gynae op as a 20-something teacher, the anaesthetist turned up and was the father of a child in my class!! He gallantly offered to find another member of staff but I felt bad and that I shouldn't make a fuss and would grin and bear it! He promised to stay up the head end but I couldn't look him in the face at parents' evening!

Sorry if this is too much information, but I was in the clinic to have a coil removed when the doctor turned out to be a father of one of my kids.

Having awkward interactions with parents can happen anywhere and everywhere, as these examples prove:

In my second year of teaching I was driving home from work after a particularly long day and I had to stop at some temporary traffic lights. After waiting for ages the lights finally turned green and I began to pull away but no sooner as I had begun to press the accelerator, a huge 4X4 suddenly appeared coming the other way. Annoyed that I had been waiting ages already and that this car had clearly jumped a red light I did something I don't normally do (I'm more of a curse-out-loud driver) and stuck my middle finger up. As the car got closer (close enough for me to see the driver, so they must have been able to see me too) I realised it was a parent of a boy in my class. I hastily tried to turn my middle finger salute into a wave but, funnily enough, she didn't wave back. I was absolutely mortified, and as I was new to teaching I was also terrified that she'd tell my head and I would lose my job! Thankfully, we both kept quiet about the matter, but I still can't look her in the eye.

I used to go to a really cheap gym – about a tenner a month, but one of the drawbacks was that the showers were just three-sided cubicles with no doors. I was having a shower when a parent of a child in my Year 1 class came into my cubicle to talk to me about how his bowel habits were making him late every day. I was naked, she was naked; changed my gym the next day!

Out for a night out dressed as St Trinian's schoolgirls and went into a bar. As I walked onto the dance floor, I suddenly heard over the microphone, 'Good evening, Miss Cable' – and there was one of the parents of a girl in my Nursery class behind the DJ decks. Needless to say, we only had the one drink in there! It wasn't a weekend, either, so I had to face his child at registration the very next morning. As I called her name, she said, 'Morning. Didn't my daddy see you in the beer bar last night dressed as a schoolgirl?' So glad I wasn't being observed that day.

Not me, but a manager of a local nursery was incredibly intoxicated on a night out and getting over a recent divorce. She got in the taxi and the driver said, 'I recognise you!'

To which she replied, 'Oh god, I haven't shagged you, have I?'

I'm sure you've guessed it, he was the father of one of the children at her nursery. Awkward!

There was a story where a male teacher was doing his parents' evening and everything was going pretty standardly. A few parents were lovely, a few had some complaints and most of them were somewhere in the middle. One by one, the teacher was ticking off his list and probably realising why some of the children in his class behaved the way they did, especially after meeting their parents. As he worked his way through his appointments he spotted a particularly attractive mum walk into the waiting area. Tall, glamorous and blonde; there was every possibility he was going to remember her and definitely tell his mates what little Billy's (not his real name) mum looked like and how he would be looking forward to meeting her again ... wink, wink ... nudge, nudge ...

It was only then that he realised that he had seen this lady before. Perhaps she was a famous presenter? Perhaps she was a famous singer that lived surprisingly locally? Perhaps she was an actress? As she came closer into sight, it turned out she was an actress, of sorts. A certain type of actress that indulged in adult-related activities in front of the camera. Yep, she was a PORN STAR!

With Billy's (again definitely not his real name) mum being a porn star, it was uncomfortable enough. I mean, she was just as entitled as anyone to have children and her lad was a pretty good child overall, but as she approached the table it became more and more embarrassing. The teacher had not only heard of the porn star mum, but he had given himself a 'treat' that morning (obviously to help alleviate the stress of the day he was about to experience). Even more embarrassingly, it dawned on him that she had featured as he performed a 'five-knuckle-shuffle' before he went to work. How could he look her in the eye? Not only was the mum about to sit and talk about Billy's reading progress, but she was still sitting in his yet-to-be deleted browser history! I mean, she'd also been sitting on something else in the video he'd watched but he needed to clear his mind and talk about Billy's (I cannot stress enough how much this is not his real name) progress in adding fractions.

I hope this chapter has achieved two things. Firstly, it has shown every teacher reading this book that awkward inter-actions with parents are inevitable and if the teachers who have shared these stories can make it through the cringe-worthy experiences, so can you.

Secondly, for any parents reading this book, please take a moment to think whether the complaint is worth making, or if you see a teacher out in the wild, question whether you need to let on or just leave them alone.

If there's anything to be learned from this chapter then it's probably that if you have some children in a class that are hilariously strange, wait until you meet their parents and it'll all probably make sense!

Let's talk about SEX, baby, let's talk about you and me ...

I'm guessing it's time for the chapter where we talk about the most cringey topic on the curriculum.

You bet!

There are plenty of words that fill teachers with dread and we all know that wet play and nits are definitely up there, but as far as topics to teach, there can't be as many that send shivers down the spine quite like SEX AND RELATIONSHIP EDUCATION (known as SRE, but we're sticking with sex ed). Some schools even have an entire week dedicated to it (depending on which schemes of work a school uses). I suppose it depends on how old you are as to the level of sex education you received. Some people are young enough to have known proper, well-thought-out sex ed lessons during their primary years with a genuinely informative approach including specific vocabulary. Some slightly older folks will remember that it was taught at least once in Year 6 and it was a morning's worth of giggling. Plenty of folks will be old enough to remember when there was no sex ed until you hit secondary school, when during a biology lesson a stuffy science teacher would wheel out the TV trolley and bang on a very dated and worryingly detailed birthing video to show a bunch of petrified Year 7s. Folks even older than this may be of the age where the boys were given a football during the summer term and they spent the afternoon having a kickaround while the girls were rounded up for 'the talk'.

One of my older mates was given a little book to read that was created by the makers of certain ladies' sanitary products by his mum and told to read it. Did he read it? Did he boll**ks!?! However you learned about the birds and the bees, it's universally understood that some kids definitely paid more attention than others. Interestingly enough, that same mate is now a supply teacher and always seems to be drafted in to teach when sex ed is on the menu. Hilariously, he works at the same school that his own children go to, and yes, he's had to teach sex ed to his kids (cringe). Fortunately, it was the lessons where they discussed personal hygiene and respecting differences, rather than 'How I Boinked Your Mother'.

Amazingly, if you didn't know already, we teach sex ed all the way down the school. The children are taught about the scientific names for body parts as young as 5. No, really! Many Year 1 kids can accurately remember the correct names of male and female private parts and have some grasp of how babies are created, including the explanation of 'When a mummy and a daddy love each other very much ...' or however you want to phrase it.

Sex ed can be, to a certain extent, a potentially controversial topic, with many elements provoking strong opinions according to a child's background, faith or upbringing. We do understand people's rights to their opinions surrounding Sex and Relationships Education, and I'm sure from reading this book you know where we stand. All we want to do in this chapter is talk about the funny sh*t that makes people giggle with embarrassment.

Sex ed is incredibly important. I can only imagine how difficult it can be for secondary school teachers who are having to deal with teenagers who are coping with urges and hormones. At least at primary school there is a lot more innocence around the topic. Stories like this one can certainly prove how challenging it can be as a secondary teacher:

This particularly embarrassing story happened a few years ago now. I was in my training year and it was towards the end of the academic year in July so I was no longer being monitored. I had responsibility for an entire class. I'd trained for this; what could possibly go wrong? It was when the European Championships were on and there was an England game midway through the day. Naturally, the kids all wanted to watch it but we'd been told we weren't allowed to, so I'm left trying to teach Year 8 (twelve- to thirteen-year-olds) some poetry instead.

I am not being funny but watching England is poetry in motion at the minute; Sir (it's only a matter of time) Gareth

Southgate has got the three lions playing like superstars. Saying that, this was the Euro 2016 tournament, which was a disaster – when we were knocked out by Iceland. So in that case poetry would have probably been a more enjoyable experience.

Naturally I had the score refreshing to keep them updated. Anyway, there is this kid who often 'made the wrong choices'. I keep seeing him looking down in his lap, which if you remember from being at school yourself generally means that you're on your phone. I was convinced that he was trying to stream the game, so when he put his hand up to go to the toilet, I really thought I'd got him. I said 'no' a few times and he started to beg, and thinking that his phone was in his lap I said, 'OK then, but stand up without moving your hands,' convinced that the phone would fall to the floor and that I would seem the ultimate detective. I should add here that there had been a sports event that morning and the students were all in PE kit. What I did not expect was for him to go beetroot red and stand up to reveal not a phone falling to the floor but a quite obvious erection. So obvious that the rest of the class started pointing and chanting 'Boner! Boner! Boner!' I've never been so embarrassed. God knows how he felt. I am a terrible person.

The overarching idea that most teachers like to impart to their children is: *The more you know, the better the choices you can make.* This also applies to things like drugs education. Teachers want the children to be as informed as possible, so when the time comes they can make the best decisions possible. Seeing kids later in life as they follow a fairly decent and wholesome path is pretty fulfilling. Modern sex ed is not just about how babies are made, but a huge amount about relationships and the fundamentals that inform family planning. Smart kids that are well informed make the best decisions ... hopefully.

One of the reasons it's such a funny topic to teach is because you have to look the children in the eye and talk about how they are all the byproduct of two humans, usually, performing the 'no-pants dance' or 'horizontal hula'. In fact, one of the most entertaining things about teaching is the hilarious names children give to the act of procreation. These include:

- making whoopee
- special cuddling
- doing the dirty deed
- ding dang do
- muffin stuffing
- bumping uglies
- rufty
- funny business
- sexy time
- boom-boom
- playing hide the sausage.

Seriously ... What do these kids watch on YouTube?

One child accidentally called it 'four-knee grating', and while four knees may potentially be grating, one can only assume he mixed it up with the act of *fornicating*. There was even a famous story online about how a kid sent a Valentine's card to his particularly attractive teacher offering to 'plough her into next week'. Fortunately (although many folks thought it was real), that was just a joke from a page called *Southend*

News Network, but you wouldn't believe how many people shared it as a real occurrence. In this day and age, it could quite easily have been true!

Whether using scientific terms for reproductive organs or some less serious variations, it's perfectly possible that they will elicit a chuckle or seven and raise a few eyebrows in a sex ed lesson. A bit of innuendo is a staple part of a teacher's day in a primary school. Most if not all of it will go completely over the children's heads but you can bet your bottom dollar that any other adult in the room will be quick to give them the eyes while trying to stifle their laughs. Here are some of our favourites:

My colleague once had a child with the surname Bates. One day, she was releasing all the children at the end of the day, calling them out by name as she saw their parents and decided on this occasion to shout 'Master Bates' instead of his first name.

During a lesson on ambitious vocabulary, I told my Year 6s, 'There's no point whipping it out if you're not going to do anything with it!'

Doing practical part/whole model addition with Year 1 with hoops and tennis balls. 'How many balls do I need to put in my hole?' Cue my LSA (learning support assistant) crying with laughter, stuffing tissues in her mouth and me having to go and stand in the cupboard, laughing hysterically.

'Whatever you do, don't lick your flaps!' Our Year 6s had just written letters to their future selves and put them inside envelopes for their yearbooks. Luckily, it went straight over their heads, only my TA gave me 'the look'!

'You're leaving me with absolutely no choice but to stand here and rub one out right now.' My teaching assistant fled

the room in bits. I was talking about removing a class point from the board.

While making felt balls, I uttered the line, 'Keep rubbing and rotating your balls in your hands until they are nice and tight!'

Today I said to the children, 'Look at my jugs. Which has more in? My right jug or my left?'

My TA once told one of our Reception class he was 'good in the sack!' She meant he was good in the sack race!

A child was playing with his cowboy doll, and he said, 'I need to put my Woody away as he's becoming distracting!' I nearly wet myself.

'I'm coming round the room to check the size of your colons.' I must state we were doing work on the punctuation mark, I was not trying to do some sort of class colonoscopy.

A colleague was teaching rhythm to my class and we were clapping in a circle. In order to stay in time she said, 'And now we're going to pass the clap round the class.' Took all her effort not to laugh, went totally over the kids' heads, luckily!

When making a Remembrance Day wreath using red handprints I asked, 'Whoever has left such a mess after doing their hand job, go and tidy up!'

I was saying to a class of Year 3s and 4s during PE, 'I do not want your balls to be flying towards my face!'

How on earth are you supposed to keep a straight face after hearing those?

So a typical day teaching sex ed will definitely vary depending on the school doing it. One way that may or may not happen at your local school is for a teacher or teachers to split the boys and girls so they are in separate rooms. If you have a male member of staff, they often get the delightful role of talking to the lads first about their journey from being boys to men.

Although we've come ... to the end of the rooooooaaad! Love a bit of Boyz II Men.

Of course you do. Believe it or not, some schools have very few males on their staff; there may be one lone fella, potentially the site manager/caretaker, but the poor chap has no interest in chatting about this stuff. He'd prefer fixing toilet seats and restoring a wi-fi router to chatting about erections. If you are the token bloke in a primary school, there's every chance you'll get drafted in to fulfil the positive male role model function ... even Adam!

While the boys are chatting about pubes and wet dreams, the girls are given the same talk but relating to the female elements, usually by a lady teacher or TA. After the input about their own gender, the groups swap to then be given the talk about the changes that happen to the other sex. It always surprises me how sensible the kids become when they have to learn about these topics. Each school will be different, but from talking to teachers in many different schools there are definitely common approaches. There used to (and may still) be a brilliant set of comics for the boys and for the girls where they get to read through them and talk about the content, including new vocabulary that they need to clarify. The 5-foot-11 Year 6 child will probably not need the concept of growth spurts explained to them as they may already be an expert in the area.

For some of the more streetwise dudes and dudettes, especially those with older siblings, there may be very few shocks in some of the new terminology. In fact, if you have an older brother or sister, they may have used plenty of the sex ed vocabulary as an insult. There are always plenty of sweet and innocent younglings that will be shocked to hear that you tend to stop referring to a boy's personal append-age as a 'willy' and either go for the more scientific 'penis' or go straight for the swear words (again, plenty to choose from if you have an older brother).

I heard them all from you and Ryan!

Well, you still act like most of them, Adam.

Just be careful when listing all the names on the board, as one teacher made this fatal mistake.

I was asking the class to tell me all the words they knew for sexual parts and writing them on the board with the aim of identifying the ones we would use. When I went to clear the board I realised I had used a permanent marker. Some of them could still be seen for months afterwards.

Or, even worse, teaching a lesson during a learning walk.

I was getting all the slang and swear words on the board at the start of the sex ed lesson to get the embarrassment and crudeness out of the way and in walked the head, chair of governors and an education minister from an African government just as the class were shouting out a C word that rhymes with runt.

There is always some child that will mishear the all-important terminology and they'll think that a penis is someone that plays a piano, testicles are made of ice and West Vagina is a state in North America. It's hard to wean the children off terms such as willy, boobies and whatever your child has been brought up to call a lady part. Every teacher has heard a wide range of names such as woo-woo, na-na and foofle. Pretty much anything you could name a pet chihuahua would apply.

Misconceptions will always raise a smile later in the staffroom during the debrief after a sex ed lesson and parents will also hear of these too. A friend of mine told me her son was so proud of himself after his first human body session. He said smugly, 'I know what the ladies' private parts are called ... a Volvo.'

A child asking what was a boner? It was explained in a professional way. The child then followed up by asking, 'So why are people in Africa dying from it?' That would be Ebola.

When I asked if the children understood what a virgin was, no one answered until one boy put up his hand and asked, 'Is that someone who doesn't eat meat?' In a weird way, technically they're right?

When discussing the word erection, a child was confused by the wording and commented, 'What, like Jesus?'

'No, that would be the resurrection!'

We were doing a World War II topic at the same time. The children got confused between the vocabulary of evacuation and ejaculation.

You have to hope the class didn't have relatives who were old enough to be evacuated during the war as that would make for one awkward conversation. 'Nan, were you excited when you ejaculated during the war?'

A Year 2 child after being taught the correct words went home to Mum and told her, 'Boys have a venus and girls have a pagina.'

When asking what name we give female parts, a child shouts, 'A black hole!'

'Miss, what's a dodo? My mom has one and she loves it!' Needless to say, I didn't correct him and say it was a dildo!

One boy was really anxious because he thought he was going to be paired up for a 'practical' session.

The misconceptions might not always be on the part of the students, of course.

If teaching sex education wasn't already an eventful topic, while teaching Year 6 before the summer I managed to mishear a girl who asked, 'How big do boobs grow?' as 'How big do pubes grow?' And proceeded to tell her they're short, bushy, black, curly and when shaved come back thicker. The look of confusion on both our faces when we each realised what had happened was real!

One thing that is always a goldmine of comedy and awkwardness for the staff involved is the anonymous questions section of sex ed sessions. Not all schools will do this but what often happens is at the end of all the input and discussions around sex and relationships education, you give the children the opportunity to completely anonymously ask a question about some of the key features of the topic. If they've learned any new words that they could do with clarifying, this is the time to ask. Obviously, in the times when the kids say things that are totally hilarious relating to their misconceptions, it's still essential that you don't laugh at them in case it makes the child submitting the question feel bad or embarrassed. What you do is store them mentally and then giggle about it in the staffroom.

Or write about them in a book!

Quite right. The way many schools do the anonymous questions is they ask the children to write all the questions they feel comfortable with asking and pop the pieces of paper in a shoebox or pencil pot. The brave grown-ups involved will draw them at random and answer the questions respectfully so the children get a good chance to better understand all the changes that will happen to their bodies and what grown-up relationships may bring. It's actually a pretty interesting lesson to be involved with, but it's a big relief when it ends – especially after the Q and A, when the teachers don't always have the answers and will often look at the other staff and say: 'That's a really good question ...'

Sometimes the questions are straightforward, like: When do periods start? What is a wet dream? When do you get pubes? Sometimes the questions amaze you and give you an insight into the kids' level of maturity. One teacher I know said he pulled three questions out in a row and they were all about AIDS. It turns out that the parents of the child (handwriting was pretty obvious) that wrote them were massive Queen fans and their lad had watched a documentary about Freddie Mercury. Fair play to him for bringing the questions forward.

Amongst the serious and thought-provoking ones come plenty of awkward ones. One question referred to a kid walking in on his parents having sex.

Wowsers!

They were going so hard that one of them smashed the light on the ceiling.

What? Really?

HE WOULD NEVER SEE THEM IN THE SAME LIGHT AGAIN!

Ffs Adam! I'm guessing that didn't really happen and you remembered it for the purpose of telling that joke. Did you get that one from your mate the Geordie PE Teacher?

Probably.

Back to the awkward ones, though. The children sometimes write down questions asking about when staff lost their virginity. It's up to the adult how they answer but it's usually answered by saying it's a personal question but they were definitely over the legal age. Sometimes you have to be diplomatic in how you approach these things. One memorable question from a boy read: 'What happens if the boy goes in the girl's weeing hole?', which is a fairly sensible question and the grown-up that selected it (a lady in her fifties) replied:

'The young lady will probably say ouch and the gentleman will have to improve his aim!'

Stuff like this definitely sticks in your mind. How on earth do you keep a straight face with that reply?

You'll get some questions from the kids that are humorously worded, humorous in general and some where you wonder what on earth the child has been watching. Here are some genuine examples that kids have written down for staff to answer (you can decide which category they fit into):

What's Viagra?

Where do you buy comdoms (sic)?

Why are condoms flavoured?

Can nannas still have sex?

What happens if my boner won't go down?

Will I go blind if I masturbate too much?

Why don't boys have periods?

Can gay people get pregnant?

Do people fart when they have sex?

Can you overdose on semen?

Is sperm friendly or will it attack me?

If you get an erection when you're looking at a tree, does it mean you like trees?

Do the 'balls' go in and if they do, do they spin?

I don't think my mum has been through puberty yet as she hasn't got any hair on her privates.

What is a tit-w*nk?

Some interesting questions, and there are plenty that are much easier to answer than others. Goodness knows where they learnt the term 'tit-wank'. Mind you, for anyone that grew up watching *Friends*, it is littered with so many sex references. Some that have aged badly and some that will resonate brilliantly. If you watched *Friends* up until the final season, you may hear the words 'Shovelly Joe' and your mind could potentially switch to a joke about a sex act that stands pretty much no chance of getting a girl pregnant. If you didn't get that reference … google it – it's a decent episode.

You are usually pleasantly surprised by the maturity of the class when you approach sex ed … well, most of the children. But one thing is for sure, you will never have as many confused, dirty looks and daggers than being pregnant while teaching a lesson on sex ed. At the moment when the penny drops and your class realise how babies are made, the communal stare that is directed towards the pregnant teacher with looks of disgust and judgement make for one interesting end of session chat.

Amongst all the discussions around intercourse and sexual wellbeing, teachers need to be very careful that they don't leave students a little disturbed from some of the more graphic details.

When showing the girls in my class some sanitary products, I held up a tampon. A girl asked, 'But what happens if it gets stuck?' To which I said, 'Oh no, don't worry, it won't.' I then proceeded to demonstrate tugging the string and it snapped off! The girls looked horrified with gasps and shrieks and I wished the ground had swallowed me up.

One thing that a lot of schools use is the DVD. Every school seems to have one, although I suspect the contents of each DVD may well be different. We have one but it only really covers the basics of puberty, whereas other schools seem to have more in-depth coverage of the curriculum.

A familiar occurrence is that there will usually be at least one child who finds the content too much and faints, so just be careful at which point you pause the DVD ...

Many years ago, I was showing the traditional sex ed DVD when a child fainted. All the children knew that if this child ever fainted they weren't to stare at him. So the child fainted, I instinctively paused the DVD and attended to the child. As I was doing so I noticed I'd paused the DVD at the point a giant 6-foot penis was ejaculating. The poor kids were just staring at the screen as they knew not to look at the child who had fainted. They are now 16 and 17 and when I see them they always mention it.

A word of warning for any members of staff whose children attend the school they work in. The sex ed lesson can lead to admissions from children that will have the rest of the staff looking at you in a completely different way.

To get the silliness out of my Year 6 class, I let them tell me any words they knew related to sex ed. So they were shouting out random things like 'cock', 'fanny', 'dick' and then someone said 'pubes'. Which prompted one child to then shout out, 'My mum's got loads of them!' His mum was the chef at the school. So I had to see her daily and have inappropriate visions.

I was a Learning Support Assistant and during PSHE the teacher was talking about myths on girls getting pregnant and mentioned withdrawing before ejaculating, so then had to explain what it meant. One boy pipes up, 'Yeah, and then you walk in and find your parents wiping it up off the living-room carpet.' His mum was a teacher at the school.

Having delivered all of the necessary learning, it was time for any further questions. One boy, who was completely deadpan and asking a genuine question, said, 'I get all of this, miss, but what part do the candles have in all of this?' Worst part for me was that his mum was a TA in the school. It was very hard to look her in the eye after that revelation.

We were talking about women having vaginas and men having a penis. A little boy put his hand up and said, 'My mum has one of them, a penis!' To which I replied, 'No, I don't think she will, she can't have one as she's a lady.' He then said, 'Yeah, she definitely does, it's a huge pink one in her bedroom drawer!' That mother was the headteacher of the school.

Once the kids are equipped with their new knowhow and understanding, you can be sure that a few kids usually spoil it for everyone by being d**kheads. This is where the boasting and bullsh**ting begins. Within a week, one doughnut will claim to have already slept with three people and have a 15-inch penis. His alpha mates will start to emerge and come up with equally far-fetched claims that could easily be disproved. It's almost like the weeks after sex ed lessons give some kids licence to try to make out that they are total studs when in reality they still wear dinosaur pyjamas and eat from plates featuring Fireman Sam. I'm pretty sure Naughty Norman Price would be in that gang, dreaming up total twaddle to try to impress his mates.

The girls can be equally as bad, mind. At times, they are even bloody worse. Making each other feel inadequate about when they start menstruating and whether they have been bought their first training bra or not. Almost in the space of a week, plenty of sweet and innocent young ladies suddenly start changing friendship groups and turning into mean girls. It's when they start wearing pink on Wednesdays and decide that everything is 'so fetch' that they need reminding to slow down and enjoy being a kid. The best part about teaching sex ed to classes in upper Key Stage 2 is that while the children are about to embark on their journeys towards adulthood, the hormones won't kick in for the majority of the class until they hit secondary school. By that point ... they won't be a primary teacher's problem any more!

We hope you have enjoyed our delightful jaunt through all things sex-ed-related. Yes, it can be the most dreaded subject to teach for some people, but it's probably the one that guarantees the most giggles in the end.

You can't really say the words penis, breasts or condom in a geography lesson, now, can you?

I mean, you can, but it may be a bit weird!

Unless you are getting paid specifically to lead them, in any walk of life or profession, I can guarantee that you will *never* look forward to a staff meeting. Whether you're an admin clerk, a firefighter or working the tills in Tesco, nobody thinks to themself: 'Yippee, can't wait for Monday's staff meeting!' We were half-tempted to name this chapter: SHOULD'VE BEEN AN EMAIL, because so much of the crap you are made to sit through could have easily been distributed to staff via email.

While a staff meeting will never be the highlight of anyone's day, ask any school staff member that is obliged to attend and they will tell you that these regular gatherings are one of the most pointless aspects of their job. This rings more true for EYFS teachers, as they have to endure staff meetings where 99.9 per cent of the content has absolutely nothing to do with EYFS. My heart does go out to them.

Don't get me wrong, I've had to sit through some shocking staff meetings, but I have had some occasional good ones, too. Especially INSET days, where as a school we have been lucky to have some incredibly inspiring training from the likes of Alan Peat, John Murray and Jane Considine. I also hope that many other teachers and school staff would say that the staff meetings and INSET training I've had the pleasure of leading in hundreds of schools over the past few years weren't a waste of time and helped in lots of ways.

One thing I have discovered from working with so many schools is how universal they all are when it comes to staff meetings. In particular, the roles each staff member takes. I will whizz through a couple of these examples. Teachers, can you recognise yourself in any of these?

There is always, always a staff member who is late to the staff meeting, awkwardly interrupting as they apologise and often explain their lateness was due to a parent arguing about a missing jumper that didn't have the child's name in.

There is always a member of SLT who has some go-to phrases that they throw out in every staff meeting multiple times. They can be very David Brent-esque – circle back, going forward, close of play, Ofsted window, hit the ground running, touch base, heads up and non-negotiables are just some I've heard on my travels. You may keep yourself entertained by tallying up how many times they are said in a staff meeting. The worst is if you have an erm-er. Someone who erms a lot. I always remember at uni we had a lecturer who was renowned for erm-ing. I once spent a lecture counting the erms and gave up at 86 after 25 minutes. I have noticed

that if I am particularly tired (which is most days) I can erm
a lot. There are some phrases that when uttered will send
shivers down any staff member's back. Phrases such as:

This won't take long.

Did I not mention this is a twilight?

Can we all sit in our phases please?

*I know I emailed everyone, but let me talk you through
the slides.*

How about an icebreaker?

Any other business?

Let's just role-play this new strategy.

I know you're all busy but ...

*Let's put this to the floor for discussion (knowing full well
whatever is said will be ignored!).*

There is always a teacher, usually busy, who is desperate
to get on the leadership team, so they nod all the way
through the staff meeting. The nodder wants to show the
utmost compliance and displays their desire to get noticed
by nodding at everything – when the register is being taken,
when the fire exits are being identified and, worse, when
something is being announced that will definitely add to
your workload. I'd end up with a severe headache if it was
me, but these teachers can go for days, it seems, like they
are the Churchill dog from the adverts bobbing away.

At the opposite end of the scale is the doodler. This is
the teacher who appears to be deep into making notes of
everything being discussed in the staff meeting but instead
is drawing a detailed picture of an eye. Their teacher
planner by the end of the year is a beautiful piece of
artwork with patterns, shading, doodles and bubble writing.
They can sometimes be caught out if a question is aimed at
them, but if carried out craftily they can pull it off to make

it look like they've noted down every word like a court reporter. I am not going to lie, I have done something similar with my iPad, made it look like I was typing notes but instead been catching up on more useful tasks, like writing this book. Yes, that's right, as I type these words I am currently sitting in a staff meeting about something to do with deep-dives and instead I am getting the word count up on this ... hang on a second, I think I have been rumbled ... 'Yes, what was the question again? How do we ensure the implementation of our subject? For me, it is ... consistency?' Phew, I got away with that one. If you want a tip, if, like me just now, you are caught out with a question, my go-to answer is always 'consistency' – it is a real buzz word at the minute and seems to be the answer to everything. If not, try 'knowledge-rich'.

I often scour everyone in the meeting to try to find the staff member on the brink of falling asleep. There is always at least one, and sometimes, depending on the subject of the meeting, you can be struggling to find a staff member still awake. My eyes normally go straight to the teacher who just returned from maternity leave or a new dad who may not yet have their little one sleeping through the night. One thing is for sure: if you clock someone on the verge of visiting snoozeville you immediately have to tell the nearest person to you, who continues the trend like a game of whispers. If that happens, though, you might as well write off the rest of the staff meeting as the battle that staff member goes through to try to stay awake is utterly mesmerising. 'Listen, can you please stop talking about that risk assessment, it is distracting us from watching Steph/Stephen fall asleep.' You might even start taking bets on how long they can last.

More often than not, despite being reminded, there will always be a mobile phone left on that will ring out in the middle of the staff meeting. Why is it always the technophobe teacher? And why do they always have the most random ringtone? Pitbull and Ne-Yo ringing out across the school hall, 'Tonight, I want all of you tonight, give me everything tonight, for all we know, we might not get tomorrow, let's do it tonight.' On one training session I did at a school, this exact thing happened, and where usually the teacher silences the phone and embarrassingly apologises for the interruption, this TA decided to answer the call and, just like Dom Joly in *Trigger Happy TV*, had a full-on conversation with her husband, Barry – who works nights by the way, if you were interested? And just like his wife, he wasn't the most confident with technology as he had to be talked through, step by step, how to use the microwave to heat up the tea his wife had left him. I couldn't help but laugh as 30-plus other staff members all turned to hear this TA explain to Barry how to heat the cottage pie. Once finished, there was no apology, just a comment of 'Bless him, he's so tired when he works nights.'

My favourite type of teacher is the one who is all talk before the staff meeting. These teachers talk the talk but never walk the walk. You may recognise this teacher from a conversation like this:

'Hi, everything OK?'

'Not really. I am up to my eyeballs in work, it can't continue, I am sick of it, someone really needs to speak up. If one more thing gets added to our workload in this staff meeting I am going to have to say something.'

'Yeah, you should.'

'Believe me, I will, I am not having this any more!'

Cut to the staff meeting where it has just been announced, 'So we feel it is going to be beneficial to use our already very tight budget to pay an external company with no links to Ofsted to come in and visit us and do a mock inspection where they will tell you all how terrible you are at what you do and get paid a lot for doing it. Is that all right with everyone?'

You shoot your eyes across the room to the teacher you had the chat with and they simply nod along in agreement. So in the staff meeting after the staff meeting, where a selective group of your colleagues have a debrief in a classroom to discuss what's just discussed, you question the teacher, who simply replies, 'I'll definitely do it next time.'

Be aware of these teachers, too, as sometimes they can manipulate you into standing up in the meeting yourself. Let's go back to the initial conversation ...

'Hi, everything OK?'

'Not really. I am up to my eyeballs in work, it can't continue, I am sick of it, someone really needs to speak up. I wish someone would speak up for us as teachers. I just don't know how long it can continue.'

You reply, 'I completely agree. I'm taking three sets of books home a night to deep mark and what is crazy is that hardly any of my students can read it! Who am I doing it for? You are right, someone should say something.'

'Well ... why don't you say that, say exactly that?' they suggest.

'I could do it, but would anyone actually listen? Maybe if everyone backed me up so I wasn't just saying it as an individual, we did it as a team.'

'We are a team, and I will back you if you say something. Honestly, I'll be with you every step of the way. I will have your back; if anyone says anything I will be defending you at every opportunity.'

'Ok, sounds good. We're going to take back teaching!'

Then, in the wellbeing and workload staff meeting:

'And relax, thank you everyone for joining in this compulsory yoga session for staff's wellbeing and workload. Just to let you know, I was on a course the other day and because Ofsted are focusing on broad and balanced, now we need to make sure we are triple-marking everything. Anyone want to add anything to that?'

With your hand shaking as you raise it, you speak up. 'Yes, I just want to let you know that most of us teachers are struggling with our workload. The expectations of following all the non-negotiables in the marking policy is overwhelming, especially when our pupils can't read what we write. It is then having a negative impact on well-being.'

'So I know I said these yoga sessions led by me aren't compulsory, but if you don't attend I will send you a passive-aggressive email letting you know you're not a team player and it's not helping your wellbeing? Well, I wonder if anyone else agrees with you. Anyone? Anyone?'

The levels of silence are deafening. You shoot daggers at that teacher who is avoiding eye contact like you're Medusa. You've been stitched up royally and now you're being left out to dry.

'Well, it seems that is a view only held by you. So thank you everyone for joining the staff meeting, it is 6pm so you're free to go. Can you stay behind, I just want a quick word.'

When you confront the teacher who tricked you into being on capabilities, they tell you how brave you are and how they were just about to say something before the SLT cut them off.

Now this might seem a far-fetched situation, but you will be surprised to realise that it is more common than you probably think.

One of my favourite staff meetings of the year happens usually around May time when the staff list by year group for the next academic year is going to be announced. The levels of anticipation go through the roof; there is more anticipation than when Gareth Southgate announces the squad for the next England tournament. It is hilarious. Some schools don't care and announce it nonchalantly in October, there are other schools who never change but there are a lot of schools who like to turn it into a TV drama and I am all over it. Firstly, you have definitely had a chat with your teacher BFF that goes along the lines of Joey and Rachel when they both discover Chandler and Monica are dating in *Friends*:

'Do you know something?'

'Do you know something?'

'I might know something.'

'Me too.'

The rumours of who is going where has dominated the staffroom for weeks and there's always that one member of staff who has the inside scoop because they carpool with a member of SLT and they do a full-blown presentation to the rest of the staffroom like they're Jamie Carragher on *Monday Night Football*. Despite having tactic boards and convincing everyone they know, they never get it right. Then comes the actual staff meeting itself; everyone is on tenterhooks, you can cut the tension with a knife. It is the one staff meeting that should be presented by Dermot O'Leary as if it is *The X Factor*. Some heads use it to up the drama, they cut to a commercial break before announcing who is going where, or prolong the moment by bringing the any other business usually done at the end of the staff meeting to the beginning. It is honestly like eviction night on *Big Brother* or recoupling night on *Love Island* with a whole range of emotions. Tears fall as year group partners who love each other are split up, TAs recouple with other teachers, some teachers are on cloud nine when they realise they are staying in the same class and so can have a summer break rather than spending all of the holiday moving classrooms and redoing their displays. I have respect for the stubborn teachers who refuse to move or leave, they make a speech like Leonardo DiCaprio in *The Wolf of Wall Street*: 'I'm not leaving!'

Then comes the big surprise, which may well be that a member of staff is moving to another school and has been able to keep the news quiet so it comes as a huge shock. Other staff may make it blatantly clear they are leaving – they've already collected the deposits for their leaving do months in advance. But some can keep that secret so well hidden you almost feel offended you didn't know. Another surprise is when a member of staff who has been a stalwart in a particular year is then thrown to the opposite end of the school – EYFS to Year 6 and vice-versa. I often feel sorry for teachers who end up moving up with the class. It is always put across as a compliment: 'You have worked wonders with this class, they have settled so well and we want you to keep building relationships.' In reality, 'You are the only teacher who has survived a full year with this class, everyone else either left or quit, and you have survived, so how are we going to reward you? Make you waste all your summer holidays moving classrooms.'

The worst staff meeting for me has to be the first one of the academic year. It is always tough for everyone involved. All the staff will be knackered as the Sunday night fear that had disappeared for six weeks is back with a vengeance. You have to go through the same conversation for the first hour before the staff meeting:

'Hi, you all right? Yeah ... you? I know, where has the time gone? It's like we've never been away! Yeah, it was quite quiet to be honest. Yeah, we managed to get away, I saw you did too, the pictures on Facebook looked lovely. Well, that's the thing about the UK, you can never guaran-

tee the weather but a change of scenery is always nice. I
know; diet starts tomorrow. Ok, lovely, yeah, catch up at
the break.' This will undoubtedly be replicated with every
member of staff you bump into that morning.

Repeat that around ten times and that's all before the
staff meeting starts. If that first staff meeting is in-house
there will definitely be some SLT who are making it up as
they go along. Why? Because they've been on summer
break too and rightfully so, it's called a break! As Ross from
Friends always said, 'WE WERE ON A BREAK!'

The first thing that will be announced is the fridge coordinator, who clearly told everyone to empty the fridge before
summer and is now raging as someone left a tuna salad and
half-eaten sandwich in there over the break. There will be a
member of staff using the time to cut out their new display,
even providing a soundtrack through the humming of the
laminator.

The staff meeting then starts properly with some house-
keeping, where, despite working in the school for nearly a
decade, you are reminded of the fire drill procedure. Any
building work that was scheduled to be completed over the
summer hasn't been finished, so you're told that it is hopefully going to be done by Christmas, but that means the wifi
will be temperamental for a while. If Ofsted is mentioned in
that first staff meeting, kiss goodbye to your hope of a
decent work–life balance. One of the most awkward aspects
of that first meeting is when new members of staff are introduced to the rest of the team and you have no idea what to
do; do I smile, but if so I don't want to come across too
keen or creepy? Or should I wave? I'll raise my eyebrows
and nod to everyone. Then there's pregnancy watch, an

update from the deputy of which staff members are expecting, returning or delivering.

One of the hardest challenges in that first staff meeting is resisting the urge to stuff your face full of cakes provided by another member of staff who has discovered baking over the break, but you've promised that you would not overindulge now the summer is over. Initially the cakes go uneaten as everyone is trying to be healthy, which can give the staff member a bit of a complex that they're rubbish at baking. However, by break time the focus of the staff meeting soon determines how many cakes have been devoured just to provide enough energy to help everyone get through the next session.

Dates for the diary is always a draining aspect of the meeting, especially when it can be done on an EMAIL!

Emailing has become such a time-consuming aspect of our job. I would always recommend using out-of-office messages and having a cut-off point each night, otherwise emails can become overwhelming. One thing I do find funny about emailing is the etiquette that everyone follows. There is a definite what I write versus what I actually mean when it comes to composing an email, and I am sure plenty of others will be able to relate:

As per my last email = Listen, you lazy sod, just scroll back through the previous thread as I have already answered that question.

Thank you for your email = Why have you bothered me about this?

I hope this email find you well = I know it won't as you're a teacher, so you'll be stressed.

I see your point = But I disagree.

Thanks in advance = This is now a legally binding document that means you have to do everything I have asked.

Kind regards = Please leave me alone.

Great = It isn't great but I can't do anything about it.

With respect = I couldn't care less how important you think you are, you are wrong.

As you are no doubt aware = Stop being clueless, we both know this.

According to my records = I have evidence, so don't even try it!

As discussed = Same complaint! Do you have the memory of a goldfish?

This is very much on my radar = Along with the 59,384 other things I am trying to balance.

Correct me if I am wrong = Which I am not ...

Just to reiterate = I am going to repeat this one more time.

Going forward = Let's make sure this never happens again.

Just checking in = When are you going to reply? I will continue to nag until you respond.

To put it more simply = I don't have time for this.

Should you require further assistance = Contact the school office so you can leave me alone.

Regards = I never want to hear from you again.

I often think that the majority of the public hold teachers in high regard and see our profession as full of highly intelligent people who use their common sense to tackle the very demanding job of educating the next generation. However, the following staff meeting stories certainly bring that into some doubt.

As someone who has sat through my fair share of staff meetings and INSET days, I always feel like two things should happen by the end of these sessions: teachers should come away empowered and inspired to improve their practice, but also they should have some practical ideas they can use in the classroom straight away to immediately impact the teaching and learning in their classroom. If that doesn't happen, what was the purpose of that 'training'? I take a lighthearted approach to this, and making the pedagogical side of my training humorous and enjoyable is an added extra, but I do believe there is real substance to what I provide, and if implemented it can improve and raise standards in the classroom. In some of the examples I will share here, though, I am not sure of the purpose or point of these sessions, especially considering that most of these have a financial cost.

I would say 99 per cent of schools I have visited to lead INSET always engage and you get the feeling the training will make a difference; however, there have been some where I can't wait to leave. Very rarely, the staff just refuse to engage; they chat amongst themselves and waste the day. I always remember a training day where I asked the staff to consider why they chose a career in education, in an attempt to remind them it is so easy to lose sight of this in the crazy, pressurised environment that so many of us find ourselves in. Expecting the usual responses of making a difference to young people, having a teacher when you were younger that had such a profound impact on you that you want to do the same for others – or the opposite, having a negative experience at school and so wanting to make sure that didn't happen to others, instead, the majority of the staff simply answered with one word: August. I mean, it is a highlight, no doubt, but that set the expectation for the rest of a tough day where the staff didn't really bother to engage.

In other situations it is the leadership who book me in to then moan about what I deliver. To make it clear, I am not, and never have been, anti-SLT, despite what some people think, and I have nothing but respect for leadership teams. I think the dedication, hard work and sacrifice that leadership teams make is nothing short of incredible. I am, however, anti-bad practice, I will call out things I don't think work, are a waste of time and have a detrimental impact. This is no reflection on people who have implemented these ideas, as more often than not they don't know a better way, and any idea I call out, I then make sure I provide solutions.

There have been a couple of occasions where SLTs become so defensive because they don't like to admit that what they do isn't necessarily the right or best way, and this can make the situation incredibly awkward. 'Who do you think you are, telling me how to run my school?' has been one response I've had when I made the point that making teachers waste time marking through ridiculous non-negotiables policy but then running a yoga wellbeing session and thinking that will have any impact on wellbeing is missing the point. The look of fear on the staff's faces when I end up saying something they are all thinking is always very telling, and it always gives me the best indication of the atmosphere and true dynamics between SLT and staff. I always appreciate when headteachers join and sit in on the training, too. I know how busy the job is, but hearing my message first hand always seems to have more impact.

I always know on leaving a school whether the training will make a positive change or not and it shouldn't really bother me as, ultimately, they are going to pay me anyway. But I do care, I want to help teachers, it really does affect me when I receive so many messages from teachers who are struggling massively with their workload or are at the point of leaving the profession due to the ridiculous expectations and pressures. The most frustrating thing is that most of it is completely pointless. I know it always seems like teachers moan about how hard their job is and people wonder, how can you moan when you get all those holidays? Surely, you know what you are getting into when you sign up? No, we don't. Most of us have fond memories of our teachers, love the idea of supporting and helping the next generation reach their potential and want to make a difference. However, the biggest difference between our teachers then and being teachers now is that teachers then were trusted. We're not, we're under constant pressure and accountability that has led to a system that is not only failing children but forcing so many incredibly talented teachers to feel dejected and worthless and it leads them to leave the profession. This is something I want to change and I hope that through my training, INSETs and CPD I can help teachers realise what matters, offer them guidance, advice and, more importantly, practical ideas to help them achieve a better work–life balance.

One of the worst INSET days I have ever had to witness involved a man who spent part of the day sharing holiday snaps and then dancing with his wife at the front of the hall like they were on *Strictly*. When I found out the amount of money charged for a day that didn't teach me anything I didn't already know but left me thinking about everything else I could be doing with my time, I was truly gobsmacked. When I reached out to my following for other examples of crap INSET, this same training session actually popped up a fair few times.

We have shared plenty of these ridiculous examples on the podcast, but here are some of my favourites:

We once had a staff meeting on art and how to encourage children to paint without judgement. We all had to spend the session creating a piece of work, then at the end the woman running it told me my artwork was sh*t!

Truly inspiring!

We had an awful man deliver a twilight presentation. I had just come back from a week off sick and still shouldn't have been in. He asked how long it took children to make up their minds about a teacher. I gave an answer and he said, no, that was how long it had taken me to decide if I wanted sex with him. Had I not felt so ill I would have given him a piece of my mind and walked out. Later, he told us that research showed women in concentration camps weren't affected by their experience. I still get wound up thinking about it. I have no idea what he was supposed to be teaching us.

The crucial information is missed off in this story, as I don't know what the main focus of this session was, but I imagine whatever it was, it became instantly lost when that comment was made. What a dick!

Some people came in to talk to us about dyslexia. They had a PowerPoint presentation with black text on white background and made us answer questions on Post-It notes and put them on the front – my idea of hell! The lady got mine and said, gosh, I didn't realise you could be a teacher and spell so terribly. I got up and said I was amazed you could have people teaching us about dyslexic children while insulting a dyslexic adult. I then pointed out how awful the PowerPoint was for dyslexic people and asked how they were qualified.

No words, simply no words.

I once went on some training where the first activity was 'Turn to the nearest person you don't know and tell them the most traumatic thing that happened to you in your childhood.'

What an awkward situation to be put in. If you ever get the opportunity to go to a conference or training day, it is the highlight of your week. Not because you are getting a day out of the classroom, or that you can have a lie in, it is the fact that usually you will get a belting lunch. If the course takes place at a fancy hotel, you can bet your bottom dollar you will be getting a decent lunch, a never-ending supply of biscuits and coffee and, more importantly, time to actually enjoy that lunch. But I would happily sacrifice all of that if it means avoiding having to either tell or hear a complete stranger's most traumatic experience. What would you say? 'Oh, I am so sorry to hear that, erm, do you want a wet paper towel?'

The head once, off the cuff, went through the teaching and learning policy that the deputy had planned to do the following week in a staff meeting. She still did the staff meeting. It was exactly the same meeting as the week before but with some pretty slides!

This further supports my theory that sometimes, every so often, headteachers just absolutely wing it!

I regurgitate this story every time I am asked this question, but it has never been topped ... we were once given training on how to open our blinds ... and then how to close them again.

I can see clearly now my blinds are open. OK, teachers, we expect you to be able to handle a class of 30 children where you are expected to nurture their curiosity, help them read, count, think and make progress despite some having a variety of needs. So despite having the intellectual capacity to do this, one thing we're not sure you'll know is how to open a flipping blind! Saying that, having to once show a teacher how to turn on a computer screen by pressing the on button, maybe I shouldn't assume. Some other similar examples:

We once spent 90 minutes discussing which cursive 's' and 'f' we should use! I bet I'm not the only one either.

The importance of wearing goggles when using a wall stapler or removing staples in display 😷. The goggles were never used.

A very long discussion on what colour pen to mark in: not red – too aggressive; not blue or black – because it doesn't show up; not purple – because the children use that for corrections; not green – because the head didn't like it.

We had one on the use of glue sticks and different ways in which we can fold paper in an exercise book.

Just before moving to our new school we were given training on how to assemble a cardboard packing box, including watching the head climb inside to demonstrate how strong they were.

Don't tell me you weren't tempted to quickly close and seal that box and post it to the other side of the world as punishment for making you sit through that meeting?

We had a meeting to establish lunch trolleys being removed as unsightly – only to have another meeting to decide how to put them back as they were actually needed!

Staff meeting on how to teach children how to pass the baton in a relay race. We all did it in slow motion in the hall to ensure we handed it over correctly!

Yeah, but did this training directly lead to the UK having huge success on the track in recent Olympics? No. Maybe it should have been a highlighter pen being passed along with my pupil's books, would have got my marking done quicker.

An hour-long staff meeting to discuss and decide who could authorise the 'pen licence'.

Don't get me started on pen licences. I hate them, mainly because I never got one as my handwriting is so bad it is almost criminal. I have harboured this hatred towards pen licences ever since, so I wonder what it must be like for every other left-hander? What a sure-fire way to make some children feel like failures because they can't share their ideas (the most important thing) in a format that once you leave school you now never publish anything in again in your whole life. That is not to say I am against teaching handwriting; before any of the traditionalists come gunning for me for suggesting we get rid of our traditional values, I still think it is a valuable skill to learn, and research has shown that if you handwrite revision notes the information is more likely to stick with you than if they were typed. Therefore, teaching it is important, but the amount of emphasis some schools put on making sure it is cursive and then rewarding that through pen licences really annoys me. Legible, yes, but having nicer handwriting isn't as important as the content and ideas you are trying to share.

We had one session that involved us watching two middle-aged men, head to toe in Lycra, doing interpretive dance. As if it couldn't get any worse, there was a moment when one of them bent down and unfortunately for him there was a quiet bit in the music and there was no disguising the noise that 'popped out'.

Surely that is a piss take? Were Ant and Dec sitting in the school office pulling the strings for one of their pranks on *Saturday Night Takeaway*?

And now for some wellbeing/mindfulness examples that just prove my point that the best thing to do if you are planning a wellbeing staff meeting is to just cancel the bloody meeting.

A whole day's wellbeing training run by a guy who'd got his act together and improved his wellbeing ... after he'd quit teaching.

A mindfulness one where we had to chew a raisin after looking at it and feeling it, then look at our toes, etc ... all the time I was thinking, I have a pile of books to mark and feeling really stressed that this training was keeping me from getting on with my work!

A friend of mine attended a 'work-life balance' meeting on a Saturday.

We had to answer a staff wellbeing survey and then were grilled and abused because of our honest answers. Key quotes from that were 'You're not happy? I'm not your mum!' and 'This isn't a Woman's Weekly *survey!' Safe to say I left that school quickly after.*

Staff development day where a consultant was paid (well) to come in and let us spend an hour and a half deciding what Winnie-the-Pooh character we were most like and examine what that meant for our wellbeing. Wt actual f!!! PS I was a Tigger. Tiggers are wonderful things. This meeting was not.

A positive-energy conference that we all had to attend, where a guy literally told us for two hours to not be a mood hoover and to smile more often.

A mindfulness meeting where we all had to do Pilates with Jet from Gladiators (she was lovely btw) – most bizarre moment of my life!

To be fair, I would probably engage with this one. I had a major crush on Jet back in the day!

A whole day (the first day of the school year) working out what type of person you are and how it takes lots of different types to make a successful team. Followed by at 14:00 'Right, so by 3 September I expect six weeks of full planning for every subject!' A TA pointed out that the day might have been spent better if the teachers could have used it for all that planning – or at least some year-group discussion. This was rebutted with, if we did not like the destination of the bus, we should get off. Many of us did!

Now one of the benefits of the recent pandemic was that most staff meetings went virtual, which was one step closer to what most teachers desire – which is that if the staff meeting can be covered in an email, it should be. Having virtual staff meetings allowed staff to attend from home, get on with more productive tasks if the staff meeting was anything like what I've mentioned above and surely, surely, there is no way you can conduct one of these ridiculous staff meetings over Zoom? Think again …

We had a mindfulness Zoom meeting and we had to take a piece of chocolate and close our eyes as we ate it.

The head then proceeded to say things like, feel it in your mouth, rub your tongue over it, roll it round 😴😂😂😂. *Needless to say his new nickname is Nigella* 🍳

All I can deduce from that is that the head has some weird food fetish, and the fact he can hide his bottom half allowed him to carry out this weird fantasy.

If you were thinking of applying for a job at a school, asking the question, 'What were the last five staff meetings you had?' would be high on the list of questions to ask. Before applying for a job at a school, many will invite prospective candidates for a walk around. You can go and see the school grounds where the member of the leadership team will explain how amazing the school is, while subtly papering over any cracks of ridiculous workload expectations. I always like the moment at the end of the walk around when the person says, 'Do you have any questions?' Now, of course you do, you have loads of questions, you want to make sure this school is a nurturing place that values and appreciates staff, ensuring they have the best environment to thrive while also providing the best education for the pupils. Questions such as:

'What is the workload like?'

'Will you make me waste time marking?'

'Will I be trusted to plan in a way that works for me or will I waste every PPA copying and pasting it into a stupid proforma that nobody will ever look at?'

'Will I even get PPA?'

'The staffroom looks lovely, but does anyone get the chance to sit in there?'

'If a parent makes a ridiculous and unfounded complaint, will you back me or hang me out to dry?'

And, of course, 'Is the Christmas party a proper piss-up?'

These are just some of the questions we should be asking, because on paper we, as trained professionals, have the power. According to a recent survey on recruitment and employment confederation data, Primary and Nursery Teaching professionals are number 5 in the list of roles with the most vacancies. The list reads as:

1) HGV drivers
2) Nurses
3) Programmers/Software Development
4) Care workers
5) Primary and nursery teaching professionals

We should be confident that we are good at what we do and schools should be begging to have a teacher like us. Therefore, we should be willing to ask these questions and not worry about the judgement that comes back. Instead, most teachers bite their tongue and say, 'No, that's great,' desperate to make a good impression and show compliance. Let's face it, the likelihood is that if you were to ask the questions your name would be blacklisted so that when you send over your CV it goes straight in the green filing cabinet – aka the green recycling bin. Nobody likes a disrupter; we can't have someone who might stand up and question the decisions we make. Some teachers are so desperate to escape the toxic environment they currently work in, the mentality is always, anything is better than this. Also, any teacher who is new into teaching is desperate to get a job. Any teacher who has taught more than five years will always comply, as they know that in the underfunded, budget-restricted system we work in, experience is used against you as you are more expensive. There's also the notion that our education system is built upon the kindness and unpaid dedication of caring staff. If a position cannot be filled, no worries, we'll just ask more of our already over-worked staff. It's flawed, but this is what is allowing so many schools to create this toxic workplace environment. We ignore all these red flags, and while people will have different types of warning signs there are always some that are universal.

Here are some red flags to look out for on your walk around that I am sure we can all appreciate:

Lifesize cardboard cutout of the headteacher in the foyer. Headteacher pops round the corner wearing the same suit.

I mean, who does that really? How much of a narcissist do you need to be to have the audacity to use some of the already tight budget to turn yourself into a 3D cardboard cutout? Jesus wept!

Triple-backed 3D displays everywhere that it looks like adults have done more work than the kids!

Websites that say 'Join us on our journey to outstanding.'

More than five job vacancies ...

Children walking down a corridor with fingers on lips.

Empty staffroom at lunch.

Being told on the walk around that if I wasn't prepared to do at least six hours after school every night then not to bother applying. Surprisingly, they have a very high staff turnover.

Told: 'The car park is always full by 7am.'

When they tell you that you have to submit your weekly planning to SLT by Wednesday 5pm so they have time to support your development and feedback to give you ideas and, quote, 'but it's really not a scrutiny process'.

A headteacher walking down the corridor and staff looking terrified and diving out of his way. He told his secretary to get out of his way and make him a drink ... I was scared of him by the end of the tour.

Having to do a Year 6 SATs paper in exam conditions as part of the interview process. The job was a part-time Reception mat cover post! No thank you!

A straight staple policy, I mean ... What?!

This last one I am not sure whether it is a red flag, but ...

I went to have a look around a school for a new position; however, my current school wouldn't allow me to do it during school time so I had to go after school. As I was being guided around the school by the headteacher I was getting a really good feel for the place until he opened the door to the staffroom where two members of staff were interrupted. It was evidently clear for the second before the headteacher slammed the door shut that one was orally pleasuring the other. The headteacher apologised profusely and ended the tour there. I ended up applying for the job just so I could get all the questions answered. They were both suspended and it turned out they were both married to separate people.

Which leaves me with the unanswered question ... did they get the job? Teaching job, that is.

Surely that last example is a potentially better (cheeky) use of a staffroom than a meeting where you spend a full 20 minutes trying to decide whether to highlight your pupil premium children in purple or orange on your tracking data! On what planet does a weekly (at least) meeting exist, just so the headteacher or SLT member that likes the sound of their own voice can bang on about new initiatives to justify their role? It really is a waste of everybody's existence ... including theirs.

Hopefully in this chapter we have managed to explore (and expose) why the humble staff meeting is such a drain on the teaching profession and a waste of most people's time.

Right, I'm off to draw loads of S-shapes on my handout and maybe do some yoga!

Teaching during a Pandemic

Covid-19 was something that I don't think anyone could have ever predicted. Well, actually, Bill Gates did, didn't he? I always remember when it first started making headlines and being discussed on the news after it started spreading in England, we were being told to be vigilant and to wash our hands. I remember making a tongue-in-cheek video about how it could help teachers. We are talking around February 2020, when there started to be guidance about not shaking hands, keeping your distance. I joked about how it could help teachers get out of staff meetings: 'Sorry guys, can't attend this staff meeting, don't want to be in such close proximity to everyone.' Refusing to mark books: 'I am sorry to say I cannot waste my evening pointlessly highlighting and writing an essay of "feedback" that my class can't read. These books haven't been sanitised.' This was in my head at the time as an exaggerated way of using this little virus to stop teachers doing the usual faff they do; little did I know that within a month our whole job would be turned upside down. We went from joking about bottles of Corona beer being the main source of the issue rather than a suspected bat at a Wuhan wet market to realising that we were not as safe as we first thought. It was starting to become serious in foreign countries, but surely (like Ebola and bird-flu in the previous decades) we were pretty safe in the UK ... surely?!?

In early March 2020, I was on the road running some conferences around the UK, still working part-time in my school and on the verge of signing with a big touring company for the podcast show. We had already booked a handful of dates and we had interest from one of the biggest tour promotion companies in the country to take the show to more venues around the UK. I had arrived at a Maidstone hotel to lead a CPD session with teachers, getting there the night before so I could do my usual routine of sitting in the bar on my Bill ordering a sort-of-but-not-really 'healthy' tea and scrolling through social media. A special news conference was broadcast where Boris made the announcement that schools were to close for the majority of children to stop the spread of the virus. WHAT THE ACTUAL F***?! was the immediate reaction of most school staff, I imagined. How would we teach kids at home? My immediate thought was around technology. Knowing the potential and the tools available, I thought OK, this is doable.

Fortunately, I had managed to implement a tool called Seesaw in our school over the past few years and instantly knew this would be the perfect way to continue learning at home. Seesaw is my favourite tech tool in the classroom at the point of writing. What I have learned in my short career of supporting schools with technology is that it can quickly change and what was the hot new piece of tech can soon become almost obsolete. Take the overhead projector, once a breakthrough piece of technology allowing hymns, slides and notes to be projected onto a wall for all to see. If you were lucky, you might have had the prefect job of sitting by the overhead projector during singing assemblies, which made you feel like you were Calvin Harris doing a set in Las Vegas. Moving the sheets at the exact right moment to ensure everyone hit the big chorus was a goosebumply rush of adrenaline that a lot of us will never again experience. So at the point of writing, Seesaw is my go-to tech tool for the primary classroom.

There are plenty of similar apps to Seesaw, including ClassDojo, Google Classroom and Showbie, but for me Seesaw was my favourite. We had originally introduced Seesaw as I was sick of teachers wasting time printing, photocopying, trimming and sticking evidence of learning in a book. What Seesaw allowed us to do was evidence learning in a much more efficient way, giving teachers time to use more effectively. I don't see why tools like Seesaw can't be used to evidence learning alongside the book. Believe it or not, there are still schools who can't allow themselves to do this and still expect teachers to evidence EVERYTHING in the book or when they do put something on Seesaw they need to print it as a QR code. This is why glue sticks are like gold dust in schools, why teachers turn into Gollum with their spare 'precious' glue sticks, why some staff will be begging, hitting the street corners just wanting one more hit of a Pritt stick – even lowering their standards for a cheap YPO brand that is like lip balm.

In those first few weeks of lockdown one I received a number of messages from schools who had me in for training and implemented ideas from the training, saying how it was a lifesaver as it made the transition to home learning straightforward and easy. Just like in my school, the children had been trained on using Seesaw in the classroom, so they were able to apply that independently at home. There were plenty of other schools in a similar position, with apps like Google Classroom or Class Dojo, but there were also plenty of other schools who for one reason or the other hadn't embraced the technology and so didn't have the means for online teaching at the beginning. With a lot of teachers putting together work packs with the photocopier – or Bob Marley as we like to call ours, as it is always jamming – working overtime. There was the usual boasting from certain schools who were already providing a full timetable for their pupils, but that wasn't going to be feasible for everyone. There's no doubt that some schools were able to provide more for their pupils but what I can say is that every teacher in every school was doing everything in their power to support their pupils.

It seems strange to think of it now but there was a sweet, innocent naivety at the beginning, as we all thought it was only for two weeks. It was incredible to see how many people stepped up to provide and share as many resources to help keep children engaged and learning; Joe Wicks had the whole country up and moving, well, the children, that is. I tried joining in and was sweating more than the time I had to do the puberty talk with Year 5 when my headteacher decided to join and a child asked, 'How does sperm get into a lady's private parts?' I got started on Joe's classes and was panting like I was about to pass out when Joe pipes up, Right, warm up over, now let's get into it. I couldn't walk for the rest of the week! Dr Chips was providing daily STEM lessons, including loads of practical investigations you could do at home, Jane Considine had her live writing sessions – to name but a few. The Oak National Academy had their teachers film lessons covering over 10,000 hours and teachers, headteachers and staff were even delivering workbooks, meals and other things to help their schools' children.

All of this showed how school staff go over and above for their pupils. There was also a period where teachers were actually praised in the media. On social media, we were inundated with messages of support from parents who for the first time were seeing what it was actually like to teach their precious little angels. 'They deserve to be paid billions', 'I have nothing but utter admiration for what a teacher does', were just a couple of comments that I remember seeing. It was so refreshing to see our profession being spoken about so positively after years of certain media outlets doing nothing but demeaning hard-working teachers and schools, which created a feeling that the general public reflected this attitude when in reality it is a small minority. It seems that the few people who have this narrow-minded view about teachers are given a platform for their voice to be heard. This certainly happened further into lockdown, but I will never forget the week where teachers' hard work was praised and recognised by parents all over the country.

Even in school, things were relaxed in the very beginning. The children who attended school (vulnerable and key worker children) had a weird freedom from the usual timetable. I was in school for a couple of weeks until I got the letter to say I was extremely vulnerable and therefore needed to isolate at home, so instead I worked remotely to support the children and staff with the online learning they were providing. I was then left with the task of doing the home learning with my own children. I love my children to death, but give me a class of thirty children over home learning with my three any day. I had no patience – and I am a teacher! – so I can only imagine some of the struggles some parents went through trying to help their children navigate their phonics work with absolutely no clue what a split digraph is. I was trying to reassure parents and school staff that doing your best was good enough. It was a confusing time for us all and actually there were so many other things children could do to continue their learning. At the same time so many parents were trying to do all this while also doing their own job. For me, I was just glad there was no home-school Ofsted inspection as I feel I would have been graded PISS POOR!

I can just imagine the inspector rocking up to my house as I was screaming at my kids to keep the noise down. I'd greet the inspector as they questioned the uniform both the staff and pupils were wearing; I'd explain that dressing gowns and pyjamas create a relaxed feeling in the learning environment. We discussed the start time of the school day and how this differed for the younger children compared to the teenager who never sees this side of the morning. In fact, the school day started at 3:30 for my fifteen-year-old. The inspector would then question the curriculum, consider a deep dive in PE – to which I'd explain that Joe Wicks is an incredibly busy person and probably wouldn't reply to his DM.

'What about reading?' the inspector would inquire.

I would then demonstrate the ultimate parenting hack of turning subtitles on for everything my children devour on the telly and clicking the mute button.

Things would then go downhill quickly when the inspector asks how maths is being covered and I demonstrate how the children are nailing their unit on converting measurements of liquids that mum and dad found themselves drinking more of each night.

With eyes rolling from the inspection team, their focus would turn to the issue of cultural capital, to which I would reply, 'Not sure whether we've got that cereal in but we've got plenty of Coco Pops!'

I can imagine they wouldn't be very impressed with the displays and the fact they have been there for a number of years, but the kids were so cute when they were babies.

'Talk to us about behaviour.'

'In the bedroom? Pretty expected standard, unless I go for the deep dive and I'm told I can get greater depth?'

Once the inspectors have stopped throwing up, they would ask about targets, to which I explain that I expect the children to be dressed at least twice a week. I would go on to explain how my biggest issue as a parent is with the teacher, and I have on numerous occasions written a letter of complaint to myself about myself from ... well ... myself, explaining how disappointed I am with the job I am doing.

Luckily, for social-distancing reasons, Ofsted didn't do home inspections.

Those two weeks soon turned into two months and at the point when banana bread no longer looked appetising, that's when it became tedious for some. We were incredibly fortunate, and despite having days when things did get on top of us, I tried to stay positive and count my blessings.

It was an incredibly scary period for my training business. In one swift night, a term's worth of bookings in school disappeared. Luckily, my website MrPICT.com, which I had set up a year earlier, was a lifesaver. After receiving so many messages from teachers who couldn't attend one of my CPD courses in person for one reason or the other – too far away, the SLT didn't value it – I decided to set up the website where I moved all my CPD online into bite-size videos to help teachers and school staff build their confidence and knowledge in using technology. The site wasn't a resource website where you can simply download a Power-Point and worksheet and off you go, that isn't my style.

Don't get me wrong, there's been the odd lesson where I've done that, but I like to have more ownership and put my stamp on things, and having a range of ideas through technology means I can take a simple idea and make it more creative and empowering for my pupils. That is what I want teachers to have from my training and website. An arsenal of tools to help and support pupils in demonstrating their knowledge and understanding. I know teachers are incredibly creative and given the time they'd produce creative lesson plans and resources ten times better than what they end up paying money for. But I wanted to help teachers gain that time back by helping them work smarter, not harder, so they could utilise that time to plan and deliver more effective lessons. The website literally saved my business; it kept things ticking over while my school bookings couldn't happen.

Alongside the website I also started running live CPD sessions over Zoom. This became a substitute for my normal face-to-face training and, while it didn't quite give me the same buzz as when I deliver training in person, it helped me continue to support and help teachers. Zoom became the go-to tool for staff meetings and, despite the technical issues that would inevitably always happen, they allowed schools to keep in touch, do any necessary training and even do live lessons in the beginning. Again, alternatives were available – Google Meet and Microsoft Teams were popular – but for the purpose of this section I am just saying Zoom.

The worst experience for me was having to do a three-hour after-school CPD session with a school where no one – and I mean no one – had a camera or microphone on. I take pride in providing the best possible training session and can usually gauge how well a session is going by the reaction of the staff in front of me. I love the sound of laughter when I do a training session and make a joke and, believe you me, my sessions are as funny as they are inform-ative ☺. On Zoom, it is more difficult when everyone is muted but if there are a few cameras on you can still see people's faces light up. However, doing a three-hour session with no interaction at all was one long afternoon.

I have had some nightmare sessions delivering training in person; the one that immediately stands out was a school that had a headteacher who just clearly hated me. I had no idea why she allowed the training, but from the moment I started she kept interrupting me, trying to undermine everything I said. You could see everyone in the room cringe every time she spoke up and objected to a point I made. Despite this, I continued to do my session and after speak-ing to the staff knew they were finding it useful. It was at the end of the training, when I had finished, that the head simply stood up and walked past me without thanking or even acknowledging me. By the time I got home she had emailed me to say she wasn't paying for the training as she felt I hadn't met the objectives of the day. I was fuming because I knew exactly the type of headteacher she was – a sh*thouse. If you've got a problem, don't wait for me to leave and then email me, speak to me while I am there. The email warriors are one of the worst types of leaders. It is weak; if you have a problem with something but are not willing to talk about it with someone face to face, you can get in the bin. I am not blowing my own trumpet and I know not everyone who attends my training will like it or me or necessarily agree with what I say, but if you book a training session, I guarantee I will deliver what has been discussed and agreed.

These experiences are few and far between, and 99 per cent of the time the training is very well received and I am always grateful for the positive feedback. However, when you are speaking to a camera for three hours with no idea of how well people are engaging, listening or caring, it is a tough gig. I remember at the end there was an awkward five minutes where I was looking for someone to speak to acknowledge they'd actually listened ... but nothing. I had to just sign off with well, thanks for having me, hopefully see you again soon, even though I had no idea what any of them looked like.

Before the end of summer, more guidance from the government came out to say that EYFS, Year 5 and Year 6 pupils could come back to school but they expected them to be socially distanced. As you will have seen in the chapter about disgusting things that happen in school, keeping their distance is something that is impossible for Reception children to do.

Summer came and went with many children falling victim to the government's 'mutant' algorithm with their GCSE and A Level results. I can't really go into too much detail about this situation, as my experience has only ever been in primary school, but what I will say is that given the situation was out of the students' hands it would have been better to give them the benefit of the doubt and the opportunity to prove themselves in the next stage of their education rather than deny them that opportunity based purely on the fact of where they lived.

After months of learning from home, I am sure plenty of parents had to have a serious conversation with their children before they did start back at school. After months of learning from home and the shortcuts or bad habits that had set in, there would have been plenty of discussions that went along the lines of this:

'OK, children, my little cherubs, the apples of my eye, we need to have a bit of a chat before you start back in school. Now you have learnt lots, and I mean lots, of new words during this first lockdown, your vocabulary has grown exponentially, but you cannot repeat a single one of those words to anyone. These are Daddy's special words that he uses to get through a day of teaching maths to you. It might be the case that you'll start hearing a lot of weird noises in your stomach area; it might sound like a whale call, but it is just your stomach rumbling. It might start at around 9.30 and go on until lunch as you will no longer be able to have the 385 snacks you've been used to at home. Remember, there is no Alexa in your classroom. Remember, if your teacher asks what you were doing at home the answer is always ... reading! That is right, not Minecraft or Among Us. If I get a phone call home to say you've been accusing other children in the class of being an imposter, I won't be happy. It might take a while for you to get used to wearing your uniform; unfortunately you'll only be able to wear your pyjamas on Children in Need day. If you don't know the answer to a question, just say "I don't know, Miss," not "I don't know as my dad did all my work at home." You can't throw Lego at the adult in the room when it comes to doing spelling. The daily wrestling match you've both had will need to stop as well: just because you'll have a crowd on the playground doesn't mean you can turn it into *Wrestlemania!* Think of all the positives: you'll be able to concentrate for longer than five minutes without being interrupted by Phil the DPD driver bringing another ASOS package of clothes for your mother that she will never wear. And remember the golden rule: What happened at home school, stays at home school!'

September started but the academic year was like no other. It was different, to say the least, the guidance was well typical of government guidance – confusing – and schools had to quickly adapt to this new normal. There were positives and negatives to this new normal, and here's a quick run through of ten things I missed and ten things I liked about the new normal:

Ten things teachers missed the most about normal school:

1) Carpet time! I never appreciated how special carpet time was until it was taken away. Don't get me wrong, it is a tough act to master and it takes time, but there is something special about having your little cherubs together in front of you, looking up at you with awe in their eyes.

2) School sports. It was all put on hold – competitions, footy leagues. I am sure some teachers were relieved not having to do those duties for the children as it was always such a huge part of their primary school career. I felt so sorry for them.

3) Having a classroom that didn't smell like your student accommodation the night after Freshers' Week. With hand sanitisers being used like they were going out of fashion, you'd be walking down the corridor, popping your head in asking how many wines your colleague had the night before. I am not going to say this smell is any better than a combination of baked bean farts and sweat from Year 6 after the Galácticos footy game at lunch with Year 5, I am just saying walking into a classroom that didn't smell like a brewery would be a good thing.

4) Classroom jobs. No longer allowing children to have the role of whiteboard monitor or register monitor was a challenge. The teacher had to do everything, you had the pressure of deciding who got given the dirty whiteboard or the pen that no longer works after a week. It was an extra pressure none of us needed.

5) Having a day when you could focus on just teaching rather than the 8,374 other things you had to make sure were in place to keep your children safe and the virus at bay.

6) Not being able to send a child to go and fetch something you forgetfully left somewhere in school, such as photocopied sheets or a message to another teacher.

7) Whole-school starts and lunchtimes. The staggered starts and lunches mess up the body clock. I usually didn't have breakfast until break time – 10.30–11 – whereas that was lunchtime for some classes. Add to the fact you couldn't then have the usual time in the staffroom with your colleagues to chat and catch up really had a negative impact on my wellbeing.

8) Hearing the children sing. Before the pandemic I would quite gladly pay to never hear certain songs being sung in assembly, whereas at that time I'd have given anything for a rendition of Cauliflower Fluffy!

9) The celebration/award assembly. It was something we all took for granted. The buzz isn't the same when it is done virtually, mainly because in an assembly there would always be some sort of incident that could be giggled about in the staffroom for the next week after.

10) Overheated classrooms. I actually missed being able to teach where it didn't feel like you were on an expedition to the Arctic. Having to keep your classroom ventilated

(which meant your windows had to be open all the time) meant there were lessons where I had actual icicles hanging off the end of my nose. Bogey icicles!

Ten things I liked about the new normal:

1) If you work at a school full of mood hoovers, the staggered start and lunch times could be used to your advantage, meaning you had little to no interaction with these negative nellies and so avoided the boring, dull chat that could engulf the staffroom.

2) Generally speaking, the fact the children had to wash their hands regularly meant they were a lot cleaner. I didn't have any child cough directly into my face for the first time in my career, and I will take that.

3) Tidier cloakrooms and lost property not looking like an actual uniform shop was a great sight. This was because the guidance stated that pupils should only bring the bare minimum and in a lot of schools this being a coat meant the cloakrooms no longer looked like a bombsite.

4) In the guidance, it was recommended that teachers shouldn't take books home to mark. Finally, some schools knocked that pointless exercise on its head, unless of course you were being told to just wear gloves to mark.

5) Children were made to be more independent. I couldn't tie any shoelaces, so the children had to do it themselves. I had to keep my distance. It was lovely not to have to touch a wet lace given the fact it hadn't been raining so therefore that lace was wet due to one thing ...

6) Staggered times and fewer children in the playground at the same time made break times a lot easier. Fewer

entries in the accident book and fewer bump notes being sent home also made break duty a lot easier.

7) As resources couldn't be shared, having every pupil have their own glue stick was dream stuff. Usually by the second week in September, there would only be a couple left in the whole class as the lids seem to disappear in the Bermuda Triangle of my classroom. Glue stick lids must be the most desired item on the dark web, as they literally go missing within minutes.

8) PE kits. This is definitely one that will stay when things do eventually get back to normal. Why we'd never thought of this before, I don't know, but it is a game-changer. Getting your class to come into school in their PE kits on the day they do PE. Mind blown! It saves you hours, you no longer have to waste half of PE getting the children changed and then changed back into their uniform. No longer are there random naked children running round the classroom looking like a Picasso painting, or wearing an item of clothing belonging to every other child in the class even though they are all clearly labelled.

9) Staff meetings being kept to a bare minimum. If they were done on Zoom they were usually short and sweet and in some cases could be done with the screens off, meaning you could get on with marking with your gloves on!

10) The best thing about teaching during the pandemic was that parents had to be kept at a distance. Obviously I am not talking about the majority of parents, who are sound, I am talking about the ones who always approach at the end of the day for a 'quick' word who actually want to treat the chat as their own therapy session. The

fact that parents' evening was done on Zoom and kept to a strict time limit was brilliant. Of course, any serious issues would be dealt with but it was the low-level interactions that could end up being very time-consuming for staff. Also, with the virtual parents' meetings, you could pretend that their signal was crap and hang up if they chatted for too long about how the letter 'z' wasn't joined that way when they went to school. 'I'm sorry, Mrs Smith ... you're breaking up a bit ...'

I felt children settled back into the new academic year pretty well on the whole. It was always a constant worry for staff being in an environment where the virus was clearly spreading. No matter what changes you made to separate children it was only going to do so much. As much as we could try to limit contact in school, we could do nothing about what they did outside of school. A parent contacted school to talk about how her little darling was feeling very anxious about returning given the fact the virus was still rampant. The teachers tried to explain it was the best place for the child and the different ways in which we have tried to keep them safe – limiting contact as best we can, washing hands every time the children do anything, etc. The teacher also commented about how wonderful it would be for her to be back with her friends after so long away from school, when the parent inter-rupted to say, 'Oh she doesn't need to worry about that, as she was at a sleepover last weekend with most of the other girls from the class.'

It was certainly a challenging start to an academic year, with so many changes but the expected outcomes staying the same. Staggered starts, staff only able to stay in their bubbles, unable to catch up, chat and interact with other staff could really make them feel isolated and fed up. It sounds silly but let me tell you, a five-minute conversation with another adult about anything other than school can keep your spirits up and morale high. I am not going to make out that school staff had it harder than any other profession. I hate the comparisons about who has it worse. Ultimately, we only know what we know, and compared to other years it was challenging. Again, I had nothing but respect for the way school staff stood up to these challenges, the constant changing guidance, bubbles bursting, and despite all this they were managing to keep their pupils learning and making progress. The message we were receiving was that schools would be the last thing to close if there was another lockdown and so the likelihood of schools closing again for the majority of children would be unlikely. Things were just done differently, nativity plays were streamed through Zoom, parents' evenings were Zoomed and staff meetings continued virtually. It was a bloody long term but the promise of a normal Christmas with family gave us all hope. This, unfortunately, turned out not to be so, and despite cases rising dramatically towards Christmas the government decided to threaten legal action against any school who decided to close earlier because of a spike in Covid cases. There were so many school staff who were told to isolate as late as Christmas Eve, completely ruining their Christmas celebrations.

Cut to January and the government continued to assure us that schools were safe for pupils. Even allowing schools to reopen for a day, millions of children were interacting and continuing to spread the virus before the government backtracked and made the decision to close schools to the majority of pupils once again. This time it was clear that this would last for a sustained period and it was expected that schools provided more structured home-learning provision.

Vulnerable and key worker children would again be able to attend school, but the government once more sold schools short by making the guidance around key worker status so flaky that anyone would think they were entitled to send their children into school. I completely understand the pressure put on parents by certain employers who weren't accommodating to the fact schools were being closed to most pupils purely for a safety reason. However, some of the requests sent to us by parents, you couldn't help but think they were really grasping at the idea of what constituted a key worker. In the beginning that was mainly NHS staff, supermarket staff and other school staff. By January, requests were coming into school that were then shared with us such as:

A Botox technician. I know the past year had been stressful for many, especially teachers, but really?

Someone who worked in Primark, a shop that was closed throughout the lockdown.

A parent who worked from home but was having the kitchen done.

A stay-at-home mum.

There was even a parent who dressed up in fancy dress as a doctor to drop the child off at school only for the children to admit that their dad worked at McDonald's.

Another cracker was, 'My partner isn't a key worker, but we are trying for another baby so if my child can come in a couple of days so we can get busy, that would be great!'

'I work in my dad's pet shop a couple of hours a week so that counts as veterinary medicine, doesn't it?'

My favourite was someone who worked in Timpson – a literal key 🔑 worker. Fair enough, you can't really complain at that request, and in all honesty, a job working as a key worker in Timpson opens a lot of doors.

As I stated before, I completely understood the pressure parents were under but the whole point of closing schools to the majority was to keep numbers down to stop the spread of the virus. Certain schools that didn't stand up to some parents' requests ended up with better attendance than when schools were normal, which completely defeated the objective.

With this third lockdown, schools had to really step up with the home-learning provision. Despite being given one evening's notice – let me repeat that: ONE EVENING – they were expected to completely transform the way in which they went about their job. Despite some tweets stating that teachers had it easy and were simply sitting back taking a wage for doing nothing, those in the know understood school staff worked harder than they'd ever worked before.

I have never been more proud to call myself a teacher than to see how our profession stepped up to every challenge faced throughout this whole pandemic, but during the spring term of 2021 it was incredible. Some schools found it easier than others – the ones who had built on their use of the technology from the first lockdown continued to utilise it to support those pupils at home. Others found it tricker, but we all got there. The amount of learning, innovation and creativity from teachers was amazing and something that deserved to be recognised. It felt at times as though we were working two jobs – continuing to teach the vulnerable and key worker children in class while also providing lessons for those children learning from home. It was incredibly challenging and difficult as teachers knew no matter what they did with remote learning, it was never going to be as good as having the children in class with us. This puts a lot of pressure on staff as we really care about our jobs and the children we teach.

Finding the right formula for remote teaching was also a struggle. Live lessons versus pre-recorded lessons became THE big debate. For me, it was never going to be a one-size-fits-all, it was so dependent on different factors. Children having access to technology was a big one; yes, the government promised all these laptops but, like most initiatives, it was good in principle but the execution left a lot to be desired. In fact, as this book comes out, I bet there are plenty of schools still waiting for their promised laptops. Everyone had an opinion on what they thought was best but ultimately schools had to consider what was right for *their* school. No one knows the children and families better than the teachers and staff at the school. For example, in our school we didn't do a full timetable of live lessons, as it wasn't feasible. The odd parent didn't agree with this approach but we felt a mix of some Zoom lessons alongside pre-recorded input and activities was best for our pupils and staff. If we had done a full timetable through live lessons and there was a family with multiple children and only one device, who gets access? At least one of the children would miss out on the live lesson. There was no research to suggest they were necessarily better than pre-recorded lessons, and when the Oak National Academy also provided hundreds of brilliant online lessons, why reinvent the wheel when we had so much on our plate?

That's the one thing I feel a lot of schools didn't consider during this time. Teachers had an awful lot on their plate just doing their job in the circumstances, but you also had to consider the challenges that staff were facing outside of school. Not being able to see their families, having their own worries and concerns about the whole situation. One thing I can say is, despite the challenges, the pressure of knowing the remote learning wasn't going to be as good as having the children in class with us, school staff did a phenomenal job. They were the reason children were able to continue making progress, and they may well have been the single reason that put a smile on so many children's faces at such a worrying time. As a profession, we should feel very proud of the way we managed the lockdowns.

One positive element of the remote-learning situation was that so many schools had to embrace technology. I was supporting a lot of schools and teachers, helping them get set up with the likes of Seesaw and getting some great feedback. What I want to make sure that schools do now is continue to build on this. If the right tech tool was chosen, it won't be a tool that can only be used for remote learning, it can also be used day to day in the classroom. Seesaw is the perfect example of that. Continuing to build on what you were doing during the lockdown can then help teachers reduce workload. Covid-19 didn't create the workload and wellbeing issues in education, they've been there for years, although the pandemic certainly didn't help and in plenty of schools probably worsened them. But when the lockdowns did happen, certain things didn't matter – marking couldn't happen, pointless staff meetings were cancelled, the amount of tick-box exercises that has plagued our profession suddenly stopped. The exciting part of this whole situation is that we now almost have the opportunity to press the reset button on a lot of things we were doing before, such as asking the question, is this going to have an impact on teaching and learning? If the answer is no, don't do it. One thing we have all learnt from this pandemic is that life is too short. We shouldn't be wasting time on things that add little or nothing to learning. At the end of the day, there won't be a teacher on this planet who is lying on their deathbed, turning to their loved ones and saying, 'I wish I had just marked more!'

As stated earlier, most parents found navigating remote teaching difficult and we all did it in different ways; however, there seemed to be certain types of parents when it came to helping their children with home learning.

1) The one who can't work out the technology. For those schools who decided that Microsoft Teams was the best tool for Year 1 children they probably had more of this type of parent.

2) The competitive one! There have been a number of occasions where I could hear parents shouting in the background when I asked questions to the class.

3) The one who can't believe what their child is actually like. They would phone the school to complain that the report they received last year was in fact a lie and the teacher has taken a lot of artistic licence as 'Callum is in fact not a pleasure to teach and doesn't always try his best. I've seen less fiction in a Harry Potter novel.'

4) The one who just doesn't get new maths. Bar models have a completely different meaning to these parents.

They argue that the old way is perfectly fine and all these new ways of working things out are just confusing!

5) The one who tries to use the age-old teacher lines, including, 'It is your own time you're wasting.' But at home this doesn't cut it; kids don't respond the same.

6) The referee. They spend most of their time splitting up the children, who are fighting each other.

7) The one with the split personality. When the teacher phones home to check in they are as nice as pie but cover the phone while they blast the children, 'WILL YOU BE QUIET! No, not you, Mrs Jones, please continue. Yes, the kids are doing brilliantly. ONE MORE TIME AND YOU'LL BE GOING TO BED!'

8) The one who invents their own curriculum. 'Forget learning about Rocks, kids, the only Rock you need to know is Dwayne "The Rock" Johnson who single-handedly saved the WWE formerly known as WWF from losing the Monday Night Wars. Look, let's see him in action as we watch Royal Rumble 1999 where he had an I QUIT match with Mankind.'

9) The one who needs a special drink to help them get through. We've all had those days!

10) The one who does all the work. You try to have all the patience of a saint but in the end your life becomes a lot easier when you just give them a helping hand. The worst part is when the work submitted receives some rather dreadful feedback from the teacher!

Expecting 30 primary school-aged children to access all this remote learning without any funny incidents would be naive to say the least. We were sent so many hilarious remote teaching mishaps, but here we'll share some of our favourites.

We were told of one child who had a full-on nosebleed during the live lesson. Imagine seeing a child's screen literally fill with blood as the teacher stopped the lesson to shout for the child's mother! It could have been worse if the mother was called Alexa; another teacher told us she set off around nine Alexa devices when she asked on a live lesson for the pupil Alexa to do question number two. 'OK, Alexa, you do number two for us.' I suppose it did answer the question my children have asked before, which is whether Alexa goes to the toilet.

Nothing quite lets you know the children are glad the lesson is over as when one leaves their mic on and utters, 'Thank God that's over, I'm desperate for a poo!' At least that child had the manners to wait. The number of stories where children logged on late to a live lesson using the excuse, 'Sorry I am late, Miss, I was just having a poo!'

There were children asking the most important of questions during live lessons: When will this end? What time is break time? Can I go to the toilet? Can I let me cat out? Are we done now? This is boring. And, of course, what time is home time? ... coming from a child at home.

Some children seem to have mistaken their live lessons for a virtual GP consultation. Imagine being in the middle of your input when a child interrupts to say:

'What is this on my foot, Miss?'

'Ask your mum after story time,' replied the teacher.

'Just have a look. What do you think it might be?' continued the child while raising her feet towards the camera.

'I really don't know, put your sock back on and ask your mum after story time.' Teacher starts story time, to be distracted the whole way through by feet slowly appearing into the camera shot.

There were plenty of parents having their own discussions in the background when children hadn't muted themselves, sometimes having arguments with each other, some even accidentally flashing while walking in the background!

Teachers also found themselves saying things they would never have dreamed of saying to their class, such pearlers as: 'Why are you waving a dead rat on the screen?' 'Can you take that snake from around your neck?' 'I want to see your face, not your guinea pig.' 'I don't think a hamster should be on your head during this spelling test.'

Here are some more cracking remote-teaching mishaps:

Pre-recording a history lesson, I had briefly looked through the PowerPoint beforehand but in the middle of recording I had to say 'fact hunt' ... never slowed down so much and spoken so clearly in all my life 😳

I asked a child at home if they had a pencil sharpener when their pencil broke. A child in class piped up that they had one here that could be borrowed! I hope they didn't arrange the delivery with Hermes, otherwise they could be waiting a while!

How about this burn from one young comedian:

I did an adjective scavenger hunt yesterday with my KS1 class. I asked them to find something old – a very enthusiastic Year 1 girl dragged in her dad. I couldn't stop laughing! Unfortunately, her dad didn't think it was quite so funny.

I can just imagine the dad going into a quiet room, sitting facing a wall and having a couple of minutes to cry at the realisation that their child thinks they're a fossil.

This one was an absolute belter:

During a live Zoom lesson, one of the Year 3 kids learning from home needed the toilet. So instead of leaving the tablet and coming back to it, the phantom pooper brought the tablet into the toilet, most likely didn't realise it was unmuted and myself and about 50 other children could hear all of the glorious toilet activities. Completely threw me off and you could see all the other kids giggling away. As I was frantically trying to scramble through the participants to find who was unmuted, we heard the toilet flush ☺️🚽 Cue a swift email from SLT reminding parents about supervising their children at all times and ensuring they are participating in the lesson in a shared, appropriate area of the family home ...

I think my favourite thing from when I had to do live lessons was having to tell an older sibling off as he kept pointing a plastic gun at his sister while she was trying to participate in the lesson. I know some children didn't like the remote learning but holding a gun to one's head was a bit excessive. It was rather off-putting as it felt like a ransom video where if I didn't pay the desired money the kid would get it. I had to interrupt the lesson to say, 'Martha, is that your brother who keeps distracting you with that toy gun?' To which Martha quickly whipped her camera round to reveal the culprit. 'OK, George, I don't think it is appropriate to be on screen pretending to be shooting your sister. Can you stop that please.'

Talking of being distracted during a remote learning lesson, my favourite story was when I tried to teach a maths lesson with a child who decided to multitask by participating in the lesson while doing his weekly shop. I didn't clock at first that the child logged in from the front seat of his car and it was only after the frantic movement of him leaving the car and entering the shop that I could see he wasn't tuning in from home. 'Are you at Tesco, Josh?' I enquired.

'No,' came the prompt reply from Josh once he had unmuted. Despite walking past a board with the slogan 'Every Little Helps,' and the tannoy explaining the social-distancing rules for the shoppers. I tried to continue with my lesson but couldn't help being transfixed watching Josh help his mum with the shopping. It was like being trolley cam on Supermarket Sweep. *He hardly looked at the device to engage with the lesson as he was off down different aisles collecting the essentials – bread, eggs and cereal. It didn't half give me a giggle and I felt it was true dedication to still take part in the lesson despite having to do the trolley dash around Tesco.*

We have shared so many more funny tales about the experience of remote teaching and I think most teachers and staff will agree it's not something we'll be rushing to do again any time soon. I wrote most of this chapter before the 2021/2022 academic year. I was considering adding more about the struggles of teaching once the Omicron variant appeared to ruin Christmas and how that pushed schools into even more despair with students and teachers isolating more than ever before during the pandemic, and how just when we thought we were coming out the other side, this new variant caused even more chaos as it spread through schools like nits on heat. The government announced that if staff shortages were critical, classes could be combined, so teachers were hosting their own concerts, standing on a school bench on the field trying to teach a lesson on adverbs to hundreds of children like Freddie Mercury's unforgettable performance at *Live Aid* because they were the only staff left in school. But the truth is, I'm too tired from teaching during it to really go into too much detail.

As I have stated, I have never been more proud to call myself a teacher than to see how our profession responded to this pandemic. I hope by the time this book is released we can look back and admire the dedication of staff, parents and pupils themselves. Everyone should be incredibly proud of the effort and hard work that went into providing the best possible education for our learners in unique and exceptionally challenging circumstances.

So, what next?

KFC?

Not for us, you banana. What's next for everyone?

Sorry, writing makes me hungry and we're near the end of the book.

Everything makes you hungry.

Anyway, on a serious note, and after at least two years of total disruption to everyone's lives (not forgetting an upsettingly large number of innocent people that didn't come out the other side), the world has properly been turned on its head. Many people, inside and outside of education, chat about what happens next. Where do we go from here? In an ideal world, this chapter wouldn't exist and our penulti-mate section would be about more classroom shenanigans, plus, if Adam had his way, even more fart jokes. But there is a new dawn on the horizon and it would be foolish not to explore how we move forward. Have attitudes towards teaching changed? Has the way people approach teaching moved forward? Will the children be given a fair shot at making up for the learning they missed? Is there some crap that teachers do that needs to be washed away like the virus? This chapter won't have all the answers, but hopefully an interesting perspective on how we move forward in education and in general.

Coming out of the pandemic, I am confident that whether you are reading this book on the day of release in 2022 or five years later, the 'Covidian era' will still be fresh enough in everyone's minds. Returning to normal or the much-hyped 'new normal' that I explored in the last chapter will take some adjustment in the long term, and as we try to get some sort of consistency back, it's almost comparable to returning to school after the summer break – otherwise affectionately known as 'the six weeks' holiday' to many British children.

As soon as 'holidays' and 'teachers' are mentioned in the same breath, it's like a red flag to the people outside of teaching that read the right-wing rags. They already have their go-to comments for running educators down. The sorts of folks that still think we work from 9am to 3pm and lazily break out the 'You get 13 weeks off a year!' line as a stick to beat teachers with. Yes, the holidays or breaks have their benefits, but I will die on the sword that school staff deserve the holidays and go one further to say the children do, too. Term time is hard, it is tiring, it is full on. Research has shown that teachers work on average 56 hours a week during term time but most folks I know easily put in 60–70.

Don't get me wrong, plenty of hours are wasted on pointless tasks that have no real impact on learning, but I think it's perfectly fair to consider the holidays as a way of cashing in on all that overtime. Teaching is one of the only jobs where you have to do work before you get into work because you don't have time to do the work while you're at work and so need to continue to work after work to make sure all of the work is done (deep breath). Holidays are definitely earned and I am sure that many school staff will agree with some of these perks about them:

- The staff night out – it might not happen every break but when it does, it's always a good way to kick off the holidays and the WhatsApp groups then continue into the holidays discussing any gossip, who was most drunk and who made a complete fool of themselves.
- Being able to read a book not aimed at children and actually have the time to enjoy it.
- Being able to go to the toilet whenever you want.
- No Sunday-night anxiety, mainly due to the fact you end up not knowing what day of the week it is – and it is bliss.
- Enjoying a **HOT** cup of tea or coffee.
- A whole day where you just wear your pyjamas. I know this tends to happen during term time on Children in Need day but we're talking about a day where you get to do what pyjamas are intended for – lounging about doing nothing.
- Day drinking or going out on a school night. Even though it is the holidays there is something a little bit cheeky about heading out on a Tuesday night.

- Brunching.
- Binge-watching a Netflix series in a day. You're lucky if you manage to watch one episode of something during term time, and if you make the dreaded mistake of one more episode during the week of teaching you are sealing your fate for the next day. But during the summer holidays you can complete the whole series.
- Turning the alarm off!
- The smug look you get when your non-teaching friends rant on Facebook about how difficult it is looking after their own children during the holidays.

And of course ...

- Being paid in August! I know teachers are paid for term time and this is spread across the year but there is something special about getting paid during a month where you haven't been in work.

But when it comes to the end of the holidays there is always this weird teacher anxiety that you go through. A similar anxiety was definitely felt as we made as much of a post-pandemic return to school life as possible. A huge apprehension that often engulfs a teacher's mindset just before they return to school. The thing is, I love teaching and I love my school, but I still go through this peculiar feeling of dread. It probably doesn't help that social media becomes awash with busy teachers posting pictures of all their brand-new displays and classrooms that look like something from the Sistine Chapel. It is worse when it is a teacher you work with, who says on WhatsApp, 'I've done no work, not even been in school.' Then you walk past their classroom and it looks like Laurence Llewelyn-Bowen has done a makeover. These people do my head in. They were the same people who when you were about to go into the exam hall for your GCSEs would boast that they haven't done any revision but come out with the best grades. Did you put 24 as the answer to question five? Erm, no, I put orange.

I think for a lot of teachers it is the fact that you go from zero to 100 in a matter of hours. You question whether you have made the most of your time off, done enough with your own children, because when term time starts it can feel like you're strangers in the night. There is also the fact that we care as teachers; we want to provide the best possible education to our pupils and so we put that pressure on ourselves. There is also the struggle of having six weeks off and then when the new term starts it is almost like you forget how to function. Simple things like sleep go out the window. I guarantee there has never been a teacher who has had a full night's sleep the night before going back to school. Having to wear trousers is also a struggle for me, as I have spent six weeks in nothing but shorts.

My handwriting is questionable at best but after six weeks of not writing a thing, trying to mark children's books, my hand is cramping after five minutes. What a hypocrite I feel when I write in a child's book 'Please take care with your presentation' in barely legible text and the child asks, 'What does this say?' I can just about remember to set an alarm, but trying to remember my laptop password at the end of the summer is like trying to break the enigma code. Reining in the swearing is hard. August is unofficially National Teacher Swearing Month – you've had weeks of being able to say what you want, but come term time you have to speak so carefully in order to make sure a naughty word doesn't slip out. This is particularly difficult during staff meetings, as is the struggle of retraining your bladder; something that needs to be discussed further, too.

But no one would ever see these struggles as I plaster on my cheery teacher face and make polite yet awkward conversation with my colleagues on the first day back. Yep, the same bloody small talk that you feel obliged to make despite not caring about the answers. As we've already established, 'Yeah, you?' is pretty much the answer to every question. Don't these people know that I have deliberately muted them on Facebook for a reason!?!

With all the anxiety and apprehension that comes from trying to return to school life, it's amazing how teaching has developed as a result of the pandemic and with a greater focus on digital literacy and using technology to make huge improvements to teaching and learning. I am constantly discussing the importance of digital literacy in the curriculum during my training sessions. Educating children from the moment they start school about how to be responsible and positive digital citizens is one of the most important things we can do as educators. I feel passionately about this and how I feel with the current curriculum we teach (2021) we don't have the right balance. I am not going to list all the reasons why I hate this current curriculum because you know, I only have 80,000 words. No, to be fair, there is plenty of it I like, I just don't feel we are getting the balance right. Wales and Scotland, however, seem to be much more progressive with their new curricula. Wales has this brilliant new curriculum (sad, I know, that I am jealous of a curriculum) but they have a Digital Literacy Framework at the forefront of it that drives everything else. In England, we are still well behind. There is an epidemic in this country of mental health issues linked to things like social media, most likely to be worsened coming out of the pandemic, and we don't even speak to children about it. Our curriculum forces us to worry about things that ultimately, in the grand scheme of life, aren't really that important, like whether a child knows the difference between the active or passive voice. I couldn't give a s*** whether my kids know the difference between the active or passive voice. In fact, I don't even know if that sentence I have just written was in the active or passive voice. But my children having a healthy and safe relationship with technology is so much more important.

From passive and active to, quite frankly, aggressive! Nothing annoys me more than when you're making small talk with someone and they ask you what you do and you say, 'Oh, I am a teacher.' Yes, some people will reply with something that makes you feel proud, like 'I honestly don't know how you manage to do it,' which at least shows some form of empathy for our profession. More often than not, however, it's something about colouring in, babysitting, or if they really want a punch in the back of the head they bring up the aforementioned holidays. What riles me even more is the people that choose to share an ill-informed and completely unsolicited opinion that often starts with 'The thing is about teaching ...' and you can almost hear an educator's blood boiling as soon as the words leave their lips. Those people feel entitled to tell you their opinion because, you know, they went to school once upon a time. In the same way, I would have the right to criticise Gordon Ramsay because I can make a belting beans on toast.

There are so many misguided ideas about teaching outside the profession, but there are plenty of teaching myths inside that definitely need to go as well. As mentioned in our story about the one and only Manc Kid, there are genuinely some teachers that still repeat the soulless idea that teachers shouldn't smile until Christmas in order to keep their class in line. *Don't smile until Christmas?!?* It's a load of boll**ks but I genuinely believe it's near impossible to do, especially in primary schools. Every day there are so many moments that make you laugh or chortle. Sometimes you have to suppress the laughter as it is not always appropriate to giggle at the time of said incident; however, it's OK back in the staffroom, which is often full of staff laughing about another day of madness.

Farting in assembly is always one that gets me. I'm a 36-year-old grown-up, yet in a quiet assembly if a child lets one rip that echoes around the hall, it is almost impossible to not burst out chuckling. Instead, though, you have to give the eyes to the culprit that it was inappropriate and not something to be laughed about.

Creating a classroom of fear does not lead to good outcomes, though. It is important to set boundaries and have clear and consistent expectations, but also to be firm but fair. Whenever I first work with a class, I always set out my expectations and try to be consistent with this so that they understand and can make the right choices. And I believe this can be done in a way where you can still smile, debunking that boring teacher myth about refusing to smile until Christmas.

As this is a chapter about moving forward, and while I'm in the process of debunking teacher myths, I feel there are a few more I should put to bed now and hopefully rid them from our profession:

1) You do not need a catchy name for a topic. If you're teaching the Romans, call it the Romans. It doesn't need to be called Roaring Romans or Ravishing Romans (I think Horrible Histories should take some of the blame for this). The amount of people posting on Facebook and Twitter asking for an alliterative title for a topic that will have no bearing on whether the children learn anything! Same for any wordplay with strategies or initiatives: don't be hoodwinked just because something rolls off the tongue. The amount of garbage I've seen being peddled to teachers and they lap it up because we go weak at the knees for alliteration, acronyms or rhyme.

2) The amount of detail you put into a lesson plan doesn't mean it will be taught better. Everyone is different: some teachers want to plan word for word, others can plan on a Post-It note. As long as the lesson is taught effectively, how it was planned really isn't important.

3) Having no aspirations to go into leadership or management does not make you a bad teacher. In fact, there is absolutely nothing wrong with wanting to stay in the classroom your whole career. It is such a weird concept that if a teacher shows real potential we then take them out of the classroom to be a leader. But that is a completely different job; teaching children is a totally different ball game to managing adults. Some people do a fantastic job, but there are some amazing teachers who don't make good leaders and some who weren't necessarily the best teachers but have a knack for getting the best out of people. Either way, if you're content with being a class teacher and that's what you want to do each year, good on you.

4) School policies should be designed to best practice, which encourages everyone to move forward instead of being designed to the lowest common denominator, which ends up holding everyone back. This is why I detest the phrase 'non-negotiables'.

5) The odd worksheet isn't going to kill anyone. Teachers don't need to reinvent the wheel but at the same time you should always have the opportunity to innovate, be creative, adapt and put your own stamp on things.

6) Being the first in school each morning and the last one to leave each evening does not make you the best or most hardworking teacher on the staff. The more time you spend doing stuff around teaching doesn't make you a better teacher.

7) No teacher is the same. We shouldn't be expected to be like every other teacher. We all bring our own individual personalities, skills, interests, talents, hobbies and humour into our schools and this should be celebrated.

8) Don't be a martyr – have a lunch break. Whatever work you normally do over lunch can wait. The impact of having a conversation with another adult about something other than teaching shouldn't be dismissed.

9) There is no such thing as an outstanding school or an outstanding teacher. It is a fallacy that creates an unrealistic expectation that leads to teachers putting a lot of unnecessary pressure on themselves. I think most teachers are capable of being outstanding on their day but we're all human, so there will be days where, no matter what, no matter how hard we try, we can't be at the top of our game. As long as we are always trying our best and learning from mistakes, that is all that can be asked of us.

10) The more you monitor and scrutinise teachers, the more you raise standards. Bollocks! The more you monitor and scrutinise teachers, the worse the teaching is. Just trust staff to do the job they are capable of doing.

Oooh, that feels good to get off my chest! If we can hopefully move on from these unnecessary teaching tropes then the next generation of teachers might have a fighting chance. Going back to the next generation, as in the children we are teaching at the present, I really feel they get an unnecessarily bad reputation before they've had a chance to embrace the world. Those same people that always goad teachers with snarky quips about 'holidays' and 'working 9am–3pm' also seem to have lazy opinions on the kids of today; ones that quite often start with lines akin to:

'Kids don't know they're born these days!'

I want to scream 'F*** OFF!'

This isn't the children's fault. They are the way they are because of us and I feel we fail them. We fail them as a generation of parents (generally speaking) and our education system fails them. Here's the thing: I would absolutely hate to be a kid nowadays. I will gladly hold my hands up and admit to you that my childhood was so much easier than what it is like nowadays. It will be the same for most of you reading this; we don't like to admit it as we always like to think that our lives are harder, but can you remember feeling an ounce of stress or pressure when you were at primary school? Did you even know what the word anxiety meant when you were 10?

I think the most amount of pressure I felt in primary school was the Year 6 local area rounders tournament. It was the semi-finals and we were playing English Martyrs or, what we used to call them, English Farters.

Nice.

I know. We were a rounder down and I was the only batter left in. We needed two rounders. I stepped up with Paddy in my hand. No, not an Irishman; this was the name of the bat that had a dent in the grip which, if you believed the myth, was caused by Paddy, a mythical giant who went to my school a few years ago and gripped the bat so hard he left a dent where the thumb would go. Most likely the bat was thrown back into the basket and hit the handle on the way in. I felt the pressure. I looked back at my teammates knowing it was all in my hands. I stepped up, and the rest is history.

You won?

No, I got stumped at first post! Only joking! Yes, I got the two rounders and we progressed to the final. You'd have thought being a lefty (both with the rounders bat and as apparently most teachers are, politically) they'd have put a fielder there, but no. There was an open field to aim for and as a result the win was in the bag. English Farters clearly weren't above us academically as well. The point I am making is that it was the most amount of pressure I felt at primary.

Whereas now we have more Year 6 children being diag-nosed with stress-related conditions because of a series of tests they have to sit at the end of their primary years that ultimately don't mean anything to them. The fact they are given all this technology at such a young age with this money-rich, time-poor approach to it, have no real educa-tion and so become addicted to these devices, craving validation through things like a like button, like that means anything. This is the world they're growing up into, and we have the audacity to say 'they don't know they're born'. What I want to do is help them, which is why I live by the mantra of 'we need to get children to be masters of technology and not slaves to it'. We see plenty of examples of children being slaves to the technology through no fault of their own, given a device at such a young age with no one setting restrictions, time limits or educating them on how to navigate these devices responsibly, because it keeps them quiet. And I am sure I speak on behalf of most primary school teachers when I say that a common issue or complaint from parents will be based around different social media platforms.

'Mr P, my daughter is having some real issues with some of the other girls on WhatsApp. Can you let me know what you're going to do about it?'

'How about you don't let your daughter have access to WhatsApp when she's six!'

I do feel we need to do more as teachers and staff, however. I am often messaged by teachers asking for advice about issues they are having with their pupils and TikTok, Instagram or WhatsApp, and I will reply with the question: when did you last spend some quality lesson time teaching them about it? Because again, we don't, and I am not having a go at teachers, it's a curriculum problem. Most schools never speak to students about social media until one day of the year ... Safer Internet Day. I want to make it clear that I admire and respect all the people, charities and companies behind internet safety day, I just hate the way schools use it as a tick-box exercise. Even as recently as this year, every February my social media feeds will be clogged up with teachers posting selfies of themselves with a piece of paper stating:

'I want to raise awareness of how dangerous the internet is. Please share this image and let me know where you are from to prove to my class how quickly things can spread online! #InternetSafetyDay.'

Now firstly I will admit I have done this thing ... in 2008! Times have moved on: these teachers are going to get the shock of their lives when they finally discover the Gangnam Style dance. What is this going to do in 2022 when most of your class have more YouTube subscribers than the well-meaning but ultimately flawed post will get? We've got to do more. The other one is when teachers say, 'Children, we are not going to talk about internet safety until internet safety day, then on internet safety day I will take an hour out of the afternoon to tell you all the bad things about the internet. How it is a naughty naughty thing and you should never ever use it. You should never ever ever speak to anyone online ever! Now we are going to make some posters!'

I'll ask these teachers, 'Where did you meet your partner again?'

More often than not, they reply, 'Oh, on Tinder!'

We have got to be doing more. Now this is hard when the educational system in this country is run by politicians, all of which have never stepped foot in a classroom as an adult. The problem with the government is that they only ever value things they can measure through testing. This current government seem to be taking this to the next level, where now there are only two year groups in primary that are not doing some sort of national assessment:

EYFS - Baseline Assessment

Year 1 - Phonics Test, sorry, Phonics 'Check'

Year 2 - KS1 SATs

Year 3 - Have a rest ... for now

Year 4 - Times Tables assessment

Year 5 - Rest up to get ready for the big one ...

Year 6 - KS2 SATs

And we wonder why these children are stressed out of their minds? This is why education always has and always will revolve around the 3 Rs — Reading, Writing and ARithmetic. I am not for one second debating the importance of these three. They are imperative, absolutely, but given this rich technological world we now live in, there are other things we need to embed in our curriculum to ensure our children can thrive in this world they are growing into. I call these the THREE Cs. Again, these are not to replace anything, but instead to work alongside what we are already doing.

1. Creativity

Controversially, he's used the big C word. This is surely going to be the part of this book that will receive the usual onslaught on Twitter from certain teachers, screaming from the top of their lungs, 'THIS IS A KNOWLEDGE-RICH CURRICULUM!'

For someone who has been teaching for 15 years, I find this 'knowledge-rich curriculum' idea to be quite patronising. It makes it out like any curriculum before this one wasn't knowledge rich, every lesson before 2014 was just a complete waste of time. I thought from the moment I stepped foot in a classroom that my job was to get kids to know stuff. For me, you can't be skilful or creative at anything without knowledge; it underpins everything. But apparently it is this revolutionary new thing, and the issue I have noticed is that it has become a bit of a bandwagon, like most things in education (learning styles, Kagan, Growth Mindset to name a few) that schools jump onto but rarely implement effectively.

It seems now that it is all about children acquiring knowledge, a death by knowledge organiser approach. While it is important and imperative that children acquire knowledge, I also think it is important to give children the chance to apply their knowledge to solve problems. Technology is making our lives incredibly convenient. I often laugh about how my teachers would mock us by saying, 'You'll never have a calculator attached to your side, so you need to know this!' The fact that I have a calculator on my Apple Watch without even getting the phone out of my pocket has left them with egg on their face for sure. I am not for one second suggesting we don't need to teach certain concepts because the technology can do it for us, the point is that no matter what advances we have with technology – and we will have them: I am currently typing this on my iPad – but by the time my children are adults, who knows what they will be using. They may nostalgically laugh about iPads the way we do about the Game Boy. So despite technological advances, what always remains is the importance and need to solve problems. To define creativity is not to split knowledge and creativity apart; instead, for me being creative is to acquire knowledge and use it to solve problems. I often think we don't necessarily get that balance right.

2. Compassion

Teaching empathy, understanding and tolerance of people who are different to us has been a staple of every school's RE and PSHCE curriculum for years. However, the big mistake we make at the minute in our current curriculum is that there is little to no education around empathy and compassion for others online. The UK is currently the worst in Europe for cyber-bullying issues by a mile. We can't buy a point in Eurovision but the hatred and ignorance we display online puts us at the top of the charts. The worst part of this ... it is killing people, people are taking their own lives due to the torrent of abuse they receive online. The biggest lie humanity has ever told itself is 'Sticks and stones may break my bones but names will never hurt me.' Well, they do, they really do.

I have only ever experienced the odd episode of trolling, but let me tell you it is horrible, really horrible. The worst part for me is that the trolling I've been on the receiving end of was from fellow teachers, the people who should be setting the example. I often think about why so many people do it, as I could put my house on the fact that most people who racially abuse footballers, send death threats to celebrities and happily mock others would never do it to their face, so why do they think it is OK to do it online? I think certain people use the same mentality they do when they are driving. When someone pulls out in front of you, what do you do? You slam on your brakes and whatever expletive comes to mind you shout angrily at the person. However, when you're walking down the street and someone walks out of a shop into your pathway, what do you say? 'Oh, sorry!' Wait a second, it wasn't your fault, yet you're apologising? So why is it when you are in your car you will call someone a nasty name whereas face to face you don't?

This is the same mentality people have with their online behaviour. They feel detached, they have no regard for the emotional impact of their words as they don't see the reaction of the person on the receiving end. They think because they can use an anonymous handle it gives them freedom to say what they like with no regard for the consequences. This is something we need to start teaching children about from the moment they start school. Not encouraging them to use these platforms but educating them so by the time they are old enough they can do it responsibly and positively. They must take ownership of their words, understand that their words can hurt and they should take accountability for their actions. I completely agree that the platforms themselves need to do more but as a teacher I have little power to change that. What I can do is embed digital literacy into my curriculum so my pupils grow up to be positive digital citizens. No one is born ignorant or racist, it is learned behaviour. I feel schools do a good job at teaching acceptance and equality, but that needs to include online behaviour too.

3. Critical thinking

There have been so many negative aspects of this pandemic. The sheer loss of life that in many cases was preventable is heartbreaking to say the least. Another aspect of the pandemic that has contributed to this is the sheer amount of fake news and misinformation that has plagued social media. This is nothing new: politicians have used the fake news tactic for a number of years, anti-vax ideas are not new, but the way that movement has latched onto this pandemic and the amount of susceptible people they have managed to dupe – and in some cases have died as a result of misinformation or fear – is unforgivable. Having the ability to navigate this vast online digital world with a real sense of truth and reliability is something that cannot be underestimated. I had my worries about how as a country we were going to deal with this pandemic when only a couple of years ago a shortage of KFC nearly sent the country into meltdown.

Bad times. I remember it well!

But some of the things I have seen so-called 'friends' spout on social media are nothing short of embarrassing. I've genuinely read stuff like: 'This isn't a pandemic, it is a plandemic. This is Bill Gates, the lizard, trying to infect us all through 5G masts so he can stick a needle in my arm and microchip me. Don't fall for it! Wake up, you sheeple!'

Facepalm indeed. The fact that most of these people are saying this through a mobile device that already tracks you everywhere anyway makes me laugh. It's safe to say the folks that share this nonsense will receive an automatic block, unfollow or mute on my timeline, but ultimately, misinformation, fake news and lies spread online SIX times quicker than anything else. This stuff gets engagement and with engagement comes monetisation. Most of these big conspiracy theory platforms don't believe half of what they say, they just know by lying and saying it, it will get so many views, comments, shares which can be monetised and profited from. From the perspective of the social media companies, it's better to keep people angry because users who are full of anger will spend more time on their platforms sharing their views and seeking approval from their online echo chamber. Adam Curtis, in his documentary *Hypernormalisation* (2016), summed it up nicely, saying 'angry people click more'. With every click, there's a potential new set of eyeballs on whatever content needs more eyeballs on it, who will hopefully buy stuff as a result. Kerrching! Again, we need to teach our young people to be aware and knowledgeable enough about the world to see through the bullsh*t that is plaguing the internet.

Obviously, not all of social media is full of anger and conspiracy theories; there is plenty to enjoy and appreciate about being better connected as a species. Most of the time I love social media, I think it is one of the most powerful ways in which you can change the world. I wouldn't be doing what I am doing now if it wasn't for social media. Unfortunately, though, it brings the best and worst out of us. I feel everyone who was involved in creating these platforms in the beginning did it with the right intention, they wanted to create platforms that would bring us closer together. The problem is we have far too many people using these platforms who don't have a clue how it works and are very naive. When you throw capitalism into the mix where you can profit off that naivety we find ourselves in a situation we're in now where it can affect our democracy. On a much smaller scale, looking at us as individuals, social media can bring us lots of positives, keeping in contact with our loved one, laughing at memes, getting a closer look at our idols, but it can also have a negative impact on our self-esteem. Here's the thing about social media ... **EVERYONE LIES**!

If you were to compare someone's Facebook or Instagram feed to their Google search it would show them to be polar opposites. We all get to control our own news feeds and feel the pressure to keep up appearances, so we only post the positives and 'perfect' elements of our lives. The full picture is often very different. I have been guilty of this myself, and over the past few years I have tried not to give in to the humble brag nature of social media. For example, a few years back we had booked a day to go to a dinosaur kingdom – a park that had different dinosaur statues dotted about for you to discover. A complete rip-off, billed as a great family day out, was effectively walking round a park with some static dinosaurs. No refunds, would you believe? Anyway, a day out with the kids and my wife is something I always look forward to no matter what we're doing. Arriving at the park, the parking was a nightmare, I think we ended up parking further away than our actual house. This was followed by queuing up like we were at Alton Towers waiting for the Smiler, but this didn't have the adrenaline rush of a rollercoaster at the end, instead an undercooked hot dog that left me doing loop the loops on the toilet for the next week. When we finally got to the entrance my wife turned to me asking where the tickets were, to which I replied 'with you'. This led to a bit of a disagreement that ended with me being wrong and doing another marathon back to the car for the tickets. When we eventually entered the park, my children literally transformed into Junior from *Problem Child 1, 2* and *3*. Yes, people, there was a third *Problem Child* movie and, just like the Parkinson brothers, the third one is the worst!

Oi! Leave me out of this. Stick to your dinosaur day out disaster!

It was a disaster. The children were tetchy with each other, I was with them, my wife was fed up with me. It was just all in all a sh*t day. Simple as. However, just before the heavens opened and we were drenched running back to our car, I managed to snap a selfie of all of us with a T-rex in the background. Once I got home and dried out, what did I do with said picture? Straight onto Instagram, posted it with the caption, 'Brilliant day out with the family!' What a straight-up lie. Why did I do it? It was at that moment I realised I had become a victim to this bullsh*t pressure of social media.

I have had it in other ways, too. I remember going to a football tournament with school a few years ago and seeing a teacher I used to work with. I hadn't seen him for ages and we were chatting away when he said, 'How do you do it, Lee?'

'Do what?' I replied.

'Your kids. They are the happiest kids I have ever met!' Just for clarity, he has never actually met them, so I was puzzled to say the least.

'What do you mean?'

'Well, whenever I see them on Facebook, they are always smiling, hugging each other. They are just the happiest kids and get on so well with each other. My two fight like cat and dog. How do you do it?'

'I don't post pictures of them when they're kicking off!'

I often get it when I am doing my training. I have had messages from teachers who say, 'How do you do it, Mr P? Whenever I see you using technology, it is always working perfectly.'

The answer is simple: I just don't post the sh*t lessons I teach. And trust me, I have taught some shocking lessons. I tend to only share things that have worked, but there are plenty of lessons that don't go to plan. I try to make it clear that I am in no way a great, outstanding teacher. I hope to think I am decent, but I am more and more conscious of not creating this image from what I post online that makes me look like I am something I am not. I hope most people know this and that is what makes my channels relatable.

The problem with this fake life we project online is that despite us all doing it, despite us all knowing everyone else does it, we still fall victim to comparing ourselves to everything we see online, and we're FULLY GROWN ADULTS. Think about our children who know nothing of the world and at a premature age are given these devices where 24 hours a day, 7 days a week they are getting a constant feed of how amazing everyone else's life is. What's worse is that now there are apps available that allow you to completely alter your appearance. Photoshopping that was once exclusive to magazine covers is now accessible to everyone with a few taps of your finger. This again can create unnecessary pressure on young people to strive for a level of beauty that isn't even attainable naturally. I always do this as a lesson with my class. I downloaded one of those photoshopping apps and took a selfie. I then make as many adjustments with the app as I can before sharing the two pictures with my class and asking them to play a bit of spot the difference and see all the ways in which the picture had been changed. This leads on to a discussion about why people are so willing to edit and filter their pictures before discussing what can be the harmful elements to this. I have yet to do this lesson with a group of children that don't manage to blow me away with their mature and thoughtful responses, although the most recent example left me speechless:

'Can anyone else think of a reason why it might be bad to edit and filter your pictures?'

Nine-year-old girl, 'You could get catfished!'

'Pardon?'

'You know, like you could be on Tinder, see someone you like, agree to meet them expecting to meet a model and a potato turns up.'

After a discussion with the class teacher, it turns out the parents of this child have recently split up and Mum was back on the dating scene and obviously sharing her struggles with her daughter!

Finding ways to build these aspects of internet safety and digital literacy into our curriculum is really important for me. Seesaw gives you the ability to embed so much of the digital literacy curriculum in a meaningful way. It's incredible how resilient teachers, children and their families had to become to use technology positively to try to keep children learning during difficult circumstances. Technological advances have played a huge part in this but so have changing attitudes. Embracing technology, including plenty of the tools and apps I have mentioned here, has meant that even the school's biggest 'digital dinosaurs' are better clued up in how to use technology to raise standards. Yes, Microsoft Teams has brought fully grown adults to tears in the early stages of remote teaching, but it's far more accepted that virtual learning will hopefully be our friend in the future.

I've chatted plenty in this chapter and the last about how teaching has changed or could change in the future and the role that digital literacy (not just for children) should play in helping everyone to move forward. Some people's perceptions will never change, but my hope is that we can at least give the next generation a fighting chance to be switched on enough to combat and embrace the brilliant yet complicated online world ahead of them.

The future is bright, the future is ... hopefully an improvement on the previous two years!

As a result of the Covid-19 pandemic, at different times the education system has had to deal with staff and student absences on an unprecedented scale. One day, we hope it will disappear off the face of the planet like glue stick lids by the second week of September (seriously, where do they bloody go?). When we released the first book, we genuinely expected the pandemic could be over by the time the second one reached the shelves. These final musings are being typed in spring 2022 and the last variant du jour was discovered in South Africa and has been given the name Omicron (Adam thought that was a Transformer). By the time you read this book, we may have run out of Greek letters of the alphabet for the different strains and variants, so according to Adam's logic we may be on Megatron or Optimus Prime.

We'll be on Power Rangers next! Especially if it keeps on morphin'.

As a result of the learning missed during the pandemic, there was a call out to teachers who had previously retired or left the profession with no intention of returning, asking them to help. The Education Secretary had tried to turn this call to action into a World War II metaphor and even dared to suggest we needed to channel the 'Blitz Spirit'. Blitz Spirit, my arse! This is often lazily referenced when politicians want to shame people into doing something through fear of being branded unpatriotic if they don't comply. It's almost, in a sense, a bit like when young men were being asked to sign up to World War I, as brilliantly depicted in Michael Morpurgo's *Private Peaceful*. Reticent lads were goaded into signing up to be soldiers by an old lady telling them they would be cowards if they didn't.

We sincerely doubt the required number of former or recently retired educators will jump at the chance to return to the places that caused them so much stress and anxiety over the last decade or so. If any ex-teacher does return to the classroom to help fill the gaps in the children's learning, it won't be because of jingoistic bulls**t, it will be because *they want to help the children*.

So much learning from home went on during the pandemic, especially during the second major lockdown where everyone except key worker/vulnerable children was doing their daily schoolwork via Teams and Zoom. The importance of understanding that educators are more than just 9am to 3pm glorified babysitters has definitely made a mark on some people, and since the release of *Put a Wet Paper Towel On It* we've had loads of non-teachers getting in touch to say how they see teachers in a much more positive light. School staff will probably never reach the level of appreciation that they deserve – not that they expect it – but it feels better knowing that so many parents appreciate the difficulty in getting their own child to learn, let alone a class of thirty.

Credit where it's not due, however, during national crises (recent events in particular) the people at the top can be excused by some from any responsibility by saying 'they are trying their best in difficult circumstances'.

If it were a child in Reception class that had managed to go a day without lodging a crayon up his nose, most teachers would deem that as 'trying their best'. As for the folks in charge of the country, if they are trying their best, I daren't think what happens when they try their worst!

Educators, as well as heroes like doctors, nurses, paramedics, carers and other amazing key workers, have no choice but to be constantly 'trying our best' because if we didn't, bad things would happen and we'd lose our jobs. Speaking of heroes, another bunch of superstars that deserved a great deal of praise during the pandemic were, of course, *the children*.

Yes, we've got a chapter dedicated to having a giggle at what a crazy bunch they are, plus they feature heavily in the stories we've shared, but it hasn't been easy for them and we probably won't learn about the long-term impacts on them in relation to lost learning and mental health issues for a while. Yet so many of the little blighters have just taken everything in their stride and kept calm and carried on. As kids of the 90s and 2000s, Adam and I have huge respect for the children of today. Everything is recorded and monitored via cameras on phones and uploaded to social media where it's hard to escape it. As mentioned in the last book, Adam's Facebook timeline from the late 2000s was accidental comedy gold, and not in a good way. Song-lyric status updates and boyband audition profile pictures. You looked like such a knob!

I'd argue, but it's true. If even half of what I got up to was in the public domain, there's every possibility I'd be in a lot of trouble! Videoing myself diving headfirst into a giant snowball at Mum and Dad's and posting it on Facebook would be the least of my worries.

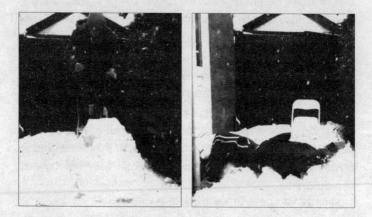

Speaking of social media, I mentioned in the final chapter about how hard it has been for the children of today but there's plenty to appreciate about how older users are influenced and even warped by what they see online. There are so many negative posts declaring how things were so much better in the 'good old days' to rile some of the older users in their opinion about the youth of today.

Nostalgia can be great, but on some of the Facebook groups our parents' generation (not necessarily our own parents) follow, there'll be posts or memes where there'll be a picture of an old cobbled street that wouldn't be out of place in an L.S. Lowry painting. The people that are reading them are almost humming the tune from the Hovis advert as they look through the lists of things they did as a child, with the tagline 'It never did me any harm,' as if to imply that the generations after them are a bunch of overly sensitive crybabies that they can brandish as 'snowflakes' or 'WOKE'.

For starters, the term 'woke' is terrible English and its definition is something close to: 'Alert to injustice and discrimination in society, especially racism' … surely that's a good thing! It's like Adam and my generation, or millennials as we've been labelled: you'll never read anything positive about us. I suppose it's only natural, to a certain extent. People in their sixties and seventies were roundly boll**ked by their parents for growing their hair long, wearing miniskirts and listening to rock and roll music. Those that vowed to 'stick it to the man' have now become 'the man' and they are only paying forward a dislike of the next generation. For every time you hear shade thrown at millennials, 'You lot are just the biggest bunch of snowflakes going. All you do is sit there getting offended at stuff,' you'll equally get 'Shut up, boomer. Thanks for buying a house for £2,000 which rose to half a million quid then crashed the economy!' We're almost as bad as each other and Adam can vouch for me in saying that I love a bit of inter-generational banter round the dinner table at Christmas.

Highlight of the year ... not!!

Don't get me wrong, there are always plenty of folks that get offended too quickly about anyone and anything, but labelling anyone born from Generation X onwards as being a 'snowflake' is just lazy. Give the kids a chance. I bet if Winston Churchill had an iPhone in 1945 he'd probably have had a few games of *Angry Birds* or watched some TikTok.

Spot on, Lee! The thing is, I believe the children are our future. We need to teach them well and let them lead the way.

Are you trying to be profound again? Where's that from?

Whitney Houston, 'Greatest Love of All' (1986).

Ffs Adam! I was trying to make a point! Go back to head-butting giant snowballs.

Moving forward to the next generation, from being in the classroom we see that lots of the children nowadays are potentially more resilient than any generation before them. This is our opportunity to give them a bit of credit. They've had to take in so much change in such a short amount of time. If they mess up, annoy someone or make a mistake ... Good! As long as they learn from it, that is. Children know way more about adult sensitivities than most so-called adults. They are far more equipped to be tolerant of people's differences. Find a few adverts from the 70s and 80s on YouTube and you'll be amazed at just how poorly they stand up. Turns out the good old days were a bit filled with casual racism, sexism and homophobia, as well as people that ended up being visited by Operation Yewtree.

Most humans will look back on their childhood fondly, and a huge part of our first two books has reflected this. Generational differences are fascinating and should be explored, but as long as they aren't being weaponised to put down others and their experiences, it's perfectly healthy. It's when folks start having a pop at modern kids for not being mentally tough or having a stiff upper lip that they are clearly missing the point. Young people are doing more to remove the stigma of mental health than 99 per cent of the humans that existed before them. Children have been heroes in recent years and they are always the best thing about working in schools.

So if there really has been a 'Blitz Spirit' during the pandemic years, it will be because of the amazing key workers that stepped up, and that definitely includes teachers, teaching assistants, office staff, lunchtime supervisors, cleaners, site managers and parent volunteers. The brilliant children have more than played their part. That spirit has been in place for years and those that seek to exploit it for political gain and cover their own arses for mistakes and bad planning, we have two words for them … **and the second word is definitely OFF!**

We hope you have enjoyed our second attempt at writing a book. We had so much positive feedback from

Put a Wet Paper Towel On It, so we hope you've enjoyed the sequel. If you didn't, how on earth have you made it this far?!?

Well ... it's your own time you've wasted.

Take care of yourselves, and each other.

Acknowledgements

Thank you to everyone at HarperCollins for putting your faith in us for another book; we appreciate the hard work and support. Thank you to Ajda, Helena, Simon, Julie and Imogen in particular.

To Paul, our agent at Headway Talent, thank you for all your hard work, managing Adam's wild expectations and helping us to gain all these amazing opportunities. To Tim (@sadlerdoodles), who has been so much more than just an illustrator, thank you for all the brilliant work and support you've put in to this second book.

To the team at Phil McIntyre and KPPR, thanks for all your support with the tour and book promotion. We are so grateful for the belief you've given us to take the podcast on the road.

To our parents, you've set the bar so high when it comes to being the best parents and role models; your work ethic and selflessness know no bounds. We hope we've done you proud. Nana Maureen, you absolute diamond – the podcast community has adopted you as their nana, and we love you to the moon and back!

We'd also like to thank the most important people – you! To everyone who has listened, subscribed, reviewed, shared a story, recommended the podcast to a friend, tuned in to one of our live episodes during lockdown, bought a ticket to a live show and/or bought the books, we both massively thank you. Your support means the world to us!

I also want to thank everyone who has supported my journey for the past ten years. I fully appreciate that the reason the podcast has grown so quickly is because of all my social media followers and supporters. So to everyone who has liked or shared a post, subscribed to my website, been on one of my training days or had me lead training in their school, again a massive thank you. You helped me build a platform, which has benefitted the podcast immensely.

I'm often asked how I find the time to do it all: teach, lead training, make videos, do the podcast, write and tour. The answer is simply having the most incredible wife who does all the unseen things. She supports and inspires me to do better in everything I do, and I will be forever grateful for her hard work, which almost always goes unnoticed. To my wonderful children – Callum, Harry, Charlie and Lily – being your dad is the best job in the world. You'll never fully understand how proud you make me for just being the kind, caring, funny and beautiful people you are. To Claire's family – Sue, Will, Leigh and Ryan – thank you for being there to help and support with the kids. The love and self-lessness you show stepping in when I'm not there is something I'm so grateful for, and I feel privileged to be part of your family.

To all my Davyhulme family, thank you for putting up with me. My colleagues, SLT and friends make it the best place to teach. The kids aren't too bad either. Having the trust, flexibility and support from you all is one of the main reasons I've been able to do all of this, and I will always be thankful. To all the other staff and children I've had the pleasure of working with over my teaching career, thank you for the precious memories and helping mould me into the teacher I am today.

Over to you, Adam ...

Once again, I will thank my darling wife, as I will surely need another ticket out of the dog house at some point. Kim, thank you for doing an amazing job holding the fort down while this adventure with my brother has taken up a lot of my time over the past year. I could not do any of this without you. To my two little rascals, Isla and Max, thank you for gracing this earth and allowing me to attempt to be the best father I can!

To my closest friends and family, there's a reason we're still close ... because you're great people and you actually put up with me!

To the first teacher I ever worked with, the infamous Cockney John, you have legendary stories to tell but you're genuinely the person who taught me the ropes, and the fact we're still mates after ten years says it all. Cheers, bruv!

To my colleagues at my wonderful school, I love doing my job and you are all such a special part of it; your support and friendship are so important to me. Thank you.

To the children I've had the pleasure to teach over the years, keep reaching high, find your passion and believe in yourselves always.